HOUSE
& GARDEN
COOKING WITH STYLE

HOUSE & GARDEN
COOKING WITH STYLE

ALICE WOOLEDGE SALMON

OCTOPUS BOOKS

TO HUGO

Editor: Marilyn Inglis
Designer: John Bridges
Production controller: Shane Lask

First published in 1987 by
Octopus Books Limited
59 Grosvenor Street
London W1
© The Condé Nast Publications Limited
© New photographs, Octopus Books Limited
ISBN 0 7064 2821 8

Printed and bound in Hong Kong
by Mandarin Publishers Limited

CONTENTS

INTRODUCTION

This book is the product of my explorations of food for *House & Garden* magazine, within which my articles have been published every other month or so during the past five years, reflecting many of my discoveries and interests throughout this period. As I review the various chapters, I find evidence of diverse flirtations and much serious involvement, a taste for simplicity as well as the suggestion that elaboration is, at times, one of life's necessities.

Each recipe, however simple or exotic, embodies a single theme: that good food is based on the best of what's available – the freshest fish and garden produce, properly prepared meat from expert butchers, decent bread made with flour of high quality. From all this excellence comes the inspiration – to buy and prepare with flair and a taste for experiment, to create something new or to re-establish classics.

I grew up in North America, in New York City, New Mexico and California, where my mother, an imaginative and epicurean cook, gave us well-planned

casseroles, crab meat, vivid salads, home-made strawberry sorbet (we called it 'sherbet') in crystal flutes. Together we made good pastry and, occasionally, big pizzas, preparing the yeasty dough from scratch. But food, in the USA of the 1950s and '60s, was something we did not make much fuss about and, when I left for London in 1970, the most exotic ingredient at my local supermarket was 'Munster' cheese, Wisconsin-produced and plastic-wrapped.

As a student I discovered how the French eat and thought the best meal in the world must be duck *à l'orange* followed by strawberries and cream in a sugar-spun cage; lunching on this at Lasserre was, to a 20-year-old in Paris, part of the ultimate gastronomy. As were, in another sense, the chewy bread on French tables – so different from the characterless wool that has largely replaced it – and the peppery *moules* dished up by my unassuming landlady.

During the 1970s, from my base in England, I often travelled to the rest of Europe, ate and shopped

with increasing curiosity, brought home recipes, read Elizabeth David, Jane Grigson, and *Mastering the Art of French Cooking*, began trying to create the dishes in these books. 'And I'll start to write about food,' I thought, 'to help pay for my travels.'

Did writing do this? Only somewhat. But it caused me to grow more attentive to both cooking and its context, French and otherwise, and by the mid-1970s I had decided to become a chef. Brief formal training, a certain audacity and a great deal of luck led me first to the kitchen of Guy Mouilleron at London's Ma Cuisine, where I made all sorts of desserts and absorbed more by watching Guy work than I ever could have done from cooking schools. I became a freelance cook, coped with temperamental employers and ovens, and eventually joined the team at the Connaught Hotel, where Michel Bourdin runs a large brigade of youthful chefs devoted to meeting the repeated onslaughts of hungry customers.

All this time I continued to write and, by the early

1980s, had made it my full-time occupation. Writing about food gives me the same degree of pleasure as buying a sparkling fresh mullet whose accompanying mayonnaise will be laced with southern garlic, or as finding that the fast froth of buttermilk is an ideal finish to a chilled soup of sweet yellow peppers.

Learning to cook is like learning how to write or to live, a lengthy process filled with speculation, in which many of the best discoveries come about unplanned. Much of this is difficult, but most of it, with luck, will be highly enjoyable; and enjoyment of cooking is increased by returning to a dish you tried years earlier and finding it easier to produce and tasting much better – or by tackling something new and deciding that you do, after all, like pumpkin or calf's brains or the business of making *gnocchi*.

In preparing these recipes, I've drawn from all aspects of my culinary travels and I've relished the experience. I hope that you too will have a long and fruitful journey.

THE BASICS

Each cook needs to acquire a repertoire of basic skills; one of the most important of these is learning to select ingredients of excellent quality, however simple their nature. The familiar parsley should always have a clean, moist, just-picked aroma, carrots the clear colour of youth, lettuce a snap in the leaf, fish a bright eye and a lustrous skin. Such good, simple elements should then be put to use in a variety of imaginative ways: nuts turning up as a stylish hors-d'oeuvre or as part of a main-course salad, garlic employed as an accent or an all-pervasive flavour, fruits sliced and gleaming across the surface of a pastry or transformed into unexpected dessert terrines.

The recipes in this section help put into practice the skills of choosing and combining ingredients, and the techniques for producing specific results. There are methods for marinating meat and preparing meat and poultry for terrines, procedures for boning fish, for making aspic jelly, for a flourless garlic soufflé, a buttery puff pastry – all adding up to a collection of favourite – and fundamental – recipes.

FOR COCKTAILS AND COOLERS

When it comes to serving drinks, I'm against run-of-the-mill accompaniments; a bit of fish paste plonked on to a biscuit, or the opulent but obvious smoked salmon bound with caviar are just not interesting. As dips can be a nuisance and toast grows soggy beneath the spread, I often use vegetables as the base for various embellishments. Some of these mouthfuls are quite complex, others fast and easy while several can be partially made in advance and briefly completed to serve.

ONION RINGS

This is a recipe adapted from the late American food writer James Beard, one that he invented more than forty years ago and which, in my view, remains without peer. Buy a large brioche from a good baker; you may have to order it specially. This recipe is not for those people who hate raw onions, though the taste of them is tempered here by quantities of parsley.

---

1 or more large brioches
mayonnaise (the best available
   commercial brand will do)
white or red onions, about 4 cm
   (1½ inches) across, peeled and very
   finely sliced into rounds
salt
large bunch of very fresh parsley,
   chopped

Chill brioche well, then slice across, very thinly. With a 4 cm (1½ inch) circular cutter, cut slices into rounds (not including any crust). Spread each round lightly with mayonnaise. Place an onion section on half the brioche rounds (to cover each completely), grind on salt, top with a circle of brioche, and press together gently. Have ready a dinner plate spread with mayonnaise and another of parsley. Roll the edge of each sandwich first in mayonnaise, then in the chopped parsley; the latter should make a fairly heavy wreath.

If not serving right away, store sandwiches on wide plates, cover well with plastic wrap, and refrigerate.

COURGETTES STUFFED WITH RATATOUILLE

The ratatouille here, unorthodox with its dashes of lemon and wine, is cut to a small scale that suits its use.

RATATOUILLE
olive oil
175 g (6 oz) onion, peeled and diced
225 g (8 oz) small courgettes,
   quartered and thinly sliced
1 small aubergine, diced
1 small red pepper, seeded and diced
1 small green pepper, seeded and diced
3 large cloves garlic, peeled and minced
350 g (12 oz) tomatoes, peeled, seeded
   and chopped
dry white wine
lemon juice
granulated sugar
salt
sprig fresh thyme
1 bay leaf
black pepper

COURGETTES
8 slim courgettes, about 13 cm
   (5 inches) in length
salt

To make ratatouille, cover base of a medium, heavy-bottomed saucepan with a film of olive oil. Add the onion and cook, covered, over low heat until softened.

Add the courgettes, aubergine, peppers, garlic and tomatoes to onions, with a dash of white wine, a dash of lemon juice and a pinch of sugar. Salt well, stir in thyme and bay leaf. Cover the ratatouille and simmer over low heat, stirring frequently, until the vegetables are cooked but neither soft nor mushy. Remove from heat, taste for seasoning, leave to cool and drain.

Take the 8 whole courgettes and boil them in salted, boiling water for 5 minutes; they should be just cooked. Drain, refresh in cold water to cool courgettes completely, dry well in paper towels. Cut ends from each courgette and halve them lengthwise. With a small, sharp knife, cut and scoop away inner flesh, not too close to the skin or each 'boat' will be unable to bear its weight in filling (use the scooped flesh elsewhere).

Drain each half, cut-side down, on paper towels until ready to use. (If preparing courgettes well in advance, keep them whole and refrigerate, covered, until ready to use.)

When ready to serve, slice each courgette half across into thirds and mound a little well-drained ratatouille into each. Makes 48.

Clockwise from top right: Courgettes stuffed with ratatouille, Vegetable kebabs, Cheese and apple turnovers, Mushrooms filled with scrambled eggs, Curried walnuts, Watercress tartlets, Onion rings

Curried walnuts

CURRIED WALNUTS

I discovered this during my travels years ago and still love it. Easy and interesting; effortlessly doubled or tripled in quantity.

---

vegetable oil
75 g (3 oz) walnut halves
$\frac{1}{4}$ teaspoon salt
$\frac{1}{4}$ teaspoon mild Madras curry powder
pinch of paprika

Lightly oil a baking dish and sprinkle on a single layer of walnuts; stir. Bake in a preheated oven at 180°C, 350°F, Gas Mark 4 for about 10 minutes until the nuts just colour. Remove to a large sheet of greaseproof paper, sprinkle with salt, curry powder, and a good pinch of paprika, gather ends of paper into a bag and shake walnuts to coat evenly with curry mixture. Serve warm.

These mouthfuls are likely to be eaten as fast as you can make them.

MUSHROOMS FILLED WITH SCRAMBLED EGGS

This is a sort of informal relation to the watercress tartlets on page 13.

---

350 g (12 oz) small, firm button
    mushrooms, very white
juice of 1 lemon
salt
3 eggs
black pepper
15 g ($\frac{1}{2}$ oz) butter
single cream
fresh chives, chopped

Carefully cut entire stem from each mushroom (use stems elsewhere); thoroughly wash and drain. Put into a heavy saucepan with lemon juice and a good pinch of salt, cover pan, and heat mushrooms over a fairly high heat. Stir carefully once or twice until just done. They will cook quite rapidly and give off a lot of liquid.

Put the mushrooms to drain thoroughly in a colander, then arrange them, stem side upward, across a work surface (use mushroom stock in soup).

To scramble eggs, whisk them well with salt and pepper, melt butter in a small, heavy saucepan. Add the eggs while pan is still quite cool, and over low heat, use a wooden spoon to stir eggs rhythmically, scraping them constantly from the pan's base, until soft, creamy curds are formed. Beat in a dash of cream to stop the cooking, taste for seasoning, and with a small spoon, fill centre of each mushroom with a little of the mixture. Transfer the mushrooms to a serving platter, sprinkle the egg with the chives, and serve immediately.

CHEESE AND APPLE TURNOVERS

I often make small turnovers of cheese pastry, around a variety of sweet and savoury fillings.

PASTRY
400 g (14 oz) plain flour
pinch of salt
275 g (10 oz) unsalted butter, chilled
    and diced
275 g (10 oz) mature Cheddar cheese
2 eggs

FILLING
1 large, firm eating apple, quartered,
    peeled and cored
mixed spice
about 400 g (14 oz) Mozzarella or
    Cheshire cheese
2 egg yolks

To make the pastry, sift the flour with the salt and rub in the butter; grate in the Cheddar cheese. Whisk the eggs together and add enough to bind the pastry without making it wet. Wrap in greaseproof paper and a polythene bag and refrigerate for 6–8 hours.

Remove pastry from refrigerator

about 30 minutes before use, roll it into 2–3 rounds about 3 mm ($\frac{1}{8}$ inch) thick and cut into circles about 6 cm (2$\frac{1}{2}$ inches) in diameter.

Slice the apple into short slivers, and dust lightly but uniformly with mixed spice. Shave the Mozzarella or Cheshire cheese into thin pieces. Mound some cheese and 1 slice of apple slightly off-centre of each pastry round, brush borders with a little of the egg yolks beaten in a dash of water, fold pastry over to make a compact turnover, pressing edges together with the tines of a fork. Trim borders, knock them up with the back of a knife, and brush tops with the egg wash. Transfer to heavy baking sheets.

Re-roll the pastry off-cuts and use all the dough. It softens quickly, so don't let it get too warm as you work. Refrigerate turnovers for 4–5 hours or overnight, lightly covered with foil.

Bake in a preheated oven at 190°C, 375°F, Gas Mark 5 for about 20 minutes until the pastry has turned a rich light-golden colour. Serve hot. Makes 30–40.

VEGETABLE KEBABS

No cocktail sticks or travelling dips in this dish; the 'skewer' is edible and the cheese is ready-spread.

---

very fresh, straight, and fairly thick
   carrots, peeled
cucumber
radishes
Boursin cheese: garlic and herb

Slice away ends of carrots to give about 13 cm (5 inch) length. Cut each length into slim, firm sticks, tapering in one direction.

Cut green skin from cucumber and cut skin into medallion-like shapes. Slice cucumber across into 3 mm ($\frac{1}{8}$ inch) circles; put these together in pairs and trim edges to neaten. Slice radishes through centre into thin rounds.

Use a metal skewer to pierce centres of a pair of cucumber slices; thread one of these on to the tapered end of a carrot stick, spread Boursin on to the other slice and push it carefully along carrot to make a sandwich with the first piece. Proceed in the same way with Boursin and 2 circles of radish; clean excess cheese from the stick, pierce a hole in the centre of a medallion of cucumber skin and thread this on to the carrot.

Proceed with more kebabs until you reckon you've had enough; they *are* rather fiddly to do, but a great surprise and very tasty. Cover the kebabs with cling film until ready to serve. Don't make them too far in advance.

WATERCRESS TARTLETS

For maximum flavour, use very fresh watercress and serve tartlets shortly after baking. The pastry is a variation on Simone Beck's *pâte à croustade*.

PATE A CROUSTADE
275 g (10 oz) plain flour
large pinch of salt
150 g (5 oz) unsalted butter, chilled
   and cut into 25 g (1 oz) squares
1 egg, beaten with 2 teaspoons water

FILLING
75 g (3 oz) Gruyère cheese
2 bunches fresh watercress
2 eggs
4 tablespoons cream
salt
black pepper

Make pastry in a food processor fitted with its steel blade or in the traditional way. Put flour and salt into the bowl and blend briefly. Add butter squares to bowl and blend, until the consistency of coarse crumbs is reached. Pour in egg and water and blend. If a food processor is being used the pastry will mass together after about 10 seconds. Turn pastry out on to a floured board and work deftly

Watercress tartlets

into a slightly moist ball. Wrap in greaseproof paper and a plastic bag and refrigerate for several hours or overnight.

Bring pastry to room temperature, roll out thinly and line tartlet moulds, round, square or boat-shaped – of either 3 cm, 3.5 cm or 6 cm (1$\frac{1}{4}$/1$\frac{1}{2}$/2$\frac{1}{2}$ inches) across. Use as many moulds as you have in the first baking, then repeat the process until you achieve the right number of shells. Refrigerate on heavy baking sheets for half an hour.

Line each pastry-covered mould with a square of foil pressed well down. Bake in a preheated oven at 165°C, 325°F, Gas Mark 3 for 15–20 minutes until the pastry has set and is just beginning to colour. Cool the shells slightly before removing them from the moulds.

When ready to finish the tarts for serving, return the shells to the baking sheets. Shave tiny slices from the Gruyère, mince watercress leaves, beat together the eggs and cream and season well. Put a shaving of Gruyère into the bottom of each shell, cover with water-cress, and very carefully spoon on the egg and cream mixture.

Bake the filled tartlets for 10–15 minutes at 190°C, 375°F, Gas Mark 5 until the tops puff and colour attractive-ly. Serve warm. Makes 50–60.

SALADES FOLLES

With salads served as a main course, you can go slightly mad, as in salades folles, letting your imagination take over. There are a few rules for improvisation: ingredients should harmonise through the careful use of contrasting textures and striking colours, and not too much should be piled on the plate. In all other ways, though, let imagination be your guide. Here are some suggestions, with possibilities for several seasons.

MEDITERRANEAN SALAD

The Middle Eastern *baba ghanoush*, made with tahini (sesame paste) and grilled aubergine, and the provençal *tapenade* of black olives and anchovies have an alluring southern pungency. Belgian chicory and the leaves of red chicory are used to hold servings of each of these, to be scooped out and spread on toast.

TAPENADE
175 g (6 oz) small black olives, stoned
9 anchovy fillets
1 tablespoon capers, drained of their
 vinegar
¼ teaspoon mustard powder
2 tablespoons lemon juice
1¼ tablespoons cognac
olive oil
black pepper

BABA GHANOUSH
1 large or 2 medium-sized aubergines
2–3 large cloves garlic
50–75 g (2–3 oz) tahini (available
 from specialist grocers)
juice of 1¼ lemons
ground cumin
salt
black pepper

TO FINISH
1 head Belgian chicory
1 head red chicory
French bread
black olives, to garnish

To make the *tapenade*, put the first six ingredients into a blender or the bowl of a food processor fitted with a steel blade. Blend to a purée and pour in enough olive oil to make a smooth, shiny paste, probably about 50 ml (2 fl oz). Grind in pepper, blend again. The *tapenade* can be stored in the refrigerator under a thin film of olive oil and cling film for weeks. Bring to room temperature and stir well before serving.

For the *baba ghanoush*, roast whole aubergine(s) under a medium grill, turning as the skin blisters and blackens all over. The flesh will soften. Allow to cool until the aubergine can be handled, lift off skin and wash flesh. Squeeze out its bitter juice, chop coarsely, and put into blender or food processor. Crush garlic cloves with the blade of a heavy knife and the aid of a little salt, add two to the aubergine, and blend. Add 50 g (2 oz) tahini, blend, add half the lemon juice, a pinch of cumin, salt and pepper. Taste and decide whether to add a third clove of garlic, more tahini, lemon juice, and cumin. Correct seasoning. The result should have a voluptuous, smoky flavour. Put into a small bowl, cover with cling film, and allow flavour to develop for one or two days in the fridge. Bring to room temperature and stir before serving.

To present, trim, wash and dry both sets of chicory leaves of appropriate size. Scoop *baba ghanoush* into red leaves and *tapenade* into pairs of Belgian chicory. Arrange leaves alternately on plates, slice French bread thinly, halve slices, and toast. Add toast to plates, garnish with black olives, and serve. Spread these creams on the toast – the *tapenade* quite thinly, as it's powerfully-flavoured and salty – then eat the leaves. Serves 2.

FIGS AND GOATS' CHEESE

As fit for a sweet-and-savoury summer's dessert as for a one-course lunch.

1 round of fresh goats' cheese; if this
 cannot be obtained, substitute a
 crumbly farmhouse Lancashire,
 Wensleydale, or White Stilton
6 ripe figs
1 fresh lime
3–4 strawberries
fresh tarragon
caster sugar

Cut round of goats' cheese into two semi-circles, slice each semi-circle thinly and arrange four or five slices overlapping down the centre of each plate.

Cut stems from figs and slice figs into quarters; arrange slices either side of cheese. Cut wedges of lime and add two to each plate; cut stems from strawberries, halve, and put beneath cheese.

Scissor tarragon leaves, sprinkle along cheese, and serve. Squeeze lime, sprinkle caster sugar, and combine flavours of strawberry, fig and cheese. Serves 2.

Clockwise from top: Zest of chicken salad, Noughts and crosses, Mediterranean salad, Brains and beauty, Figs and goats' cheese, Fusilli and red pepper salad

Fusilli and red pepper salad

cheese, but if these are too hot you will end up with a stringy mess and have to dice the cheese all over again!

Remove pasta to a bowl, add tomato and garlic, scissor on cress, and toss.

Divide the mixture between two plates, leaving enough space for two lines of red pepper strips along each, as shown. Cut up the chicken livers and distribute over salads. Grind on pepper and serve. Serves 2.

ZEST OF CHICKEN SALAD

Roast chicken is well-steeped here in a wonderfully piquant Italian sauce.

*1 roasting chicken 1.5–1.75 kg
   (3½–4 lb) oven-ready weight*
butter
dried tarragon
2 sweet red peppers
*350 ml (12 fl oz) homemade chicken
   stock (see page 100)*
16 anchovy fillets
*2 large cloves garlic, peeled and
   chopped*
1 tablespoon wine vinegar
3 tablespoons peanut oil
salt
black pepper
interesting salad leaves
cherry tomatoes or walnuts

Truss chicken, smear inside and out with butter and tarragon. Roast in a preheated oven at 190°C, 375°F, Gas Mark 5, turning and basting frequently, until done (about 80 minutes).

Meanwhile, prepare the sauce. Roast whole peppers under a medium grill, turning as the skins blister and blacken all over. Cool under wet paper towels to trap steam which will help loosen skins. Peel off all skin, cut peppers open and remove core and seeds. Cut up peppers and put into a blender or the bowl of a food processor. Add chicken stock, anchovy fillets and garlic and purée all to the consistency of a thickish sauce.

FUSILLI AND RED PEPPER SALAD

1 large sweet red pepper
175 g (6 oz) Mozzarella cheese
salt
olive oil
225 g (8 oz) fusilli (corkscrew pasta)
vegetable oil
black pepper
3 fresh chicken livers, never frozen
*3 small tomatoes, peeled, seeded and
   chopped*
*1 large clove garlic, peeled and finely
   chopped*
small handful of fresh mustard cress

Grill and peel red pepper as in recipe for Zest of Chicken Salad. Slice into strips. Cut Mozzarella into tiny cubes. Bring a large saucepan of water to the boil, add salt and olive oil, boil pasta until *al dente* or just cooked.

While pasta is boiling, heat a thin film of vegetable oil in a small sauté pan, season cleaned chicken livers and toss in pan over a high heat for about 2–3 minutes until just pink inside. Remove from pan to cool.

When pasta is ready, drain thoroughly, return to saucepan, season liberally and toss pasta in a tablespoon of olive oil. Let cool for about 2 minutes and then toss with the diced mozzarella. The heat of the pan and pasta will slightly melt

When chicken is roasted and partly cooled, skin and shred the flesh from half of it (use the other half for something else). Put shredded flesh into a bowl and pour in enough sauce to coat chicken liberally. Refrigerate overnight, turning chicken in sauce occasionally.

To serve, make a vinaigrette with the vinegar, oil, salt and pepper. Wash and dry whatever leaves you like; turn in vinaigrette and shake off excess so that leaves are barely coated, and arrange them in an attractive pattern around each plate. Pile shredded chicken in the centre, add a little freshly-ground black pepper to the remaining red pepper sauce, and spoon a bit over the chicken. Top with cherry tomatoes or with walnuts. Pass extra sauce at the table. Serves 2.

NOUGHTS AND CROSSES

Smoked fish, avocado, wild mushrooms, and a crisp greenery are a persuasive mixture.

50 g (2 oz) slim French beans (ie, 24 perfect specimens), topped and tailed
50 g (2 oz) smoked sprat, smoked eel or smoked herring fillets
1 ripe avocado
juice of 1 lemon
225 g (8 oz) wild mushrooms; oyster mushrooms, chanterelles or caps
vegetable oil
1 large clove garlic, peeled and finely chopped
elderflower, tarragon, or sherry vinegar
salt
black pepper
1 tablespoon dry white wine
3 tablespoons peanut oil
a mixture of interesting leaves

Bring a saucepan of salted water to the boil and parboil French beans for 2–3 minutes, until just tender. Refresh in cold running water to stop cooking and set colour. Drain and dry in paper towels.

Slice fillets of smoked fish into strips.

Cut avocado in half, remove stone, peel one half and hold it in a bowl of cold water laced with half the lemon juice.

Wash, drain, and cut up wild mushrooms, not too small since they shrink a lot in cooking. Heat vegetable oil in a pan, add mushrooms, and sauté over fairly high heat for several minutes. When cooked, add the chopped garlic and a good splash of flavoured vinegar to the pan, add salt and pepper and remove mushrooms from pan to cool.

Make a vinaigrette with the white wine, peanut oil, salt and pepper. Wash and dry leaves. Turn leaves, beans and fish in the vinaigrette.

Arrange 12 beans and 6 strips of smoked fish in a criss-cross pattern, as shown, down the centre of each plate. Pile the garlicky mushrooms either side of centre cross, and arrange leaves in the four 'corners'. Remove avocado-half from water and lemon, slice thinly, turn in the remaining lemon juice and put slices to flank the mushrooms. Grind black pepper over and serve. Serves 2.

Zest of chicken salad

Noughts and crosses

BRAINS AND BEAUTY

2 sets calf's brains, or 3–4 sets lamb's
  brains, depending on appetites
4 tablespoons wine vinegar
1 onion, peeled and sliced
1 carrot, peeled and sliced
1 large garlic clove, unpeeled
1 bay leaf
salt
3 peppercorns
10 slim asparagus spears
4 large, thick carrots
firm-textured bread, slightly stale
about 40 g (1½ oz) butter
vegetable oil
3 tablespoons olive oil
black pepper
1¼ teaspoons mild Madras curry
  powder
75 g (3 oz) mayonnaise
2–3 tablespoons double cream
juice of 1 lemon
2 cup-shaped salad leaves

Brains and beauty

Soak brains for 1–2 hours in cold water and 1 tablespoon of wine vinegar; this will loosen the membrane of blood vessels in which each is encased.

While brains soak, fill a large saucepan with water, add onion and carrot, garlic, bay leaf, and a large pinch of salt. Boil for 15 minutes to make a court-bouillon.

After brains have soaked, carefully lift away their membranes. Wash off blood thoroughly and add peppercorns and 2 tablespoons of wine vinegar to the court-bouillon. Return it to the simmer. Gently slide brains into the liquid.

Simmer 10–15 minutes; test by inserting a skewer into centre of one brain, apply skewer to back of hand and if hot the brains are done. Transfer the brains and the court-bouillon to a bowl and let them cool in the cooking liquid.

Wash asparagus, cut off tough ends of stems, and with a swivel peeler, scrape off thick skin. Tie stalks in a bundle with string and bring a large pan of salted water to the boil. Simmer asparagus about 6 minutes or till they test done; drain, and refresh under cold water.

Quarter the 4 large carrots and carve into 16 small elongated olive shapes; wash and boil in salted water for about 3 minutes, until just cooked but still slightly crisp. Drain the carrots, refresh, dry and if necessary, chill them covered, until used.

Make croûtons by cutting thin slices of bread, then cut slices into thin fingers and cut fingers into tiny cubes. You will need 30–40 of these. Put butter and a little oil into a small sauté pan, melt butter over low heat, add cubes, and fry gently, tossing often, until croûtons become pale golden-brown. Remove from pan and cool.

Make a vinaigrette with 1 tablespoon of vinegar, olive oil, salt and pepper. Beat curry powder, salt, and pepper into mayonnaise, stir in double cream to taste and a few drops lemon juice to sharpen.

To assemble salads, halve asparagus spears lengthwise, turn in vinaigrette and shake off excess, place seven of the most perfect halves, trimmed to fit, in a circle radiating from the centre of each plate. Remove brains from court-bouillon, slice crosswise thinly and trim away any ragged edges. Turn the brains in lemon juice to keep white, shake off excess, and arrange the slices between asparagus spears.

Fill two cup-shaped salad leaves – I've used red chicory – with generous measures of curried mayonnaise and place in the centre of each circle; slip seven of the best carrot olives underneath each. Toss on croûtons and serve, dipping the various elements into mayonnaise as you eat. Serves 2.

GARLIC, STRONG AND SUBTLE

There is little I need say to introduce garlic, except that for devotees like me, a long plait of the season's bulbs is essential kitchen 'equipment'. In these recipes, garlic is variously used as a strong or elusive seasoning, as the significant ingredient of a soufflé, and finally, for true fanatics, as a highly desirable end in itself.

CAESAR SALAD

For this well-known Californian salad, the cloves are infused in olive oil, which is later drained and poured over croûtons and lettuce. The effect is subtle.

2 large cloves garlic, peeled and sliced
120 ml (4 fl oz) olive oil
day-old French bread
1 large head cos lettuce
6 anchovy fillets
½ teaspoon salt
generous grindings of black pepper
¼ teaspoon dry mustard
2 tablespoons wine vinegar
1 egg
3 tablespoons grated Parmesan cheese

Steep garlic for 24 hours in olive oil.

An hour or so before making salad, slice bread, minus crust, into enough cubes to make up 50 g (2 oz) croûtons; dry these in an oven preheated to 150°C, 300°F, Gas Mark 2 for 20–30 minutes or until turning golden-brown. Dribble hot croûtons with 2 tablespoons of the garlic oil.

Discard the ragged outer leaves of cos lettuce, tear the remainder across into manageable pieces, wash thoroughly, dry, and place the leaves in a salad bowl.

Drain anchovy fillets of their oil and chop finely.

Bring 7.5 cm (3 inch) depth of water to the boil in a small saucepan; in the meantime, scatter lettuce with salt, pepper, and mustard, spoon on vinegar and remaining olive oil, drained of garlic.

As the water boils, remove from the heat and lower in the egg. Cover pan and leave for 1 minute. Drain egg, run under cold water and break it over the salad, tossing leaves once more. Strew with croûtons, anchovy and Parmesan, toss briefly and eat. Serves 4 as a light lunch with good bread and a cool wine.

GARLIC SOUFFLE

Alice Waters' famous garlic soufflé from her *Chez Panisse Menu Cookbook* (Chatto & Windus), has a roux and cream base, and though delicious, is extremely rich. I've worked out a version based on puréed cauliflower as support for the garlic. The result is buoyant while the flavour of the cauliflower is recessive.

1½ large bulbs garlic
olive oil
thyme
1 bay leaf
salt
black pepper
75 g (3 oz) cauliflower florets
15 g (½ oz) butter
2 egg yolks
75–100 g (3–4 oz) Gruyère cheese, grated
25 g (1 oz) Parmesan cheese, grated
4 egg whites

Peel outer skin from garlic bulbs and break up into cloves, leaving these unpeeled. Put cloves into a small heavy saucepan, add water to cover, a dash of olive oil, a large pinch of thyme, a bay leaf, a grind each of salt and pepper. Cover the pan, bring water to simmer, and poach the garlic for about 15 minutes, or until the cloves test tender when pierced by a trussing needle.

Meanwhile, boil the cauliflower in salted water for 3–5 minutes or until cooked. Drain and cool slightly then purée in a food processor until smooth. Season, then dry out in 15 g (½ oz) butter by stirring for several minutes over a low heat. Transfer to a medium bowl.

When garlic is ready, drain well; as soon as you can handle it, peel off skins, cut away any brown ends and push the soft innards through a sieve into same bowl as the cauliflower. The garlic will have lost most of its fire and become quite mellow.

Butter and lightly flour a 25 cm (10 inch) gratin dish.

Add egg yolks to the garlic base, season well and beat thoroughly. Mix the cheeses and have them to hand. Whisk the egg whites to peaks. Stir a third of these into the garlic and yolks, pour back on to remaining whites and swiftly fold all together, incorporating the cheese as you go. Turn into gratin dish, spread the mixture smooth and bake on the top shelf of a preheated oven at 220°C, 425°F, Gas Mark 7 for 15 minutes until soufflé has risen and its top has browned. The interior will remain a soft contrast to the darkened crust. Eat immediately as the soufflé quickly deflates. Serves 2.

*Clockwise from top right: Grilled fish and Calabazines rellenos, Garlic soufflé, Baked garlic,
Cassoulet, Caesar salad*

CASSOULET WITH GREEN LENTILS

This is a classic, wintery dish from the southwest of France, made shockingly unorthodox to a native of Toulouse, Carcassonne, or Castelnaudary by the use of dark green Puy lentils, whose smoky flavour I prefer to the traditional haricot beans. *Lentilles du Puy* hold their shape much better than red or yellow types and, like preserved goose, can be found in speciality food shops or brought back from a trip to France. If you can't get goose, increase the weight of lamb and sausage.

450 g (1 lb) lamb shoulder, boned weight
450 g (1 lb) Puy lentils
small bouquet of parsley and 2 bay leaves
4 tomatoes, quartered and seeded
medium onion, peeled and stuck with 2 cloves
450 g (1 lb) Toulouse sausages (coarse-cut, pure pork)
freshly made breadcrumbs
100 g (4 oz) salt pork or fat bacon
3 large cloves garlic
1 canned thigh of preserved goose (confit d'oie)
salt
black pepper

Cassoulet with green lentils

Roast the lamb in a preheated oven at 160°C, 325°F, Gas Mark 3 for 25 minutes. Wash and drain lentils, place in a large, flameproof casserole, cover with 1.5 litres (2½ pints) water and bring slowly to boil. Remove from heat and stir in bouquet, tomatoes, and onion, lay on sausages. Cover casserole and bake in an oven preheated to 145°C, 290°F, Gas Mark 1 for 1 hour, removing sausages after 40 minutes; prick these in several places to release fat, and allow to cool completely.

Meanwhile, make breadcrumbs (I usually use about half a granary cob, minus crusts), slice lamb into 1 cm (½ inch) cubes, remove rind from the pork or bacon and cut flesh into dice. Sliver the cloves of garlic. Take the goose from its tin, scrape off fat (save this), and chop the thigh, with skin and bone intact, into small sections. Skin and slice sausages.

Remove casserole from the oven, drain the lentils, and reserve their liquid. Discard herbs and onion, press the tomatoes' flesh through a sieve into the lentil stock.

Clean the same casserole or take up another large one, and spread half the lentils over the base. Season well, add all of the meats, intermingled with garlic, season again and cover with remaining pulses. Moisten with 250 ml (8 fl oz) of the reserved liquid. Put on a good layer of breadcrumbs and dot these with some of the reserved goose fat (or a little olive oil if not using *confit d'oie*). Bake, uncovered, at 150°C, 300°F, Gas Mark 2 for 2 hours. Twice during cooking, stir the crust, as it forms, into the lentils, moistening with reserved stock, adding a layer of breadcrumbs and dotting with more goose fat at each time. Any fat which remains from the *confit d'oie* is excellent for making sautéed potatoes.

Eat bubbling hot and serve copiously for a weekend lunch, accompanied or followed by a green salad. Serves 6–8.

CALABAZINES RELLENOS

Otherwise known as stuffed courgettes, this Gibraltarian recipe is of Genoese origin. The traditional cheese ingredient has been Spanish ewes' milk *queso*, when available; hard goats' cheese, though, is a good alternative. I've added a tomato and cucumber sauce.

COURGETTES

8 medium courgettes, each 15–18 cm
    (6–7 inches) long
olive oil
3 large cloves garlic, peeled and minced
salt
black pepper
1 teacup fresh breadcrumbs
milk
1 egg
small handful fresh chopped parsley
grated goats' cheese
pinch of dried oregano

TOMATO AND CUCUMBER
SAUCE

225 g (8 oz) cucumber flesh, skinned
    and seeded weight
salt
15 g ($\frac{1}{2}$ oz) butter
2 cloves garlic, peeled and minced
350 g (12 oz) canned Italian plum
    tomatoes, weight without juices
salt
black pepper

Grilled fish and Calabazines rellenos

Boil washed, unpeeled courgettes in simmering, salted water for 5 minutes; make sure you have enough water to cover the courgettes completely. Drain, refresh and dry. Cut away most of each stem, halve courgettes lengthwise, and carefully cut and scoop out flesh of the six best pairs, being careful not to tear shells. Invert shells on to paper towels to drain off excess moisture.

Finely chop the remaining halved pairs (minus stems) and the scooped courgette flesh, put into a sieve, and squeeze away as much moisture as possible. Heat a splash of olive oil in a medium sauté pan and sauté the courgette, with the minced garlic and seasoning, for about 5 minutes. Cool in a bowl.

Reserve a tablespoon or so of the breadcrumbs, and soak the rest for several minutes in a little milk. Squeeze, and add most of these to the courgette and garlic. Beat in the egg and parsley, grate in the goats' cheese to taste (it should be quite strong), season with oregano, salt, and pepper, and judge whether to add remaining breadcrumbs. The mixture should be moist but not wet, and quite savoury.

Dry the shells inside and out with paper towels and fill with mounded stuffing mixture. Place the shells in a large, lightly-oiled baking dish with low sides. Strew tops with reserved breadcrumbs and dribble with a little olive oil.

Bake in a preheated oven at 220°C, 425°F, Gas Mark 7 for 20–30 minutes until the tops of the shells are browning. Serve with spoonfuls of sauce made as follows.

Take cucumber flesh, chop coarsely, salt lightly and drain in a sieve for 1 hour to expel moisture.

Wash the cucumber, dry in paper towels and sauté in butter until half-cooked. Stir minced garlic into the cucumber, and after several minutes, add the tomatoes and break up with a wooden spoon. Simmer the sauce uncovered, until most of liquid has evaporated. Cool the mixture slightly and purée in the food processor, not so thoroughly as to lose all trace of the cucumber's texture. Season and reheat the sauce. Serves 4–6 as a vegetable.

GRILLED FISH WITH SWEET PEPPERS AND GARLIC-CHILI MAYONNAISE

The contrasts of texture and temperature are good here: freshly grilled fish, just-sautéed garlicky peppers, pungent mayonnaise. As an alternative to red mullet, which is delectable but can be hard to come by, try sea bass or bream.

MAYONNAISE
2 fresh chili peppers, plump if possible
2 large cloves garlic, peeled
salt
1 egg
1 tablespoon lemon juice
olive oil

FISH
6 × 175 g (6 oz) red mullet
salt
black pepper
olive oil

PEPPER GARNISH
2 medium-sized sweet peppers, 1 red,
*   1 yellow; halved, seeded, sliced*
1 large clove garlic, peeled and minced
olive oil
salt
black pepper

Grill chilis until skins loosen and char; cool. Take the garlic cloves and break them down to a paste on a board with the aid of salt and a heavy knife blade.

Wearing rubber gloves if you think that the oil of the chilis will burn your fingers, skin, seed and slice them. Put one of these peppers with garlic into a food processor, steel blade in place.

Add egg, process for 30 seconds, add lemon juice, process for 10 seconds, and through top opening, slowly pour in olive oil, blending at high speed, until mayonnaise becomes creamily thick. Taste, and judge whether to blend in part of the second chili; mayonnaise should taste rather fiery but not aflame. Salt, if need be, and set aside.

Scale, gut and de-fin the red mullet, preserving the livers if you like them. Wash, dry, season, and oil mullet all over.

Thoroughly pre-heat grill and grill mullet, 5 minutes per side, under high flame. Meanwhile, sauté sweet peppers and minced garlic in a splash of oil across one or two wide pans until just tender. Season.

Serve 1 mullet per person, flanked by the sweet peppers and a good spoonful of garlic-chili mayonnaise. Serves 6 as a first course.

BAKED GARLIC

The apotheosis. I think nothing quite equals cloves of tender garlic – cooked more slowly than in the Garlic Soufflé (see page 19) squeezed on to buttered toast and well-seasoned.

1 bulb of garlic, with sizeable cloves,
*   per person*
salt
olive oil
butter
wholemeal or granary bread
black pepper

Carefully peel outer skin from each bulb, leaving cloves attached to base with skins intact. Put heads base down in a baking dish with salt and a dribble of oil. Bake, uncovered, in a preheated oven at 150°C, 300°F, Gas Mark 2 for 30 minutes.

Baste garlic, add water just to coat the bottom of dish, cover with lid, and bake for a further 45–60 minutes, or until cloves are soft.

Serve a bulb to each person, with plenty of hot, buttered toast; squeeze the contents of each clove on to toast, spread, and grind on pepper.

Baked garlic

TERRINE TECTONICS

These are six terrines, in the widest sense. Each has been moulded into an earthenware dish or terrine, or a metal equivalent, and all but two have some connection with meat and poultry. The tomato jellies and pear *bavarois* are also included here because of their use of gelatine.

TERRINE OF SWEETBREAD WITH WATERCRESS SAUCE

This is pale and elegant, a sweetbread surrounded by a forcemeat of veal and calf's brains, flavoured with tarragon and served with a watercress sauce.

TERRINE
*275–350 g (10–12 oz) pork back fat,
    cut into thin sheets by your butcher*
*1 'heart' sweetbread of about 300 g
    (11 oz)*
a set of calf's brains
salt
lemon juice
75 ml (3 oz) dry white wine
¼ teaspoon dried tarragon
*750 g (1½ lb) braising veal, from
    shoulder*
1 egg, beaten
black pepper
butter
*6–7 large leaves from a round-heart
    lettuce*
75 g (3 oz) pork back fat
fresh parsley, chopped

SAUCE
2 bunches fresh watercress
soured cream
salt
black pepper

Line the base and sides of a 1.5 litre (2½ pint) terrine (I use a rather wide bread tin) with a single layer of back fat in sheets, leaving some for the top.

Soak sweetbread and brains in several changes of cold water for 2 hours, to draw out blood. Rinse very well after soaking.

Put sweetbread into a pan, cover with fresh water, add salt and a dash of lemon juice, bring to boil and simmer for 5 minutes. Remove sweetbread with slotted spoon, refresh and dry it, peel away fat, tubes, and outer membrane. Place between sheets of paper towels on a board, cover with another board and some heavy tins and weigh down for 2 hours.

Meanwhile, peel as much membrane as possible from the uncooked brains, simmer for 10 minutes in sweetbread's poaching liquid. Drain and cool.

Boil together wine and tarragon until reduced to 2 tablespoons. The flavour of the tarragon becomes pronounced.

Remove excess nerve and connective tissue from veal shoulder, cut into cubes, put these into the bowl of food processor with brains and process until smooth. Add cooled wine and beaten egg, mix and season well. Fry a little of this forcemeat in butter, and when cold, taste for seasoning; adjust salt and pepper if necessary.

Blanch, refresh and dry lettuce leaves, cut the 75 g (3 oz) of back fat into lardons 7.5–10 cm (3–4 inches) long by 5 mm (¼ inch) thick. Roll lardons in chopped parsley.

Dry sweetbread, slice into 4–5 pieces, season these and wrap each in lettuce. Press forcemeat to fill a third of the terrine, lacing with half the lardons.

Lay the sweetbread down the centre. Cover the sides and top with the remaining forcemeat, interspersed with the rest of the lardons. Smooth the surface repeatedly with a wet hand, tap the container on a work surface to settle the contents, lay the top with a sheet or two of back fat.

Cover the terrine with a double thickness of foil, place in a bain-marie. Bake in a preheated oven at 180°C, 350°F, Gas Mark 4 for about 2 hours, turning around once, until contents test hot through middle.

When terrine is done, remove from bain-marie and cover foiled top with a board or brick that fits into rim. Weight this, and when filling is cold, remove all but foil and refrigerate terrine in its tin, well-wrapped, for 4–5 days to mature flavours.

When planning to eat, prepare sauce by puréeing watercress leaves in food processor. Stir in soured cream to make a fairly loose consistency and season.

Cut terrine carefully, serve 1 slice per person, with an exotic leaf and some sauce. Serves 6–8.

Clockwise from top right: Chicken liver pâté with calvados, Tomato jellies and coriander sauce, Terrine of guinea-fowl, Terrine of sweetbread with watercress sauce, Pear and caramel bavarois with pear sauce, Pâté de porc en brioche

CHICKEN LIVER PATE WITH CALVADOS

Calvados and apple are the intriguing dimension to this delectable 'pâté', based on an invention of the late Michael Field. It was one of the first 'grown-up' things I learned to make, and remains top of my preferred list.

450 g (1 lb) fresh chicken livers, never frozen
salt
black pepper
215 g (7¼ oz) unsalted butter, softened
50 g (2 oz) onion, peeled and finely chopped
1 large shallot, peeled and finely chopped
50 g (2 oz) apple, cored, peeled and chopped
50 ml (2 oz) Calvados
2–4 tablespoons double cream
1 teaspoon lemon juice
clarified butter, to seal (see method)

Clean livers, cut away connective tissue and any discoloured parts, dry. Cut each liver in half. Season with salt and pepper. Melt 25 g (1 oz) butter in a large sauté pan, add onion and shallot and sweat over low heat, stirring occasionally, until soft and lightly coloured. Stir in apple, cook until easily mashed with back of a spoon. Transfer all to a food processor fitted with a steel blade.

Clean the pan, melt 40 g (1½ oz) butter, and as foam from butter subsides, throw in livers. Toss for about 3 minutes over high heat until browned but still pink inside. Meanwhile warm calvados and when livers are done, remove these from the heat, set spirit alight and pour it, flaming, a little at a time on to livers, shaking sauté pan until flames have died. Add the livers and calvados to the apple and onion.

Moisten with 2 tablespoons of cream and blend at high speed, adding rest of cream if mixture seems too thick. Process until very smooth. Rub resulting paste

through a sieve, cool and return to processor. Add remaining softened butter. Blend completely, add lemon juice, salt and pepper to taste (remember that chilling will blunt flavour). Put mixture into a terrine of 750–900 ml (1¼-1½ pints) capacity, smooth top, refrigerate till firm, and seal as follows. Melt 100 g (4 oz) butter, spoon away foam and run the clear yellow liquid beneath (free of its milky solids) over the pâté. Refrigerate until set and allow to mature for 4–5 days before scooping out to eat with toast. Serves 6–8.

TERRINE OF GUINEA-FOWL

If you like game terrines, a good way to enjoy one out of season is to use guinea-fowl, which are now bred on farms, available the year round, and classed as poultry. The effect here is highly-flavoured, with some truffle as an added flourish.

1 guinea-fowl, about 1 kg (2 lb), dressed weight
port
cognac
1 whole truffle, not too small
750 g (1½ lb) belly pork, weighed without rind or bone
100 g (4 oz) green streaky bacon, without rind
¼ tablespoon coarse salt
8 black peppercorns
5 juniper berries
2 large cloves garlic, peeled and chopped
1 egg, beaten
enough green, streaky, rindless bacon to line and cover a 1.25 litre (2¼ pint) terrine
butter
1 bay leaf
lard

Roast the guinea-fowl in a preheated oven at 200°C, 400°F, Gas Mark 6 for 10

minutes; cool. This will aid skinning.

Skin carcass and cut breast meat into enough thin strips to make up two layers in a 1.25 litre (2¼ pint) terrine. Put these to marinate with 1½ tablespoons each port and cognac. Pare the truffle (reserve parings), cut into batons and add these to marinade. Refrigerate overnight, turning occasionally.

Pull remaining fowl from bones, de-nerve it and chop flesh by hand, not too finely. Cut excess nerve and connective tissue from pork belly, cut up bacon; mince latter two in food processor to a coarsely-chopped consistency. Combine the three meats in a bowl.

Meanwhile, make a stock with the stripped carcass, skin, and giblets (minus liver) of the guinea-fowl by simmering all in lightly-salted water for several hours. Strain the stock and boil to reduce to 85 ml (3 fl oz), then cool.

In a mortar, crush salt, peppercorns, juniper berries, and garlic to a paste, add to the forcemeat with egg, chopped parings from truffle, 1 tablespoon port and 2 tablespoons cognac. When the reduced stock is cold, work this in. Put to mature overnight in refrigerator.

Next day, line the terrine with bacon, drain guinea breast and truffles of their marinade and add the marinade to the forcemeat; make a test for seasoning as in the Terrine of Sweetbread (page 24).

When satisfied, press a third of the forcemeat along the base of the terrine and lay on half the strips of breast and truffle. Cover this with a third of the forcemeat, then the rest of the truffle and breast and finally the remaining forcemeat. Smooth with a wet hand, rap terrine on work surface, put a bay leaf in the middle, and add a slice or two of bacon.

Cover terrine with foil and its lid and bake in a bain-marie at 160°C, 325°F, Gas Mark 3, for 1½-2 hours, turning around once, until the meat tests hot through the centre. When the terrine is done, weight and cool as in Terrine of Sweetbread. Refrigerate overnight. The next morning remove the bay leaf and seal surface with melted lard. Refrigerate for a week to allow the terrine's flavours to mellow. Serve sliced with toast, butter, and gherkins. Serves 6.

TOMATO JELLIES AND CORIANDER SAUCE

These are for vegetarians who will eat gelatine, or for those who want something lighter than the previous recipes. I originally made this as one jelly in a loaf tin with layers of different vegetables; the result collapsed into disaster on slicing. Individual moulds, however, provided a rapid solution.

JELLY
2 × 794 g (1 lb 12 oz) tinned peeled
    Italian plum tomatoes, with their
    juices
1 large onion, peeled and finely
    chopped
2 carrots, peeled and finely chopped
2 large stalks celery, with leaves,
    finely chopped
1 bay leaf
pinch of dried tarragon
2 good pinches of paprika
2 teaspoons granulated sugar
½ teaspoon salt
1 tablespoon red wine vinegar
vegetable oil
1 celeriac, peeled
salt
lemon juice
6 leaves gelatine
black pepper
20 leaves coriander

SAUCE
2 bunches fresh coriander
50 g (2 oz) walnuts
2 tablespoons walnut oil
150–200 g (5–7 oz) natural yogurt
salt
black pepper

Tomato jellies and coriander sauce

In a large saucepan, simmer together all jelly ingredients, up to but excluding oil, for 30 minutes.

Lightly oil 10 × 75 g (3 oz) oval moulds; chill until needed.

Cut the celeriac into 4 cm × 5 mm (1½ × ¼ inch) batons, boil these for a few minutes in salted, acidulated water until cooked through; drain and dry.

Soak gelatine in a jug of water until soft.

Strain all juices from the finished tomato sauce, pressing solids firmly against sieve (use the solids as a soup base); you should have about 1 litre (1¾ pints) of liquid. Drain gelatine and dissolve it completely in this amount. Season to taste.

Cool jelly, stir it well, take off a small quantity and stir this over ice till thickening. Immediately ladle a thin layer into the bottom of each mould and refrigerate. Take 10 handsome leaves of coriander and put one face down into every mould; spoon on more thickened jelly, let set, put a layer of four celeriac batons over the centre of each (later, toss remaining celeriac in hot butter and eat as a vegetable). Finish each mould with two layers of jelly that sandwich another leaf of coriander. Chill until firm; use any spare jelly elsewhere.

Make a sauce by puréeing all but a handful of remaining coriander leaves with walnuts and walnut oil; stir in yogurt to make a fairly loose sauce, add more oil and if need be, season.

To serve jellies, run a blunt knife round the sides of each, dip moulds briefly into hot water and turn out. Present each with a spoonful of sauce and a shoot of coriander. Serves 10.

PATE DE PORC
EN BRIOCHE

This is easy and quite impressive: the centre is quickly made of pork and liver, while the brioche is adapted from Simone Beck's supersonic *jet brioche*.

FILLING
225 g (8 oz) pig's liver, minced
75 g (3 oz) pork back fat, minced
350 g (12 oz) pork fillet, minced
1 large onion, peeled
butter
50 ml (2 fl oz) red wine
2 medium cloves garlic, peeled
salt
25 g (1 oz) fresh breadcrumbs
1–2 tablespoons double cream
fresh dill, chopped
black pepper
75 g (3 oz) piece boiled fresh or pickled
   ox tongue

BRIOCHE
200 g (7 oz) strong plain flour, plus
   extra for kneading
pinch of salt
pinch of sugar
15 g (½ oz) fresh yeast
2 tablespoons tepid milk
90 g (3¼ oz) unsalted butter
2 eggs
vegetable oil
1 egg yolk
home-made aspic jelly (see page 47)
fresh dill

For the filling, ask your butcher to put the first 3 ingredients, separately, through the medium blade of his meat mincer, telling him that each weight required should be the total after grinding.

At home, take a large sauté pan, melt 25 g (1 oz) of the back fat, mince onion and sweat this slowly in fat till soft and colouring. Add pork fillet and stir over a medium heat for several minutes, until greyish; add liver and cook until its red just goes. Remove from heat to a bowl.

Pâté de porc en brioche

Butter a 24 × 14 × 7.5 cm (9½ × 5½ × 3 inch) loaf tin.

Meanwhile, reduce the red wine to a generous tablespoon. Add to the meat with the rest of the back fat, garlic cloves crushed in salt, breadcrumbs, 1–2 tablespoons cream, depending on consistency of mixture (it shouldn't be too loose), lots of fresh dill, salt and pepper. Fry a little of the forcemeat in butter to test flavours; it should be quite savoury.

Cut tongue into lardon-like strips and roll these in chopped dill.

Spoon pork mixture into a rectangle on to foil, lay the tongue strips over it, lengthwise, and form the whole into a sausage shape about an inch shorter than your tin. Wrap 'sausage' and refrigerate.

To make the accelerated brioche, sift together dry ingredients and stir yeast into warmed milk until liquefied. Melt and cool butter and beat with eggs and yeasty milk. Work these well into the flour. Turn the dough, which is soft and sticky, on to a floured board and for 3–4 minutes scrape, knead, and manhandle it, adding more flour, until dough becomes elastic but is still rather yielding and only slightly sticky when it pulls away from your hand.

Form into a ball, lightly oil the top and put into a medium bowl set into a bain-marie whose water is kept at 35°C, 95°F. Cover bowl with a plastic sheet and weight this with a bread board. Leave dough to rise until more than double in bulk (takes 60–90 minutes).

Meanwhile put sausage to firm in the freezer for 30 minutes.

When brioche has risen, deflate it on to a floured board, press it into an even rectangle, unwrap sausage, and place it in the centre. Fold sides of brioche to meet round sausage and firmly pinch the seam. Fold over ends, cutting off excess dough there. Lower brioche into tin, with seam underneath. Make three holes along top, insert a small, rolled piece of cardboard into each as a 'chimney' for steam to escape, and build up a little circle of excess dough round the three cards. Cover all loosely with plastic and let brioche rise, in a warm place, until it fills the pan.

When ready, brush dough with egg yolk beaten in a little water. Bake in the centre of a preheated oven 220°C, 425°F, Gas Mark 7 for 20 minutes, then reduce the oven temperature to 180°C, 350°F, Gas Mark 4 for 35 minutes more. Cool sausage completely in tin, remove 'chimneys' and refrigerate.

To fill the gap between baked, chilled sausage and brioche, melt 300 ml ($\frac{1}{2}$ pint) of aspic jelly; pour this into a bowl set over ice and stir liquid until it starts to thicken. Swiftly remove bowl from ice and spoon the jelly, via a funnel, into each chimney hole, tilting pâté in all directions to spread it evenly, until jelly will go no further. You will probably not use quite all of it. Refrigerate for several hours to set.

Unmould pâté, slice with a bread knife and present with chopped aspic and fronds of dill. Serves 8.

PEAR AND CARAMEL BAVAROIS WITH PEAR SAUCE

Stretch a point and call this dessert a terrine; the smooth caramel contrasts well with the grainy-textured pears and the sauce.

CARAMEL LAYERS
175 g (6 oz) granulated sugar
600 ml (1 pint) milk
5 leaves gelatine
8 egg yolks
85 ml (3 fl oz) double cream

PEAR LAYER
50 g (2 oz) granulated sugar
120 ml (4 fl oz) Sauternes or similar sweet wine
1 firm pear, about 200 g (7 oz), quartered, peeled and cored
2¼ leaves gelatine
1 generous tablespoon eau de vie de poire – or kirsch, if unavailable
6 egg yolks
50 ml (2 fl oz) double cream

SAUCE
1½ tablespoons granulated sugar
85 ml (3 fl oz) Sauternes
3–4 firm pears totalling 500–550 g (18–20 oz), quartered, peeled and cored
eau de vie de poire
lemon juice

Butter a metal loaf tin of 24 × 10 × 7.5 cm (9½ × 4 × 3 inches) and press a piece of greaseproof paper, cut to size, against base. Refrigerate.

Make a caramel with sugar and a little water, bringing it up to a good colour (about 188°C, 370°F). Meanwhile, scald milk, soak gelatine and beat yolks with a hand-held beater until thick.

When caramel is ready, remove from flame; cover hands, pour on a little of the hot milk. The mixture will froth wildly; whisk well, carefully add remainder. Return milky caramel to heat, bring to boil to dissolve any sugar that has stuck to pan.

Beat this into egg yolks. Pour all into milk pan, whisk mixture over a high heat, just bring to first boil, and immediately sieve into a bowl. Drain gelatine and beat this into custard to dissolve it completely.

While custard cools, prepare the pear layer. Melt sugar in the Sauternes in a heavy saucepan. Poach the pear quarters, covered, in the wine-syrup until cooked. Meanwhile, soak the gelatine in water.

Drain pear quarters well, purée in food processor while reducing syrup to

just under 120 ml (4 oz). Add to this the eau de vie de poire and the drained gelatine; whisk to dissolve.

Put egg yolks into a large heatproof bowl, set this above a small pan of simmering water, and beat with electric beater for about a minute. Slowly pour on wine-syrup and continue to whisk until mixture is thick and expanded in volume. Remove bowl from heat and beat the contents till cool. Fold in puréed pear mixture.

By this stage the caramel custard should be cooled but not setting. Stir well, measure off a generous 300 ml ($\frac{1}{2}$ pint), and when this is cold, use a fork to whisk 25 ml (1 fl oz) double cream to the same consistency. Fold the two together and quickly pour this along base of the loaf tin. Refrigerate to set.

Place bowl containing pear mixture inside a larger bowl of ice and water and stir pear constantly until cool. Whisk 50 ml (2 fl oz) cream with a fork to same consistency, fold the two together and pour all but about 150 g (5 oz) of this in an even layer atop the firm custard. Refrigerate again and eat the maverick 150 g (5 oz), on the spot, to keep you going.

When pear layer is firm, remaining caramel custard may have started to set; simply stir it over hot water until completely loosened but not warm. Fold with 50 ml (2 fl oz) whisked cream and fill mould to the top. Refrigerate for at least 4 hours.

To make the sauce, dissolve sugar in wine as before. Poach the pears until just cooked, drain and purée. Then reduce the syrup to a tablespoon and add this to the purée with eau de vie de poire and lemon juice to taste. Cool and refrigerate until ready to serve.

To serve the *bavarois*, carefully run a blunt knife round inside of mould, dip this briefly into hot water and turn out the contents. Peel off paper. Slice 'terrine' with a sharp carving knife, present 2 slices per person with a ribbon of sauce and some cigarettes russes. Serves 6.

NUTS GALORE

At the end of my first visit to Turkey, I brought home bags of walnuts, pine-nuts, hazelnuts and pistachios. Although Turkish nuts, of excellent quality and concentrated flavour, are imported commercially to Great Britain, I was challenged by this private windfall and began experimenting. I also added nuts from elsewhere, like almonds, chestnuts and macadamias – all of which can be bought in different forms in our shops.

BANANA BREAD WITH MACADAMIA NUTS

A classic, made a little exotic by the addition of crushed coriander and a handful of Hawaiian macadamia nuts, with their subtly-sweet, rather smoky flavour. If macadamia nuts are not available, substitute walnuts.

BREAD
100 g (4 oz) macadamia nuts, either salted or unsalted, as available, or walnuts
100 g (4 oz) unsalted butter, softened
100 g (4 oz) dark brown sugar
2 eggs
3 ripe bananas
2 tablespoons soured cream
1 tablespoon lemon juice
150 g (5 oz) plain flour
1½ teaspoons baking powder
½ teaspoon baking soda
large pinch of salt
150 g (5 oz) wholemeal flour
¼ teaspoon coriander seeds

CREAM CHEESE BUTTER
100 g (4 oz) unsalted butter, softened
50 g (2 oz) cream cheese, softened

To prepare the bread, slice macadamia nuts into thirds and place on a baking sheet. Toast in a preheated oven at 180°C, 350°F, Gas Mark 4 for 5–10 minutes, until nuts turn golden brown. Cool and set aside.

Butter a 20 × 13 × 9 cm (8 × 5 × 3½ inch) loaf tin and line the base with buttered greaseproof paper.

Cream together the butter and sugar. Whisk the eggs and beat into the butter. Mash the bananas thoroughly with a fork and add with the cream and lemon juice to the butter and egg mixture.

Sift together the plain flour, baking powder, baking soda and salt. Combine well with the wholemeal flour. Crush the coriander seeds with the side of a large knife blade and add to flours.

Beat the dry ingredients into the banana mixture, then fold in the macadamia nuts.

Pour the mixture into the loaf tin and bake in the oven at 180°C, 350°F, Gas Mark 4 for 60–70 minutes or until the bread tests done. Cool in tin for 15 minutes. Turn out, peel off the greaseproof paper and leave to cool completely.

The bread is moist, and good sliced fairly thick and toasted for tea, as a snack, or even at breakfast, accompanied by butter whisked with cream cheese until perfectly smooth, or put through a sieve if necessary.

WATER CHESTNUTS WRAPPED IN BACON

Not really nuts at all, but like nuts a kind of fruit, water chestnuts are imported in cans from the Far East, and can be bought from Chinese grocers. The crunch of chestnuts wrapped in hot, crisp bacon makes cocktail savouries which guests eat as fast as you can grill them. They should not be served with a dip.

a large can of water chestnuts, weighing about 500 g (19 oz)
green streaky bacon, thinly-sliced

Drain however many chestnuts you decide to use, dry with paper towels, cut in half across and in half again. Cut rinds from bacon, halve each piece across its centre, slice each half lengthwise into two equal strips.

Wrap a piece of chestnut in a strip of bacon and secure with a wooden cocktail stick. You can make about 120 mouth-fuls with this quantity of chestnuts, preparing them in advance and refrigerating, or you can hold the uncut chestnuts in a bowl, refrigerated in their water, for a week or so, and make up small clusters as required.

To serve, grill first on one side and then the other until bacon cooks and crisps, then rush to eat them while still piping hot.

From top of left column: Banana bread with macadamia nuts, Hamsi tarator, Smoked salmon crêpes, Marron-caramel ice cream with hazelnut custard, Chicken liver pâté with cream, Water chestnuts wrapped in bacon, Roast chavignol on toasted rye and corn bread

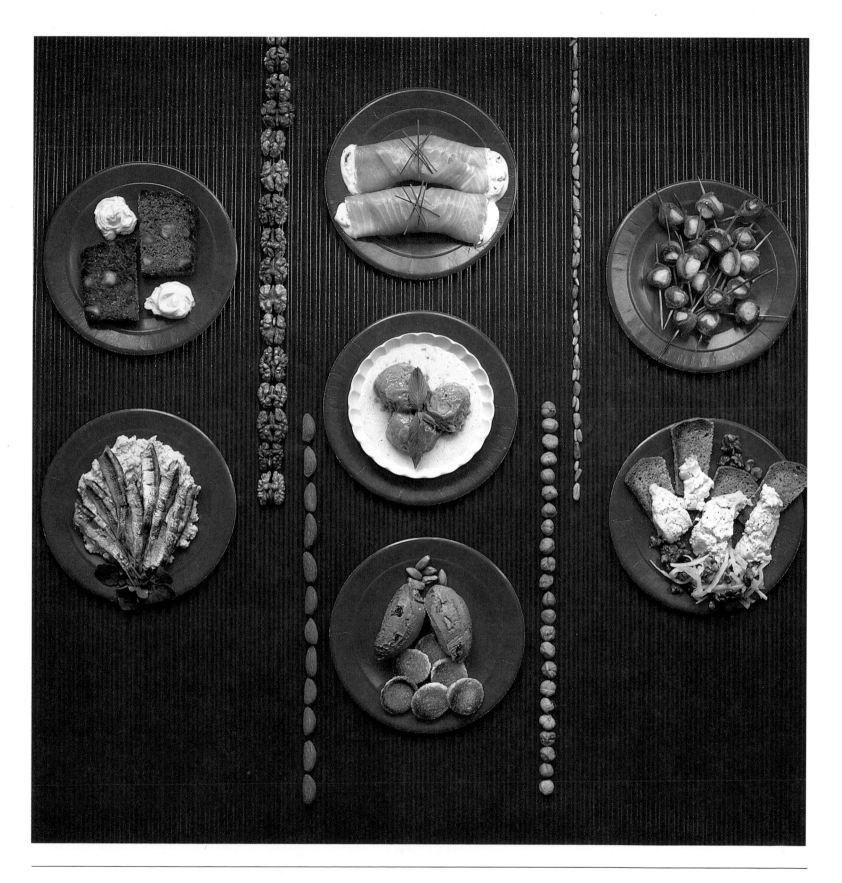

SMOKED SALMON CREPES

A way of refreshing a popular first course, and of spinning a few slices into something substantial. *Fromage blanc* is a thick, skimmed milk soft cheese; if you can't get it, soured cream will substitute, but the result is richer.

---

40 g (1½ oz) hazel and pine-nuts,
    mixed
225 g (8 oz) fromage blanc
100 g (4 oz) natural yogurt
mustard cress or watercress
fresh chives
salt
black pepper
8 slices best smoked salmon, Scotch if
    possible and very thinly cut

Roast the whole pine-nuts for about 5 minutes in an oven preheated to 180°C, 350°F, Gas Mark 4 until nuts turn golden-brown. If hazelnuts have not been skinned, roast in the same oven for about 10 minutes; the skin will flake and can be rubbed off. If the hazelnuts are already skinless roast for 5 minutes and then chop coarsely. Allow to cool.

Whisk the *fromage blanc* until smooth, and beat in enough yogurt to make a rather loose, but not liquid, mixture. Add cooled nuts, some leaves of mustard cress or of chopped watercress, some snipped chives, and salt and pepper to taste.

As the slices of salmon are probably narrow, overlap them in pairs to form four more or less square pieces. Put a large spoonful of *fromage blanc* mixture across one end of each square and roll up to form crêpe, tucking 'selvage' underneath. These can be prepared hours in advance and refrigerated. The filling will seep slightly at either end, and you will have some left over after all four crêpes have been rolled.

Thirty minutes before serving remove crêpes from refrigerator and transfer to small plates. One per person is ample, as this is a filling dish. Decorate with chives and place a spoonful of the *fromage blanc* mixture beneath each crêpe as a little extra sauce. Serves 4.

HAMSI TARATOR

This is a Turkish dish, *hamsi* being the Turkish word for anchovy, to which the Turks are devoted, and *tarator* a sauce for fish based on nuts and garlic, or sometimes garlic alone. I've used almonds here (ready-ground almonds from the supermarket, frowned on by some), and toasted them in the oven, which is not traditional but improves the flavour of the sauce. The whole anchovies which you'll find at the fishmonger (you may have to order them specially) may have been frozen and imported from Italy or elsewhere, but they work perfectly nevertheless.

---

225 g (8 oz) ground almonds
2 thin slices bread, granary or
    wholemeal if possible
2–3 large cloves garlic, peeled
olive oil
2 large lemons
salt
black pepper
32 whole anchovies, ungutted, heads
    and tails on
vegetable oil
watercress

To make *tarator* sauce, place ground almonds on a heavy baking sheet. Toast in a preheated oven at 180°C, 350°F, Gas Mark 4 for 10–12 minutes, stirring almonds round two or three times, until they have turned golden and begun to brown slightly. Cool.

Cut the crusts from the bread; white bread is the orthodox choice, but granary or wholemeal gives a more interesting texture. Soak in water and squeeze dry. Take 2 cloves garlic and with the aid of some salt, reduce them to a paste with the side of a knife blade. In a mortar or small, sturdy bowl, pound together almonds, bread and garlic. Add a little olive oil, the strained juice of a lemon, and a little water; beat to make a paste. Taste, and add more olive oil, juice of the second lemon (probably all of it), some

Smoked salmon crêpes

more water, and the third garlic clove, peeled and crushed, if like me, you love garlic. Grind in salt and pepper. The paste should have the consistency of a fairly thick sauce; if it should start to separate, pound in some more soaked and squeezed bread. The final flavour should be sweetly almond and sharply lemon-garlic. This can be made in advance, covered, and refrigerated; bring to room temperature before serving.

This is a recipe for 4 people, and the notion of cleaning and boning 32 small fish may seem discouraging, but in fact it is an easy job which is quickly and deftly done.

Wash the anchovies. Hold each by the back of its head. Gut by running a small knife down the belly almost to the tail. Scrape out the innards with your thumb and pull back the head and gills, innards attached, snapping off the head where it connects with the backbone. Carefully open the fish out flat; the backbone will almost pop out. Grasp it and peel it off the flesh, taking side bones with it, and cut it away above the tail. Remove any visible small bones, trim fish if necessary, leaving tail intact. Rinse well and move on to the next fish. They can be prepared hours ahead of time and refrigerated, under foil, until you are ready to grill them.

To serve, put a round of sauce on to four small plates. Dry fish on paper towels, flap them shut, and brush both sides with a little oil. Salt and pepper them and grill 2 minutes per side. You will doubtless have to grill in two or three batches; keep fish warm in a very low oven as they are ready.

Arrange 7 or 8 fish on each round of sauce and bring to table, garnished with watercress; have plenty of napkins and some finger bowls at the ready. With one hand, grasp a fish by the tail, have a teaspoon of sauce in the other hand, and take a bite of anchovy alternating with a bit of sauce. Serves 4 as filling first course or the same number as an informal luncheon dish.

Chicken liver pâté with cream

CHICKEN LIVER PATE WITH CREAM

---

25 g (1 oz) dried currants
25 g (1 oz) shelled pistachios
450 g (1 lb) chicken livers, fresh if possible
100 g (4 oz) butter, softened
4 tablespoons brandy
4 tablespoons dry sherry
1 clove garlic, peeled and chopped
½–1 teaspoon salt
black pepper
pinch of mixed spice
pinch of dried thyme
pinch of dried basil
pinch of dried oregano
150 ml (¼ pint) double cream
toast
butter

Wash currants and plump them by simmering for about 1 minute in boiling water. Drain and dry. Skin pistachios by blanching them for a minute in boiling water, draining, and rubbing away their skins in a towel. Toast the nuts in a preheated oven at 180°C, 350°F, Gas Mark 4 for 5–7 minutes until they begin to colour. Cool.

If the livers have been frozen, drain very well after thawing. Clean them, cut away connective tissue and any discoloured areas and dry. Melt 25 g (1 oz) butter in a large sauté pan and toss livers over a high heat for about 3 minutes until cooked but still pink inside. Remove livers to a blender or food processor fitted with a steel blade.

Add brandy and sherry to pan juices, bring to boil, set alight with a match and, gently shaking pan, flame away all the alcohol. Pour liquid into processor, add garlic, ½ teaspoon of salt, pepper, spices and herbs. Blend until smooth, let cool, add remaining butter, and blend again until very smooth. Add rest of salt if necessary, remembering that flavour mellows with chilling.

Remove pâté to a bowl. Whisk cream until it forms soft peaks, and fold, with currants and pistachios, into mixture. Pour it into a 900 ml (1½ pint) terrine or if serving pâté in *quenelles*, into a medium bowl. Cover tightly with cling film and refrigerate overnight. The flavour improves with age and is at its best three days after making.

If serving from terrine, make rounds or wedges of toast, butter them, and scoop out pâté with a small knife. But if wanting a less informal presentation, form one *quenelle* per person and serve on small plates with buttered toast.

To make these, have pâté at room temperature and three dessertspoons in a jug of very hot water. With your right hand, remove a spoon from water, shake off excess moisture, and immediately scoop out a rounded mass of pâté. Roll this mass repeatedly against side of bowl, turning pâté round and round in spoon to shape and compress *quenelle*. Transfer spoon to left hand; with right hand remove a second spoon from water, shake, smooth top of *quenelle*, and with a third hot, damp spoon, scoop *quenelle* smartly from first spoon and drop slightly above centre of a small plate. Clean spoons and continue this process for the remaining portions. Put toast underneath. Serves 6–8.

MARRON-CARAMEL ICE CREAM WITH HAZELNUT CUSTARD

Puréed sweet chestnuts combine with caramel and an Italian meringue to make a light, fluffy and delicious dessert. Caramel – which lowers the freezing point of ice cream – the cooked meringue, and the farinaceous quality of chestnuts contribute to a lack of obvious ice crystals, though the cream is still frozen.

ICE CREAM
440 g (15½ oz) can unsweetened
*   chestnut purée*
6 eggs
400 g (14 oz) granulated sugar
1 tablespoon caster sugar
2 tablespoons dark rum

CUSTARD
75 g (3 oz) shelled hazelnuts
1 split vanilla pod
600 ml (1 pint) milk
8 egg yolks
100 g (4 oz) caster sugar
a dash of Kirsch

GARNISH
sprigs of fresh mint

To make ice cream, sieve chestnut purée and beat it very smooth. Separate eggs.

Make a caramel with 225g (8 oz) of the granulated sugar and a little water, bringing it up to a good colour (188°C, 360°F). Meanwhile, beat yolks, with a hand-held electric beater if possible, until thick and pale.

When caramel is ready, remove from heat and, covering hands with a cloth, add to it a little boiling water, which will cause it to roar up alarmingly. Beating egg yolks hard with electric beater, pour in caramel. As you whisk, it will dissolve into yolks and cause them to expand in volume. Beat until they are very thick and cold; then whisk in the chestnut purée.

For the Italian meringue – egg whites into which a sugar syrup, cooked to the firm ball stage, is beaten – melt 175 g (6 oz) granulated sugar with a little water. When it starts to simmer, beat whites to peaks, beating in a tablespoon of caster sugar at the end to stabilize them slightly. They should be ready as the syrup reaches 118°C, 245°F. Using a large whisk, beat the syrup in a rapidly falling stream into the whites and continue beating until whites are cold. A light, shiny meringue will result.

Fold this into the chestnut base, stir in rum and freeze overnight in one or two large plastic boxes.

To make custard, skin, roast and coarsely chop hazelnuts as in recipe for smoked salmon crêpes (see page 32).

Infuse them, with split vanilla pod, in milk brought up to simmering point, while beating yolks and sugar until thick and pale. Pour milk into yolks, beating fast. Put the mixture back into milk pan through a sieve.

Over a high heat whisk vigorously until custard just boils. This happens suddenly; to prevent curdling, immediately remove from heat and sieve into a bowl. Whisk in hazelnuts, add a dash of Kirsch, wash vanilla pod and put it aside to dry. Cool and then chill custard.

Move ice cream from freezer to refrigerator about 30 minutes before serving. Pour a little custard on to dessert plates, pile on ice cream, and garnish with sprigs of fresh mint. Serves 8.

ROAST CHAVIGNOL ON TOASTED RYE AND CORN BREAD

In certain French restaurants for some years it has become fashionable to serve small roast or grilled goats' cheese on fried bread or toast. The cheese is usually a chavignol, known familiarly but inaccurately as a *crottin*, from the Berry district near the River Loire, and prepared in this way it is an interesting variation on the cheese course.

If you can't buy the chavignol at home from a good cheese importer, bring them back on your next trip to France and store them, if necessary, under olive oil in a jar. But be careful, after several weeks in oil they may begin to ferment, so don't plan to keep them too long before use.

This is a recipe best made for two as it's fiddly and needs to be eaten piping hot. Toast from home-made bread and a garnish of walnuts and apple add new dimensions.

RYE AND CORN BREAD
275 g (10 oz) strong plain flour
75 g (3 oz) rye meal, stone-ground if
*   possible*
75 g (3 oz) corn (maize) meal, finely
*   ground*
generous 15 g (½ oz) fresh yeast
1 tablespoon salt, preferably rock salt
about 300 ml (½ pint) water
vegetable oil
50 g (2 oz) Cheddar cheese

TO FINISH
¼ small, tart apple
lemon juice
4 slices toasted rye and corn bread, as
*   recipe*
butter
50 g (2 oz) broken walnuts
2 chavignol cheeses, 5 cm (2 inches)
*   across × 2.5 cm (1 inch) deep, firm*
*   but not hard or dried out*
black pepper

To make bread which is moist, close-textured and agreeably sour, mix the three flours in a large bowl and cream yeast in a little warm water. Put salt into a measuring jug with a tablespoon or two of boiling water, and stir until salt is dissolved. Add about 275 ml (9 fl oz) cold water.

Pour liquid yeast into centre of flour, add some of salted water, stir, and mix in all but about 25 ml (1 fl oz) of remaining water. Work ingredients with hands and judge whether to add more water, or if too wet, more plain flour. When consistency of dough seems right, elastic and not too damp, form a ball and knead vigorously on a board, flouring as necessary, for 5 minutes.

Wash and dry the bowl, pour in a drop of oil, smear one surface of dough with this, and turn it over; the oil will inhibit formation of a crust as dough rises. Put bowl aside in a cool place; slow rising makes for better bread. Cover bowl with a plastic sheet and weight this with a bread board. Let dough rise until triple in bulk, which takes 3–4 hours. At this point, punch down, knead briefly but thoroughly, clean bowl, oil it, and allow dough to rise again – it will take less time – under plastic and board. This double rising and slow ripening of gluten in the dough will result in a bread of good character.

When ready, grate cheese and oil two loaf tins of 750 ml ($1\frac{1}{4}$ pints) capacity each (about $18 \times 8 \times 6$ cm/$7\frac{1}{4} \times 3\frac{1}{4} \times 2\frac{1}{2}$ inches deep). Strew clean board with corn meal, place dough on board, and by folding and kneading, work in cheese. Knead dough for 2–3 minutes after cheese is incorporated, divide into two oblongs of equal weight, shape with folds underneath and place them in tins. Turn each oblong out and over to oil tops; return to tins. With scissors, make a cut the length of each loaf and widen cut with hands. Cover loosely with plastic and let rise until dough passes slightly over tops of tins.

Bake the loaves in centre of a preheated oven at 230°C, 450°F, Gas Mark 8 for 15 minutes, then reduce temperature to 190°C, 375°F, Gas Mark 5 for 15 minutes more. Turn out loaves and return them, upside down, to the oven at 160°C, 325°F, gas mark 3 for 10 minutes. Cool loaves on wire rack.

These loaves freeze well, slice thinly, and make excellent sandwiches.

To assemble this dish, peel, core and shred the apple quarter; immerse in lemon juice to prevent discoloration, then set aside while you complete the preparations. Cut four thin slices of bread, toast and butter these, and keep them warm. Toss walnuts over medium heat in a little butter until browned; keep warm. Place cheeses (drained and well-dried with paper towels, if they have been stored in oil), on a heavy baking sheet in a preheated oven at 240°C, 475°F, Gas Mark 9 for about 3 minutes, or until melting around the edges. With a very sharp knife, cut each cheese into four or five slices, return them to oven for about 2 minutes. Cut toast in half down the middle, place four pieces on each of two small heated plates and, with the aid of a palette knife, arrange the melted cheese on toast. Strew with nuts and some shredded apple, quickly dried on paper towels, grind on pepper and serve piping hot. Serves 2.

Marron-caramel ice cream

Roast chavignol on rye and corn bread

FRUITS OF THE WORLD

Here are fruits from several countries: English strawberries and raspberries, Brazilian figs, Cape gooseberries, Italian pears, New Zealand kiwis – and more besides. Some are in guises as simple and refreshing as the terrine of orange jelly. Others, such as the mango-studded Bavarian meringue, are more complex. Cherries are used as garnish, while wine has been turned into a sorbet that can lighten the end of a copious meal but is tart enough to revive the palate between courses.

In two of these recipes, I've recast old favourites; the Tarte Tatin is made with pears, and a rich chocolate mousse is served in *quenelles*.

BAVARIAN MERINGUE WITH RED-FRUITS SAUCE

This is a vanilla bavarois, or Bavarian cream, turned out on to a puff pastry base and covered with meringue. Red-fruits sauce flavoured with Kirsch, is served separately.

225 g (8 oz) puff pastry made with unsalted butter (see page 47)

BAVARIAN CREAM
5 leaves gelatine
600 ml (1 pint) milk
2 split vanilla pods
7 egg yolks
90 g (3½ oz) caster sugar
Kirsch
1 mango, peeled
150 ml (¼ pint) double cream

MERINGUE
4 egg whites
100 g (4 oz) caster sugar

RED-FRUITS SAUCE
225 g (8 oz) raspberries
225 g (8 oz) strawberries
225 g (8 oz) loganberries
juice of 3 large lemons, strained
caster sugar
Kirsch

For Bavarian cream, oil interior of a 24 × 10 × 7.5 cm (9½ × 4 × 3 inch) loaf tin with good quality vegetable oil and line bottom with an oblong of greaseproof paper pressed well down.

Soak the gelatine in water to soften. Scald the milk with vanilla pods. Beat the yolks with sugar for 5 minutes until light and thick, whisk in scalded milk, pour mixture back into the milk pan and beat over high heat until the first boil. Swiftly sieve into a bowl, wash and dry vanilla pods. Drain gelatine and beat this into custard to dissolve it completely. Add about a tablespoon of Kirsch. Cut half the mango into slices, then cut the slices into small cubes.

Set the bowl of custard over ice and water and stir until cold. Remove the bowl from ice, half-whip the cream then return custard to ice, stir continuously and when almost set remove from ice and thoroughly fold in the cream. Cream and custard should be of the same consistency in order to blend properly. Add more Kirsch if necessary, but the flavour should be subtle. Add half the mango cubes, pour into the mould and place remaining cubes by hand into the bavarois so that the fruit is evenly distributed. Refrigerate for at least 4 hours, until well set.

For puff pastry base, roll pastry into a 30 × 18 cm (12 × 7 inch) strip (it will shrink considerably, particularly in the predominant direction rolled, on bak-ing), place on to a heavy baking sheet, prick all over with a fork and refrigerate for at least 1 hour. Bake in a preheated oven at 190°C, 375°F, Gas Mark 5 for about 35 minutes, turning over after 25 minutes. The pastry should be deep golden-brown and well-risen. Cool.

Shortly before serving dessert, turn oven up to 230°C, 450°F, Gas Mark 8. Cover a heavy 30 × 23 cm (12 × 9 inch) baking sheet with foil, place pastry on foil, run a blunt knife round inside of bavarois mould, dip it briefly into hot water and turn out on to the puff. Peel off paper, trim pastry to edges of cream.

For meringue, beat egg whites to soft peaks, then beat in sugar by the tablespoonful until all the sugar is incorporated and meringue stands in stiff peaks. Using a palette knife, thickly mask cream and visible puff pastry base with meringue, to insulate them from the oven's heat. Smooth surface and put all into oven for 3–5 minutes until meringue has browned lightly.

Remove, with foil intact, to a flat platter, crinkle foil into a ruching all round to catch possible leaks from inside, and slice into 2 cm (¾ inch) slices with a very sharp knife.

For sauce, purée, in blender or food processor, the red fruits and lemon juice, plus the caster sugar and Kirsch to taste. Put sauce through a fine sieve. Serves 6.

Clockwise from top right: Bavarian meringue with red-fruits, Tart of kiwis and strawberries, Orange terrine with quenelles of chocolate mousse, Coeur à la crème, Toasted Sally Lunn, Claret sorbet, Tarte Tatin with pears

TOASTED SALLY LUNN WITH CHERRIES

Sally Lunn is a kind of light brioche. The name is derived from either a corruption of *soleil lune* (sun and moon) or the name of an eighteenth-century cake seller in the city of Bath.

SALLY LUNNS
250 ml (8 fl oz) milk
100 g (4 oz) unsalted butter
75 g (3 oz) caster sugar
2¼ teaspoons salt
25 g (1 oz) fresh yeast
3 eggs, well-beaten
500 g (1¼ lb) strong plain flour
1 egg yolk

CHERRY GARNISH
120 ml (4 fl oz) fruity red wine
350 g (12 oz) whole black cherries, stemmed and pitted
350 g (12 oz) morello cherry jam
lemon juice
caster sugar

To make Sally Lunns, heat milk, butter, sugar, and salt to about 60°C, 120°F, whisk to melt butter and dissolve seasonings. Pour into a large mixing bowl. Dissolve yeast in a little warm water, stir into milk mixture with the eggs. Sift flour and by hand, beat 425 g (15 oz) of it into bowl until blended with base. Add remaining flour and beat for 5 minutes by hand, turning bowl and constantly bringing dough in from sides. This is a soft, sticky batter which, with beating, becomes very elastic. Scrape sides of bowl, cover with a plastic sheet and weight this with a bread board. Set aside in a cool place until dough is triple in bulk – a process which will take several hours.

Butter the interiors of three 900 ml (1½ pint) Parisian brioche tins. Punch down dough, divide it into three equal portions (this may be difficult, as it is sticky and tenaciously elastic), and put each portion into a tin. Smooth over tops, cover with a cloth, and let rise in a cool room for an additional 1–2 hours, until blooming over tops of tins.

Brush each cake carefully with egg yolk beaten with a little water. Put the cakes into the middle of an oven preheated to 190°C, 375°F, Gas Mark 5. After 15 minutes turn oven down to 180°C, 350°F, Gas Mark 4, and then watch from time to time, as the tops can burn easily. Cover with foil to prevent this if necessary.

After 30–35 minutes, test cakes with a trussing needle thrust into centres. If needle emerges piping hot, the Sally Lunns are done. If not, bake longer.

Turn each cake out of tin, invert on to a heavy baking sheet and return upside down to oven for 5 minutes to crisp bottoms. Cool right side up on cake rack.

Three Sally Lunns are too much for this particular recipe, so when cakes are cool, wrap one well and freeze it for future use.

To make the cherry garnish, reduce red wine in a small, heavy saucepan to a few tablespoons, add whole cherries, plus morello jam. Cook over low heat, stirring occasionally with a wooden spoon, until jam has melted. Add lemon juice, and sugar if necessary, to taste. It should not be too sweet. Remove cher-

Toasted Sally Lunn with cherries

ries with a slotted spoon, and reduce jammy liquid until fairly thick. Slice Sally Lunns just over 1 cm (½ inch) thick, toast slices on both sides, butter one side lightly, and cut larger slices in half. Arrange on dessert plates, return cherries to their sauce, reheat, and spoon over toast. Serves 6.

TART OF KIWIS AND STRAWBERRIES

shortcrust pastry as Tarte Tatin
175 g (6 oz) redcurrant jelly
brandy
100 g (4 oz) apricot jam
225 g (8 oz) strawberries, uniform size
3 kiwi fruits
175 g (6 oz) wild strawberries

Using two-thirds of shortcrust recipe described under Tarte Tatin, line a 23 × 2.5 cm (9 × 1 inch) flan ring set on to a heavy baking sheet. Refrigerate for 1 hour. Line pastry with greaseproof paper weighed down with dried beans. Bake in a preheated oven at 180°C, 350°F, Gas Mark 4 for 30–40 minutes, removing the paper and beans when pastry has set, leaving pastry in oven until golden, and completely cooked. Cool.

Bring redcurrant jelly and a little brandy to simmer in a small, heavy saucepan, pass through a fine sieve and brush part of this glaze liberally over interior of pastry case, reserving remainder for top. Reheat to use.

Simmer apricot jam and a few drops of brandy in another saucepan, sieve, and reserve. Reheat to use.

Halve strawberries lengthwise, peel and slice kiwis thinly, and together with wild strawberries, make an attractive arrangement to fill pastry. Brush both kinds of strawberry with redcurrant glaze, brush kiwis with apricot.

Assemble this tart within a few hours of eating, as moisture from fruit progressively softens the crust. Serves 6.

TARTE TATIN WITH PEARS

An unorthodox version of a classic French tart, usually made with apples. As in the Pear and Caramel Bavarois with Pear Sauce, the grainy texture of pears is a good foil to the sweetness of caramel.

SHORTCRUST PASTRY
225 g (8 oz) plain flour
2 tablespoons icing sugar
large pinch of salt
150 g (5 oz) unsalted butter, softened
1 egg

CARAMEL AND PEARS
150 g (5 oz) granulated sugar
3–4 round medium-sized pears, a little
*   under-ripe, quartered, peeled and*
*   cored*
40 g (1½ oz) unsalted butter
25 g (1 oz) caster sugar
½ teaspoon brandy

To make shortcrust, sift flour, sugar and salt together on to a pastry board and make a well in the centre. Put butter into the well, make a trough in the butter and break in the egg. With one hand, work butter and egg swiftly together until they form a sticky mass. Then, with a spatula, toss and chop flour gradually into butter and egg until it begins to look like pastry. With both hands, bring pastry together, add a few drops of cold water if necessary to make adhere, knead briefly and form into a homogeneous ball. Wrap in greaseproof paper and a plastic bag and refrigerate overnight if possible. Only about a third of this amount is needed for the Tatin; when ready to use, cut off this third, bring it to room temperature, and save remaining pastry for another use, like the kiwi and strawberry tart.

When ready to make the Tatin, have to hand a clean, straight-sided 20 × 4 cm (8 × 1½ inch) aluminium cake tin. Make a caramel with the granulated sugar and a little water, bringing it up to a good colour (188°C, 370°F). Pour carefully

Tarte Tatin with pears

over the bottom of the tin, tilting to cover completely. Cool in refrigerator until hard.

Slice each pear-quarter lengthwise into four equal parts, melt 15 g (½ oz) butter in a heavy sauté pan and toss half the slices, sprinkled with 15 g (½ oz) of caster sugar, over high heat for 1–2 minutes until beginning to cook but still firm inside. Turn on to a wire rack over a bowl to cool and drain thoroughly. Repeat with remaining pear slices, sugar and 15 g (½ oz) butter. As pears are watery by nature, it is important for the success of this dessert that they are well drained.

When the caramel is hard and the pears cool, arrange the slices closely overlapping in two alternating circles in caramel, starting from outside of tin, with outside edge of fruit against bottom of tin. Melt the remaining ½ teaspoon of butter, add the brandy, and pour it over the pears.

Roll out pastry, cut into a circle that just fits inside tin, and place over fruit. Refrigerate for an hour.

Bake in the centre of a preheated oven at 220°C, 425°F, Gas Mark 7 for 35–40 minutes, checking after 20 minutes to see if the pastry is browning too much; if so, cover with foil. The crust should be a deep golden brown and the syrup boiling and heavy round edges of the tin when the tart is ready.

Cool tart for 15 minutes in tin, place a metal round from the bottom of a two-piece cake pan or a circle of heavy, foil-covered cardboard inside tin, and invert tart on to a cake rack set over a clean bowl to catch excess syrup. The pears will have absorbed the caramel and turned a mellow golden-brown.

Transfer the tart with its circular support to a flat serving plate, pull away support, and slice tart into six equal portions (which will be small, as this dessert is rich and sweet). Spoon some extra syrup, drained after baking, over each slice and serve with half-whipped cream. Serves 6.

CLARET SORBET

Served without vine leaves, this sorbet cleanses the palate beautifully between courses of a large dinner. Make at least 36 hours in advance of serving, as wine-based mixtures take a long time to freeze.

---

225 g (8 oz) granulated sugar
350 ml (12 fl oz) water
3 leaves gelatine
900 ml (1½ pints) good, inexpensive claret, such as Premières Côtes de Bordeaux, not more than five years old
juice of 1½ large lemons, strained
1½ egg whites

Boil the sugar and water for 10 minutes while soaking gelatine in a jug of water to soften. Drain gelatine, remove the hot syrup from heat and dissolve gelatine in it. Cool completely.

Combine cold syrup, wine, and lemon juice, whisk together and pour into deep plastic box. Cover with tight-fitting lid and place in freezer. After several hours, when mixture is semi-frozen, beat egg whites to soft peaks, fold and whisk into wine-ice and re-freeze. After two hours, scrape sides of box and whisk ice thoroughly. Repeat scraping and whisking at intervals during the day to encourage uniformity of texture.

When set, the sorbet will be a rather soft, crystalline mass. Scoop into grapes with a melon baller and fill six tall wine glasses. Put into refrigerator for 5 minutes, to frost glasses. Serve the sorbet without delay (as alcohol-based ices melt very quickly) on dessert plates garnished with black grapes and vine-leaf shortbreads. Serves 6.

VINE-LEAF SHORTBREADS

---

100 g (4 oz) unsalted butter, softened
200 g (7 oz) caster sugar
1 egg
50 ml (2 fl oz) milk
370 g (12½ oz) plain flour
2 teaspoons baking powder
large pinch of salt

Cream the butter using a wooden spoon until light, gradually beat in the sugar, creaming after each addition. Whisk the egg to break up and beat into butter in two pours, then beat in milk. Sift together dry ingredients and beat into mixture. The dough should hold together well and be moist but not damp; if necessary add further drops of milk. Roll into a ball, wrap in greaseproof paper, and refrigerate until firm but not hard.

Break off pieces of dough, roll out on floured board to thickness of 3 mm (⅛ inch), and using drawings of vine leaves as inspiration, cut free-hand leaf shapes – about 10 cm (4 inches) square – with a sharp knife. It may seem difficult at first to get a good likeness, but persevere.

Place leaves on to unbuttered heavy baking sheets. Bake in a preheated oven at 180°C, 350°F, Gas Mark 4 for about 10 minutes until the edges are golden-brown. Cool for 1–2 minutes on the sheets before removing with spatula to wire racks. Makes 24–30 leaves.

ORANGE TERRINE WITH QUENELLES OF CHOCOLATE MOUSSE

TERRINE
11–12 medium seedless oranges
4½ leaves gelatine
scant 100 g (4 oz) granulated sugar

MOUSSE
250 g (9 oz) semi-sweet dark chocolate
150 g (5 oz) unsalted butter
dash of dark rum
4 egg yolks
6 egg whites
scant 25 g (1 oz) icing sugar

To make terrine, use a small sharp knife to peel, segment and completely de-pith and de-membrane 6 oranges, putting segments on to a cake rack to dry out slightly. Squeeze juice from membranes of the 6 oranges, strain it, and make up liquid to 450 ml (¾ pint) with strained juice of remaining 5–6 oranges. Soften gelatine in water.

Heat the juice with sugar and drained gelatine over a low heat until both are dissolved; remove from heat.

After the orange segments have dried for about 6 hours, oil the inside of a 19 × 8 × 6 cm (7½ × 3¼ × 2½ inch) loaf tin, line the bottom with a strip of greaseproof paper pressed well down. Carefully and closely overlap orange segments – being careful not to squeeze – in one layer the length of the tin. Melt orange jelly and pour on just enough to barely cover oranges. Refrigerate until almost set, repeat one layer of oranges, pour on jelly, refrigerate, and continue until segments are used up. Cover with jelly to top of tin. Chill until set.

Meanwhile, make the mousse. Melt chocolate with butter in a small, heavy saucepan set, covered, into a larger pan of just-boiled water. When ready, beat smooth, remove pan from water, and beat mixture for 1–2 minutes to cool slightly. Add about a tablespoon of rum and the egg yolks. Beat again, to thicken and cool. When cool, beat egg whites to soft peaks, beat in icing sugar until firm peaks form. Beat about a quarter of the whites into the chocolate base to lighten it, then pour chocolate on to whites, folding them together quickly. Pour mousse into a wide mixing-bowl and refrigerate for several hours.

When ready to serve, dip terrine mould briefly into hot water, run a knife round sides, and turn out jelly. Peel off paper. With a very sharp, straight knife, cut carefully into 1 cm (½ inch) slices, serving two per portion, side by side.

To make *quenelles* of chocolate mousse, have ready several dessert spoons and a jug of very hot water. With your right hand, dip one spoon into hot water, shake off excess moisture, and immediately scoop out a rounded mass of mousse. Roll this mass again and again against side of mixing-bowl, turning mousse round and round in spoon to shape and compress *quenelle*. Transfer

spoon to left hand, with right hand dip second spoon into hot water, shake, smooth top of *quenelle*, and with a third hot, wet spoon, scoop *quenelle* deftly out of first spoon and drop on to dessert plate beneath orange slices. Place another *quenelle* beside first and continue.

COEUR A LA CREME WITH FRUIT

The cheesy acidity of yogurt is an important element in this deliciously light dessert.

---

300 ml (½ pint) double cream
275 g (10 oz) natural yogurt
4 egg whites

TO SERVE
figs, Cape gooseberries, or soft fruits
*   like raspberries and strawberries*
optional: double cream, caster sugar

Prepare six white-glazed, hole-pierced coeur à la crème moulds by lining each with a square of muslin; the muslin should line the mould as smoothly as possible without crease or fold.

Whip the cream until stiff, beat the yogurt smooth and fold into the cream; beat egg whites to soft peaks and fold all together.

Spoon mixture into each mould until slightly too full; rap moulds on the work surface to settle their contents, fold over each cloth to cover cream, and place moulds on flat plates in the refrigerator or larder to drain overnight. The cream will set into compact heart shapes.

To serve, carefully fold back cloths and invert each mould on to the centre of a dessert plate. Lift off mould, gently detach cloth, smooth any ragged edges, and serve with peeled, sliced figs and Cape gooseberries, or with soft fruits like raspberries and strawberries, and optionally, with unwhipped double cream and caster sugar. Serves 6.

Orange terrine

Coeur à la crème

METHOD AND TECHNIQUE

I'm not an advocate of kitchens full of equipment. The best cooking, in my view, is done with a reasonable number of first-rate essentials like good pots, excellent knives, a reliable oven, and an ever-increasing knowledge of how they are best used. Techniques can be taught, but their mastery comes with practice. So in this chapter I'll run through a few fundamental procedures.

PIMENTO SOUP WITH POLENTA AND AIOLI

A few years ago, I ate some of the most delectable food of my life in Berkeley, California, at the Fourth Street Grill and Chez Panisse, Alice Waters' restaurant. At Chez Panisse we had a lovely pimento soup with *polenta* and *aïoli* and I came home determined to make my own version. Techniques in this recipe include: grilling peppers, emulsification by machine and an unusual way with *polenta*.

SOUP
*2 onions, about 225 g (8 oz) each,
    peeled and finely chopped*
*2 carrots, about 50 g (2 oz) each,
    peeled and finely chopped*
*4 large cloves garlic, peeled and finely
    chopped*
25 g (1 oz) butter
25 ml (1 fl oz) vegetable oil
500 g (1¼ lb) tomatoes
salt
dry white wine
*6 sweet red peppers or 'pimentos',
    weighing total of about 1 kg (2 lb)*
*1.75 litres (3 pints) home-made
    chicken broth (see page 100)*
black pepper

POLENTA
750 ml (1¼ pints) salted water
*150 g (5 oz) medium-grained polenta
    (maize meal), available from most
    Italian grocers*
salt
black pepper

AIOLI
2 large cloves garlic
salt
1 egg
1 tablespoon lemon juice
olive oil

Make soup in one very large pot or two saucepans of 2.75 litre (5 pint) capacity each. Sweat the onions, carrots and garlic, covered, in butter and oil for 10 minutes, or until softened. Peel, seed and chop the tomatoes, add to the vegetables with salt and a good splash of white wine. Bring to boil, and simmer until the liquid is almost evaporated.

Meanwhile wash and dry the peppers, place on grill pan about 2.5 cm (1 inch) away from strong heat, and grill, turning with metal tongs or spoons, until skins blister and blacken all over. This charring brings out the smoky sweetness of the peppers' flesh.

Cool under wet paper towels to generate skin-loosening steam, and when cold, halve peppers lengthwise, cut out stems, drain juices, remove ribs and seeds. Peel off all the skin with a small knife, wash and slice peppers into saucepan(s). Add the broth, a little salt, bring to the boil and simmer for about 10 minutes, until the peppers are tender. Cool a little, purée in blender or food processor, season, and cool completely.

To make *polenta*, bring salted water to a brisk simmer and very slowly add maize meal, whisking to prevent lumps. When all the maize is in, stir well with a wooden spoon and cook gently for about 15 minutes, stirring frequently and thoroughly. The *polenta* is done when mixture comes away from sides of pan. Season *polenta* and spread it evenly, 1 cm (½ inch) thick, with a wet palette knife across a wooden board. Cool.

I don't like the tedium of mayonnaise-making by hand, and I refuse the labour of *aïoli* – the garlic mayonnaise – pounded and stirred in a mortar with pestle. Long live the food processor for production of rapid emulsions!

Have all the *aïoli* ingredients at room temperature, peel the garlic cloves and break down to a paste on a board with salt and the side of a heavy knife blade. Put into a food processor (or blender), add the whole egg, and process for 30 seconds, add lemon juice, and process for 10 seconds more. Through the top feeder, very slowly add olive oil, blending at high speed, until *aïoli* looks like a medium-thick mayonnaise. Taste it for salt and transfer to a bowl.

To serve, slice *polenta* with a sharp knife into 'chip'-like shapes and toast these on two sides under a hot grill till slightly charred. Reheat the soup, ladle into bowls, swirl through spoonfuls of *aïoli*, float on grilled polenta and serve immediately. Serves 7–8.

Clockwise from top right: Marrow lemon preserve, Caramelized apple with crisp pastry and Calvados sauce, Grilled skirt steak, Trout stuffed with julienned vegetables, Pimento soup with polenta and aïoli

TROUT STUFFED WITH JULIENNED VEGETABLES

This subtle dish provides good practice in the techniques of boning a trout through its back and the cutting of fine juliennes – thin strips – of vegetables. Adapted from a Gault-Millau recipe.

150 g (5 oz) carrot, peeled
75 g (3 oz) fennel bulb
225 g (8 oz) button mushrooms
butter
vegetable oil
275 ml (9 fl oz) double cream
salt
black pepper
chopped fresh chives
chopped fresh fennel leaves
1 medium shallot, peeled and minced
85 ml (3 fl oz) dry white wine
85 ml (3 fl oz) home-made fish stock
  (see page 101)
4 trout, 275 g (10 oz) each, ungutted
dry white vermouth

With a long, slim knife, thinly slice the carrot, fennel and mushrooms. Stack several slices and cut into fine strips, reserving a number of the longest strips of carrot for use as decoration; blanch the latter for 10 seconds in boiling water, refresh, drain, and reserve. Wash remainder of julienne and sweat, covered, for 15 minutes in a little butter and oil in a large saucepan. Add 120 ml (4 fl oz) double cream, a little salt and simmer julienne, uncovered, until almost all cream is absorbed. Season well, add chives and fennel leaves to taste.

Put the shallot into a small saucepan with wine and fish broth. Simmer briefly, add the remaining cream and reduce by a third. Season the broth well and reserve.

Meanwhile bone each trout. With a small, sharp knife, cut down either side of dorsal (back) fin and in along the backbone to release the two fillets, working from the head almost to tail, without piercing belly.

Work the backbone and ribs free of flesh, and with a pair of scissors, sever backbone at the head and tail and remove. Cut out the side bones and pull out the viscera.

Pull back the trout's head, grasp each gill in turn and wrest it free. Snip off remaining fins and rinse fish thoroughly. Proceed with the other three. This is not a difficult technique and gets easier with each try; if you simply can't face it, ask your fishmonger to bone the trout by this method.

Dry and season them well inside and out and spoon a sensible amount of julienne into cavity of each fish, but do not overfill them. Put the trout into a heavy, oval, buttered baking-dish into which they will just fit in a single layer, spoon on remaining julienne, pour on cream sauce. Bake, uncovered, in a preheated oven at 220°C, 425°F, Gas Mark 7 for 10 minutes or until fish have just cooked.

Transfer them carefully to a serving platter and keep warm; reduce the sauce in a small saucepan until it lightly coats the back of a spoon. Season well, add a few drops of vermouth *just* for accent, arrange the reserved carrot strips and some fresh chives along each fish, and serve with a little sauce poured round and the rest passed separately. Serves 4.

Trout stuffed with julienned vegetables

Grilled skirt steak

GRILLED SKIRT STEAK

Rump skirt is a cut of steak that few people eat, as such – except for Americans, who use a near-equivalent for a method called London broil, and the French, who know their way around obscure cuts. The uninitiated miss an excellent, long-fibred, very lean meat of reasonable price. The technique featured here is marinating, to give an already flavoursome choice some extra dimensions. Order the cut in advance from your butcher.

---

275 ml (9 fl oz) can lager beer
1 tablespoon clear honey
1 tablespoon dark soya sauce
1 tablespoon grated fresh ginger root
2 tablespoons peanut oil
2–3 spring onions, minced
2 large cloves garlic, minced
½ fresh chili pepper, seeded and minced
handful of chopped fresh coriander
  leaves
750 g (1½ lb) piece rump skirt steak,
  about 2–2.5 cm (¾–1 inch) thick
salt
black pepper
Dijon mustard

Thoroughly mix the beer, honey, soya sauce, grated ginger, peanut oil, spring onions, garlic, fresh chili and coriander. Lay the steak in a glass or china container into which it fits snugly, cover with the marinade and turn over. Refrigerate the meat, covered, for two days, turning and basting the steak about every 8 hours or so.

When ready, bring meat to room temperature and thoroughly preheat grill to high heat. Drain and season steak and grill it, about 4 cm (1½ inches) from heat, for 3–5 minutes each side. It must be very rare. Let it rest for a few minutes, then carve it, across the grain at an angle, into very thin slices. Serve accompanied by Dijon mustard. The meat has an elusive, sweet pungency imparted by its long marination. Serves 2–3, liberally.

CARAMELIZED APPLE WITH CRISP PASTRY AND CALVADOS SAUCE

A restaurant called Adlard's was opened a few years ago in Wymondham, Norfolk, by David Adlard and his American wife Mary. David was a chef with me at the Connaught Hotel in London, and he is an inspired cook, whose delicate apple dessert exploits two properties of the egg: whites as a binder for airy pastry and yolks whisked as the base of a sweet sabayon mousse. The resulting combination is delicious and unusual.

PASTRY
50 g (2 oz) unsalted butter, softened
65 g (2½ oz) icing sugar, sifted
50 ml (2 fl oz) egg whites
50 g (2 oz) plain flour, sifted

APPLES
3 firm, sweet, eating apples, 90 g (3½
  oz) each, halved, peeled and cored
Calvados
soft light brown sugar
dry white wine

SABAYON
3 egg yolks
1 tablespoon dry white wine
1 tablespoon caster sugar
½ tablespoon Calvados

TO FINISH
icing sugar

To make the pastry, cream the butter and sugar in a small bowl and when very light, slowly add the egg whites (if the mixture starts to separate, beat in a little of the flour); fold in all of the sifted flour.

Cover heavy baking sheet(s) with baking parchment and, using the base of a ramekin as guide, trace on the parchment a series of 7 cm (2¾ inch) circles. Drop spoonfuls of batter into these and spread very thin with back of a wet dessertspoon.

Bake in a preheated oven at 160°C,

325°F, Gas Mark 3 for 10–12 minutes until the biscuits are golden and browning at the edges. Remove carefully from paper with a palette knife and allow to cool. The recipe makes about 22 discs; 12 are used here, and the rest are delicious as biscuits some other time.

To prepare the apples, slice halves thinly lengthwise, and keeping slices of each half together, place them inside-downward in an ovenproof dish. Sprinkle with a little Calvados and brown sugar, cover the base of dish with wine. Bake at 180°C, 350°F, Gas Mark 4 for 15–20 minutes, or until the apples are cooked but not disintegrating. Remove from the oven, baste fruit with liquid and let cool completely.

Although a sabayon pot is certainly not an essential piece of kitchen equipment, whisking warm yolks across its rounded bottom ensures that none of the yolk congeals lumpishly into corners, and if you make a lot of egg-based sauces mounted over heat, the pot could be a useful investment. In any case, when ready to complete the dessert, whisk sabayon ingredients together in a heatproof bowl or the special pot. Set apples in their dish to heat at 160°C, 325°F, Gas Mark 3 for 10 minutes, (in cooling, they will have absorbed surrounding liquid and thus acquired a marvellous flavour). Sieve the icing sugar over four pastry discs.

Set the bowl or pot over a pan of barely simmering water and whisk its contents well for 2–3 minutes, until the mixture forms a light, thick mousse. Watch carefully and don't overcook into scrambled eggs.

Pour sauce immediately onto four slightly warmed dessert plates. Fan the sliced apple across eight pastry discs and with these, construct four double-decker sandwiches, topping with sugar-dusted rounds. With a palette knife, carefully place each stack of sandwiches in middle of sauce, and serve. The contrast of textures in this dessert is part of its attraction. Serves 4.

MARROW LEMON PRESERVE

This recipe, from *The Wine & Food Society Menu Book*, which I wrote with my husband, shows how lemon curd can be transformed into something unusual by substituting the light crunch of vegetable marrow for eggs. Using a jam funnel makes this an easier, neater task.

1 very large, firm vegetable marrow, or 2 smaller ones, to yield 750 g (1½ lb) flesh after seeding and peeling

350 g (12 oz) granulated or preserving sugar

75 g (3 oz) unsalted butter

pinch of salt

grated zest and juice of 2 large lemons

Halve the marrow across its middle, halve each half lengthwise, scoop out and discard seeds, pare off rind. Cut flesh into 1 cm (½ inch) dice and steam in several batches over boiling water until soft and translucent. Each round takes about 20 minutes.

Drain and dry marrow thoroughly and purée it in a food processor – just enough to eliminate all lumps but not until ultra smooth. It should retain an interesting texture.

Transfer the marrow to a heavy saucepan, add sugar, butter, salt and the grated zest and strained juice of the lemons. Bring to the boil and simmer for 20 minutes, stirring the mixture occasionally to prevent sticking. Pot the preserve without delay into hot, dry, sterilized jam jars and cover immediately. Makes 3 small pots.

Marrow lemon preserve

A FEW BASICS

In addition to basic techniques, there are certain recipes which every cook will find useful to attach to the fundamental repertoire. The following recipes are important both in themselves and for completion of dishes described in the text: *beurre blanc* appears with fish and vegetables in parchment (see page 66), puff pastry is part of Bavarian meringue (see page 36) and of Twist-of-grape Tarts (see page 105), while the aspic jelly is a necessary element of the Pâté de Porc en Brioche on page 28.

BEURRE BLANC

1 shallot, peeled and minced

4 tablespoons dry white wine

4 tablespoons white wine vinegar

salt

black pepper

225 g (8 oz) unsalted cold butter, cut into small cubes

lemon juice to taste

Put the shallot, wine and wine vinegar, with a good grinding of seasonings, into a small saucepan with a heavy base. Boil and reduce the liquids until you are left with 1 tablespoon of liquid. Remove the pan from heat and quickly whisk in 2 cubes of butter. As they melt, beat in another piece.

Continue in this way with the remaining butter, adding piece by piece and returning pan to the heat three or four times as you whisk, letting each cube almost dissolve into the emulsion which is being formed before you add another. A foamy sauce will result.

Remove pan from heat when all butter has been absorbed, check seasoning, add lemon juice to taste; its presence should be subtle. Pour sauce into a warmed boat and serve without delay. Serves 4–6.

PUFF PASTRY

450 g (1 lb) plain flour, plus extra
½ teaspoon salt
500 g (1 lb 2 oz) hard unsalted butter
about 250 ml (8 fl oz) cold water

Sift the flour and salt into a bowl, cut 75 g (3 oz) of the butter into cubes and cut these into the flour, using two butter knives. Pour in enough water to bind ingredients; you may need the entire 250 ml (8 fl oz), but don't add it until you've judged how much the flour will absorb.

Make the pastry into a ball and knead this vigorously on a large floured pastry board for 5 minutes. This dough is called the *détrempe*. Reshape it into a ball and wrap it in greaseproof paper; refrigerate to relax for 1 hour.

Put the rest of the butter between two sheets of greaseproof paper and use a rolling pin to beat it into a slab of about 15 × 15 cm (6 × 6 inches). Wrap and keep cool, in lowest part of refrigerator if necessary.

When the *détrempe* has rested, flour the pastry board again and roll the dough into a circle or square, keeping it slightly higher in the middle than at the sides. Put butter in the centre, fold the *détrempe* around the butter to enclose it completely, and seal the dough with your fingers. Turn it over.

Flour the board and pastry and roll the dough into a rectangle of about 40 × 20 cm (16 × 8 inches). Fold it into three from bottom to top, like a business letter. Give this a 90° turn so that one end of the letter is towards you, and flour it if necessary. Roll the pastry into a rectangle once more, fold it into three again, make two light dents in the side of the dough to indicate it has had two turns, and chill it for 1 hour, wrapped in greaseproof paper.

Give the pastry two more turns as above – always flouring it if the butter starts to break through, or resting it in the refrigerator if the dough becomes too elastic or the butter too soft. Make four dents to indicate four turns, wrap the pastry airtight and chill it overnight. Or if you wish to freeze it, wrap it for the freezer and do that.

When you are ready to make whatever is appropriate, thaw the pastry, if necessary; cut off the weight you will need, and give the dough its final pair of turns before rolling it out. Makes about 1.5 kg (3 lb) of pastry.

ASPIC JELLY

2 calf's feet
ingredients for basic meat broth (see
   Cold Asparagus, Spinach and Basil
   Soup on page 102)
salt
black pepper
2 egg whites and their crushed shells
75 g (3 oz) very lean minced beef
   mixed with a chopped green leek
   top and a handful of chopped fresh
   parsley
cognac to taste

Order the calf's feet in advance from your butcher. Ask him to remove the bone from each foot at its joint and to split feet in half lengthwise.

Assemble ingredients for the broth. Scrub the calf's feet in cold water. Soak them in several changes of cold water for 8 hours. Rinse the feet, add them to a stockpot with the broth's meat and bones and proceed to make broth as in recipe. Strain and refrigerate as instructed. The broth should set to a firm jelly.

To use this jelly in something such as the Pâté de Porc en Brioche (page 28), it is necessary to clarify it. Scrape all fat from top of the bowlful of set broth and sponge away its traces with a paper towel wrung out in hot water. Melt the jelly, season it carefully, and measure the quantity of resulting liquid. For every 1.2 litres (2 pints), assemble the specified amount of egg whites, shells, and beef-with-aromatics.

Pour all but 300 ml (½ pint) of the liquid jelly into a very clean pot, and place this over a medium heat. Mix the beef and egg whites with the remaining 300 ml (½ pint) of jelly. As the liquid comes towards the boil, whisk in the beef and egg whites mixture and continue whisking, slowly and thoroughly, until the broth comes to the first simmer.

The whites will be rising to the surface and the surface itself will rise to the top of the pot. Remove immediately from the heat and let stand for 10 minutes. Then bring contents of the pot just to the boil, twice more, without whisking, leaving 10 minute intervals between each boil. The egg protein forms bonds with the stray meat particles in the liquid jelly and draws these out of solution; doing this in concert with the addition of the minced beef and aromatics will give the flavour a boost.

Line a large, fine sieve with a triple thickness of muslin and very gently ladle through the clarified jelly, keeping the base of the sieve well above the surface of the strained liquid. Let contents of the sieve drain undisturbed for 5 minutes. Discard whites and all the debris, check the seasoning of the jelly – which should be crystal-clear and of good colour – and flavour to taste with cognac, whose impact should not be overpowering.

When the jelly is cool, check its setting potential by pouring a depth of 1 cm (½ inch) into a chilled saucer. Chill in refrigerator for 10 minutes; the jelly should set firmly. Chop this and leave it at room temperature for 10 minutes more; if the pieces hold their shape, the jelly has set correctly. If not – a case which is highly unlikely – thoroughly whisk a leaf or leaves of dissolved gelatine into the bowl of liquid jelly and continue testing.

Before the bowlful of cooled jelly has set, ladle it, in small quantities, into freezer bags, seal these, and freeze until ready for use.

STRETCHING THE HORIZONS

Travelling abroad brings spice, both literally and in the form of fresh ideas, to the cook's basic repertoire – inspiring an unusual new dish, or a way of enhancing a long-time favourite with alluring and novel ingredients.

In these chapters I explore the cooking of France, Turkey, and the USA, regions I know well and continue to search for intriguing gastronomic ideas. Italy, with her appealingly straightforward country food, makes a passing appearance, as do Bulgaria, Morocco, and Denmark, adding their diverse accents to an exotic collection.

The market-place in an unfamiliar city is a wonderful source for discovery; but the cook's horizons can be stretched without once leaving home, by taking a new look at unjustly-neglected ingredients such as buttermilk, *polenta*, or chicken livers and remembering how good these can be.

COOKING IN PROVENCE

We usually spend a magical part of each summer in Provence, staying with friends near the square clock-tower of a hilltop village between Grasse and Cannes. The heat and the sounds, the garden full of flowers, the markets of Cannes, Nice and Menton where we find superb raw ingredients to turn into vivid outdoor meals – all of these things rouse us early each morning and send us, eventually, back to England, unable to believe our time could have gone so quickly. These dishes are among my favourites.

A LUNCH-TIME SALAD

After a late-morning market visit, we often have a terrace lunch of fish or cold meat and a large salad of whatever we've been unable to resist buying. The favourite is sliced tomatoes strewn with basil leaves, without dressing, or a dish of just-cooked new potatoes. If we're feeling ambitious, however, we might stuff tiny round courgettes, or, as in this case, tomatoes. There is no recipe besides improvization.

Take, say, one or two perfect tomatoes per person, skin them in just-boiled water, halve, and scoop out the insides. Crush several cloves of peeled garlic to a paste, with salt and the aid of a heavy knife blade. Combine with 1 part wine vinegar to 4–5 parts olive oil, salt and pepper, and a little peeled and grated fresh ginger root. Brush the tomatoes inside and out with some of this.

Take a few small aubergines (allow about 75 g (3 oz) per tomato), slice unpeeled into 1 cm (½ inch) cubes, season, and sauté in a wide frying pan with several tablespoons of olive oil until the aubergine is tender but still firm. Turn into a bowl and sprinkle with dry white wine, coat with the vinaigrette you've just made, and cool.

In the meantime, top, tail, blanch and refresh slim French beans (in Provence, as elsewhere, the best ones, when not garden-grown, usually come from Kenya). Dry them, and toss in vinaigrette. Cube some firm goats' cheese and toast a small handful of pine-nuts under the grill.

Cover a platter with lettuce leaves, lightly-dressed, and combine the aubergine with the cheese and nuts and a fresh herb like chervil. Season the mixture to taste, add more vinaigrette if needed and put this into the tomato halves. Arrange on lettuce and intersperse with the *haricots verts*.

'MERDA DE CAN'

These are green *gnocchi*, as made in Nice with Swiss chard leaves. The Niçois eat huge amounts of chard, and while I really prefer *gnocchi* of potato and flour only – see page 132 – these are an interesting variation and amusing to make. Serve as a dish on its own or as accompaniment to the Pintade en Salmis.

---

225 g (8 oz) Swiss chard leaves (use ribs to make a gratin)
salt
750 g (1 lb 10 oz) floury potatoes
2 teaspoons olive oil
½ beaten egg
about 200 g (7 oz) plain flour
black pepper
Parmesan cheese, freshly-grated
butter, heated

Remove any large veins from the chard leaves and boil in briskly-simmering salted water for 2–3 minutes, until tender. Refresh, squeeze as dry as possible and chop finely.

Meanwhile, boil the unskinned potatoes in salted water until done; drain, and peel as soon as you can handle them. While still hot, purée through a food mill or ricer, and combine immediately with oil, egg, and chard.

With one hand, work about 175 g (6 oz) flour into the potato base and knead this smooth. You may require more flour if the potatoes are particularly absorbent, but stop when the mixture feels soft, smooth, and still a little sticky. Season well, work in some Parmesan and form dough into rolls about as thick as your thumb. Leave to rest for 30 minutes.

Cut each roll into 2 cm (¾ inch) lengths, and between floured hands, roll the lengths into oblongs, tapered at each end. Poach in two pots of boiling salted water, not overcrowding *gnocchi*, until they rise to the surface. Drain carefully on to a hot platter, season, and pour on foaming butter and liberal Parmesan. Or if serving with guinea-fowl, baste *gnocchi* with a little of sauce.

Serves 4 as an unaccompanied dish, or 6–8 when escorting Pintade.

Clockwise from top right: Vin d'orange, Tarte aux prunes, Lunchtime salad, Pintade en salmis, Courgettes 'en spaghetti', Merda de can

COURGETTES 'EN SPAGHETTI' LA MOURRACHONNE

This dish is exacting to make, but showy and delicious. Have at least one dress rehearsal and limit your numbers to four.

TOMATO SAUCE

100 g (4 oz) onion, peeled and chopped
2 large cloves garlic, minced
25 g (1 oz) celery, chopped
25 g (1 oz) carrot, peeled and chopped
1 tablespoon olive oil
794 g (1 lb 12 oz) can Italian plum
    tomatoes and their juices
3 tablespoons dry white wine
2 teaspoons granulated sugar
1 bay leaf
pinch of thyme
a few parsley stalks
salt
black pepper

CREAM SAUCE

50 g (2 oz) butter
25 g (1 oz) carrot, finely chopped
1 large celery stick, finely chopped
1 shallot, peeled and minced
1 sprig of fresh thyme
1 small bay leaf
120 ml (4 fl oz) dry white wine
400 ml (14 fl oz) double cream
salt
about 2 teaspoons lemon juice
black pepper
fresh chives

TO FINISH

4 plump courgettes, about 75 g (3 oz)
    each
1 tablespoon clarified butter from cream
    sauce recipe
about 8 large fresh basil leaves,
    shredded
salt
black pepper

The sauces and the preparation of the courgettes can be done in advance and refrigerated, while the finishing and assembly should be carried out at the last minute. The flavours will benefit from this advance preparation.

To make the tomato sauce, sweat the first four ingredients with the olive oil in a medium sauté pan, covered, over a low heat, until the vegetables are soft but not coloured. Add the remaining ingredients to the pan. Break up the tomatoes with a wooden spoon, stir well, bring to boil and simmer briskly, uncovered, for 15–20 minutes, stirring occasionally, until the sauce is reduced to an interesting but still fairly liquid consistency.

Let it cool slightly, liquidize, and push the sauce through a coarse sieve to be rid of the seeds and debris. Check the seasoning.

The result is about 600 ml (1 pint) of sauce; only a small amount of this is needed here, but the remainder can be frozen for repeats of this dish or used elsewhere. Cool and refrigerate until required.

To make the cream sauce, clarify the butter, (see Chicken Liver pâté with Calvados on page 26 for method) which will give you about 3 tablespoons of clear, yellow liquid. Take a small heavy saucepan, add a tablespoon of the butter, plus the carrot, celery, shallot, thyme and bay leaf to the pan, stir, and place over a low heat.

Cover, and let the contents sweat gently for 7–10 minutes until the vegetables are soft but not browning. Add the wine, raise the heat, and simmer briskly until about 1 tablespoon remains. Whisk in the cream, a little salt, and boil lightly for 2–3 minutes.

Strain the sauce through a fine sieve – pressing the vegetables to extract maximum flavour – into another small saucepan. Add the lemon juice – probably as much as 2 teaspoons – plus salt and pepper to taste. Cool and refrigerate until just before you prepare the courgettes.

Top and tail the courgettes. If you have a mandoline, use it to slice the vegetables lengthwise into spaghetti-like sticks; otherwise, use a long, slim blade – like a carving knife – to cut the courgettes lengthwise into pieces 3 mm ($\frac{1}{8}$ inch) thick, and these, lengthwise again, into long, 3 mm ($\frac{1}{8}$ inch) strands.

If doing this operation in advance, place the resulting courgette 'spaghetti' in a bowl, cover with damp paper towels and refrigerate.

When ready to begin, put four 23 cm (9 inch) plates to heat in the oven, snip about 1 tablespoon of chives and shred the basil leaves and set aside. Place two small bains-marie to heat on burners, put the pan of cream sauce in one and a generous 5 tablespoons of tomato sauce in a pan in the other. Whisk and gently heat both liquids before finishing courgettes.

Meanwhile, take a 30–33 cm (12–13 inch) sauté pan and heat in it 1 tablespoon of the clarified butter. When hot, add courgettes and toss or stir over high heat – adding a *little* more of the butter if you think necessary – for 2–4 minutes until just cooked but still *al dente*. Season the courgettes well, extinguish the heat beneath. Whisk the chives into the cream sauce.

Immediately line up the four plates and in the centre of each loosely pile an attractive nest of 'spaghetti'. Spoon round the cream sauce, drop a spoonful of tomato sauce into this pool, and deftly swirl each edge. Garnish the courgettes with basil and eat without delay. Serves 4 as a first course.

PINTADE EN SALMIS

One of our Provençal friends is Simone Beck, of *Mastering the Art of French Cooking* and two volumes of *Simca's Cuisine*, whose pastry and *jet brioche* I've adapted for use elsewhere in this book.

No one is a better cook than Simca, and this dish of guinea-fowl in a winy, smoky sauce is one which she taught to me and the friend in whose Provençal house we stay.

Courgettes 'en spaghetti'

Pintade en salmis

2 guinea-hens, about 1 kg (2 lb) each,
  dressed weight
350 ml (12 fl oz) stock made from
  guinea-hen carcasses
salt
1 small carrot, peeled
1 small onion, peeled
about 75 g (3 oz) best lard
2 medium onions, finely sliced
100 g (4 oz) salt pork or unsmoked
  streaky bacon, without rind
4 large cloves garlic, peeled and finely
  chopped
1 bay leaf
1 sprig of thyme
a few parsley stalks
40 g (1½ oz) plain flour
750 ml (1¼ pints) dry red wine
1 clove
black pepper
thick slices of stale white bread without
  crusts
butter
small handful fresh parsley, chopped

The day before you plan to serve the birds, cut them into a total of eight serving pieces. Make a stock from their carcasses, using salt, the carrot and small onion.

Melt 15 g (½ oz) lard in a large, heavy sauté pan and lightly brown half the guinea sections on both sides. Remove and brown the remaining pieces, adding a little more lard if necessary. Reserve.

In a heavy, flame-proof casserole of a size that takes the poultry comfortably, melt 15 g (½ oz) lard, add the onions and the pork or bacon, cut into lardons. Brown both lightly over a low heat. Add 3 garlic cloves and the 3 herbs.

Melt 40 g (1½ oz) lard in a heavy medium saucepan, beat in the flour and let cook over a low heat, whisking, until the roux turns a nutty, golden-brown.

Off the heat, whisk in the wine and 350 ml (12 fl oz) of the strained stock, and beat until smooth. Add the clove and a little salt, bring to the boil and simmer, half-covered, over a very low heat for 40 minutes, skimming regularly.

Arrange the guinea pieces in the casserole. Season and strain the mellowed sauce and add to the casserole. Cover with buttered greaseproof paper and the lid. Braise in a preheated oven at 190°C, 375°F, Gas Mark 5 for 35 minutes, turning and basting the birds once.

Remove the casserole from oven, and either strain the sauce of its onion, or simply leave the pot to cool. When cold, cover and refrigerate overnight.

The next day, spoon the fat from the surface, add a few tablespoons of water to the pot, and gently reheat its contents, covered, over a low flame, for 10–15 minutes, or until birds are completely cooked through. Taste and correct the seasoning.

Meanwhile, cut the bread into cubes and toss in a little butter over a fairly high heat. Add chopped parsley and remaining garlic when croûtons are turning golden-brown.

Present the guinea-fowl on a hot platter, spoon over the sauce and garnish with croûtons. Serves 6–8.

TARTE AUX PRUNES

Being surrounded by excellent pastry shops, we sample their variety with dedication and have never been known to make a dessert. We particularly like the homely plum tarts of a pâtisserie in the village of Mouans-Sartoux, of which here is an approximate recipe. The flavour is sharp and sophisticated.

275 g (10 oz) rich shortcrust pastry, as
*   for Tarte Tatin on page 39*
500 g (1¼ lb) tart dessert plums, ripe
*   but firm*
granulated sugar
ground cinnamon
juice of ½ lemon
butter
crème fraîche or cream whipped with
*   lemon juice*

Roll out the pastry and use it to line a 23 cm (9 inch) flan ring set on to a heavy baking sheet. Chill the pastry. Bake blind in a preheated oven at 180°C, 350°F, Gas Mark 4 for about 25 minutes until the pastry is golden and browning and almost completely done.

Wash and dry plums and halve them through their natural indentation; remove the stones and put the fruit, cut side up, in one layer across a baking dish. Sprinkle liberally with sugar, some ground cinnamon, and the lemon juice. Dot with butter. Bake in a preheated oven at 190°C, 375°F, Gas Mark 5 until the plums are tender but still hold their shape. Remove from the oven and let cool in their dish for 10 minutes. Take up halves with a slotted spoon and arrange snugly inside the tart shell, making a second layer with any extras.

Simmer juices from baking dish into a syrup and pour this over the fruit; bake tart at 180°C, 350°F, Gas Mark 4, for 10–15 minutes to finish cooking.

Let dessert cool for 15 minutes and serve warm, with *crème fraîche* or cream that's been fortified with lemon juice. Serves 6.

Tarte aux prunes

VIN D'ORANGE

This recipe was given to me by Madame Annette Bernhard, whose family lives perched dramatically beside the gorges of the river Loup, east of Grasse, in an area once thick with trees of *oranges amères*.

The blossoms of these trees were formerly used in perfumery and their fruits candied. Many local families still prepare the bitter-sweet aperitif described below. It is excellent iced and enlivened with Perrier. In colder climates, buy Seville oranges to make the drink in January, then store it away in bottles that are well stoppered, in a cool dark place until summer. Serve from an attractive carafe, with plenty of ice and Perrier to taste.

2.5 litres (4½ pints) still, dry rosé
*   wine, like a Côtes de Provence*
475 ml (16 fl oz) eau de vie de fruits
*   (best bought on a trip to France)*
3 bitter oranges, washed, dried and cut
*   into eighths*
pinch of nutmeg
475 g (17 oz) caster sugar
Perrier water
ice

Combine all the ingredients, except the Perrier water and ice, in one or more large airtight containers. Shake well, and leave at room temperature for 45 days, shaking occasionally.

Pour the wine carefully through a sieve and ladle into bottles that can be tightly stoppered.

MARKET FORCES

I can't resist lingering in good fruit and vegetable markets; the best draw me back, time and again, to particular cities and quarters, and more than one dull town has been saved for me by seeking out its better efforts in the way of produce. These recipes accommodate ingredients from the comfortable onion to the much more elusive blueberry.

CABBAGE POUCHES STUFFED WITH SCALLOPS AND FOIE GRAS

Fredy Girardet's book *La cuisine spontanée* gave me the idea of stuffing cabbage leaves on a smaller but snappier scale than that leaf's usual fate of mince, rice, or leftovers. The sweetness and varied textures of *foie gras*, scallops and carrot make an agreeable combination for eating in the early spring, when cabbage and fresh scallops coincide.

1 green cabbage, preferably Savoy
salt
6 large scallops with coral, never frozen
dry white wine
black pepper
1 large carrot, peeled and finely-diced
granulated sugar
50–75 g (2–3 oz) unsalted butter, cut into squares
75 g (3 oz) pure foie gras, en bloc
1 shallot, peeled and minced
1 tablespoon double cream

Blanch 12 large and handsome cabbage leaves in boiling, salted water for 3–4 minutes until completely cooked. Refresh in cold water, dry well, and cut away thick part of each central rib.

Wash and dry scallops and slice the white muscles diagonally into small medallions. Cut the coral into halves or thirds, put the fish into a small, heavy saucepan and barely cover with white wine. Season, bring the wine to simmer and gently poach scallops for 2–3 minutes until *just* cooked. Drain the fish, reserving its liquid.

Simmer the carrot briefly with seasoning, a good pinch of sugar, a little butter and a spoonful of water until just done; drain the carrot, add its 'stock' to that of the scallops.

Cut *foie gras* into 5 mm ($\frac{1}{4}$ inch) dice.

Spread eight of the best cabbage leaves on to work surface (reinforce each with an extra half-leaf if need be), mix the scallops, carrots, and *foie gras*, divide these among the eight, centring the mixture. Season, wrap each leaf round its contents to make up a smart pouch. Put the eight packets, seam side down, into a low-sided baking dish into which they will fit snugly, place a scrap of butter on top of each, pour on a couple of tablespoons of the fish stock. Slide dish into centre of an oven preheated at 220°C, 425°F, Gas Mark 7.

Reduce 75 ml (3 oz) of the remaining stock to the volume of 2 tablespoons, add the cream, bring to boil, and off the heat, begin to incorporate the butter, whisking and returning the saucepan to the heat after each incorporation, as for a *beurre blanc*. When the sauce is ready, season and keep warm until ready to serve.

The pouches are done after 15–20 minutes, when the contents are hot throughout; test with a knife or trussing needle. Serve 2 parcels per person, accompanied by spoonfuls of sauce. Serves 4 as a first course.

PEPPERS AND AUBERGINES

Another summery salad. The sliced aubergines are served warm and both vegetables are dressed with lemon juice and garlicky oil.

2 large cloves garlic, peeled and minced
75 g (3 oz) first-pressing olive oil
2 slim aubergines, about 225 g (8 oz) each
salt
2 yellow and 2 red sweet peppers, of good size and shape, with thick flesh
1 egg
black pepper
wholemeal or granary breadcrumbs, freshly-made
lemon juice
flat-leaf parsley

One day ahead, stir minced garlic into olive oil; cover and set aside at room temperature.

About 5 hours before eating, slice each aubergine across into 5 mm ($\frac{1}{4}$ inch) rounds, no thicker, or the results will be tough. Strew slices with salt and weight under a large, heavy chopping board until shortly before the meal. The aubergines will lose a lot of brownish liquid.

Meanwhile, rub the peppers with oil and place on a grill pan an inch or so from strong heat. Grill, turning peppers with spoons or metal tongs, until the skins blacken and blister. Remove from the heat and cool under wet paper towels to loosen the skin. When each is cool enough to handle, peel off the loosened skin, halve flesh lengthwise, cut out stems, drain away juices and scrape out seeds. Wash and dry peppers and slice

Cabbage pouches, Peppers and aubergines

into wide strips. Arrange these, inner surfaces downwards, across one or two serving platters remembering to leave enough space for the aubergine.

About 30 minutes before serving, thoroughly wash the aubergines and dry the slices on paper towels, but don't wring these or they will be as tough as cardboard when you chew them. Beat the egg with ground pepper, then strew a lot of breadcrumbs on to a plate. Dip the slices into the egg, coat lightly with crumbs, and slowly grill on both sides, about 10 cm (4 inches) from a low heat, until the aubergine slices are tender inside and rather browned. Keep warm in a slow oven until all of the aubergine is ready, then quickly distribute among the peppers. Grind on black pepper, dribble over lemon juice, spoon on olive oil and garlic mixture, add sprays of parsley and eat as soon as possible. Serves 4 as a substantial first course.

TOURIN BLANCHI AUX ESCARGOTS

Gilles Marre is a young French chef whose name will be celebrated. He has undergone ten years of preparation and training, including military service in the kitchens of the Elysée Palace and a period with Paul Haeberlin of l'Auberge de l'Ill in Alsace, whom Gilles considers as his mentor.

In 1984 'il s'est installé' as the French put it, in his family's Hôtel Terminus in Cahors, calling his restaurant La Balandre, the canal barge. Here I've eaten two refreshing excellent lunches, one as part of Cahors' Fête de la Truffe in January, where we started with Gilles' embellishment of the south-western onion and garlic soup known as *le tourin*.

I've juggled his amounts of milk and cream, as I find equal quantities of each too rich (though there's ample cream remaining); the *escargots* add smoky depths to the soup.

---

4 large white onions, about 1.5 kg (2 lb 2 oz), peeled, halved and thinly sliced
50 g (2 oz) butter
1 large or 2 medium bulbs garlic, peeled
2 litres (3½ pints) milk
salt
black pepper
grated nutmeg
72 escargots
900 ml (1½ pints) double cream
3 egg yolks
fresh parsley, chopped
small croûtons

Sweat the onion with 40 g (1½ oz) butter in a large, heavy pot with lid ajar. Halve garlic cloves, remove the slim green stalk at the centre of each, add the garlic to the onion and sweat, semi-covered, 4–5 minutes further to soften. Add a drop of water if necessary to prevent the garlic burning.

Pour in the milk, season, and grate on a little nutmeg. Bring liquid to simmer and leave barely to shudder, over a very low heat, for 30 minutes, stirring occasionally. Drain the garlic and onion (return milk to pot) and purée smooth in food processor. Whisk purée back into the milk.

If the snails are tinned, drain these of water, rinse well under running water – canned snails are very salty – dry and season; toss in 15 g (½ oz) butter to heat through, put aside to keep warm.

Beat the cream briskly into the yolks while separately bringing the soup to first boil; remove pot from the heat and slowly whisk in the egg-and-cream to liase the mixture.

Quickly roll the snails in parsley to coat evenly and divide among eight heated soup plates. Ladle in *tourin*. Strew with more parsley and croûtons which have been made by drying cubes of stale bread in a 150°C, 300°F, Gas Mark 2 oven until the cubes turn golden brown. Eat without delay. Serves 8.

WARM SALAD OF PASTA, CORN AND POLENTA

---

65 g (2¼ oz) medium-grained polenta (maize meal)
375 ml (13 fl oz) salted water
salt
black pepper
walnut oil
peanut oil
450 g (1 lb) small, dried Italian pasta shapes; ideally in 3 colours
2 ears fresh young sweetcorn
green or purple basil

Measure the *polenta* and bring the salted water to boil in a small, heavy saucepan. Turn heat low and as water simmers, very slowly add maize meal, whisking to prevent lumps. When all the maize is in, stir well with a wooden spoon and cook gently for about 10 minutes, stirring frequently and thoroughly. *Polenta* is done when it comes away from the sides of pan. Season and pour out, scraping pan sides, on to a wooden board. By means of a wet palette knife, spread *polenta* into a flat square about 5 mm (¼ inch) thick. When cold and firm, slice into rectangles about the size of half a postage stamp.

Shortly before the salad is to be served, bring 2 large pots of salted water to boil, add a pour of walnut oil to one. Heat a large serving bowl in a low oven, take a wide sauté pan and pour into it a coating of peanut oil in which to fry the *polenta* dominoes (peanut oil will not give these an unpleasantly greasy coating). Drop pasta into the pot with the oil when the water is at full boil, stir well to separate, boil for about 10–12 minutes or until pasta is just past *al dente*.

Meanwhile, heat the oil in a sauté pan, add *polenta* slices and fry on both sides till a crisp but transparent crust forms on each. Drain on paper towels.

When pasta is about half done, plunge husked corn into second pot and boil for the few minutes necessary to cook. Drain the cobs of corn and as soon as you can touch them, slice away kernels with a small, sharp knife. Put these into the heated bowl with a little walnut oil. Season, toss, and keep warm until ready to use.

When the pasta is ready, drain well, add to the corn with more walnut oil, season and toss; gently mix in fried *polenta*, strew with basil leaves and serve. Serves 4–6.

PUMPKIN BRULEE WITH STRAWBERRIES AND RASPBERRIES

Pumpkin *brûlée* is the brilliant invention of American cookery writer Marion Morash: I've reinterpreted her recipe and served spoonfuls of the custard accompanied by the crushed, sugared strawberries and raspberries. I think that the result is memorable.

475 ml (16 fl oz) double cream
2¼ teaspoons dark rum
6 egg yolks
5 tablespoons caster sugar
200 g (7 oz) cooked pumpkin purée; if you can't find a fresh pumpkin with which to make your own, the canned variety is fine here
¼ teaspoon ground cinnamon
generous pinch of ground cloves
generous pinch of salt
75 g (3 oz) soft light brown sugar

TO SERVE
fresh strawberries
fresh raspberries
icing sugar

Scald the cream and rum while whisking yolks with caster sugar until thick and light. Combine the yolks with pumpkin, spices and salt and slowly beat in the hot cream. Pour mixture into a Pyrex baking dish of 1.5 litres (2½ pints) capacity and bake contents in a bain-marie at 180°C, 350°F, Gas Mark 4 for 1 hour, or until the custard is set and a trussing needle thrust into centre tests very warm. Cool and chill overnight.

To caramelize the top, sieve on brown sugar, pressing it down to an even layer. Place Pyrex dish inside a grill pan filled with cold water and put the custard under a medium to low heat, about 10 cm (4 inches) away from source if possible. Watch the dish carefully and turn it as the sugar melts, blisters, and browns. Remove from the grill, cool for 15 minutes, repeat until brown has deepened and glazed. Try not to burn the sugar! Chill the *brûlée*, uncovered, for several hours. The caramel must not sweat or it will begin to soften.

To serve, bring the pumpkin mixture to room temperature, and with a fork, crush the strawberries and raspberries – also at room temperature – and dust them with sieved icing sugar. Serve with piles of the mixed, sugared berries. Serves 6.

Salad of pasta, corn and polenta, Tourin blanchi aux escargots

RAFT OF PEARS AND BLUEBERRIES

Fresh blueberries have a short, late season; I can't get enough of them. The pastry for this 'raft' is made with cream cheese.

PASTRY
200 g (7 oz) unsalted butter
75 g (3 oz) cream cheese
3 tablespoons soured cream
225 g (8 oz) plain flour
large pinch of salt

FILLING
1 kg (2 lb) ripe but firm pears,
  quartered, peeled and cored
25 g (1 oz) unsalted butter
75 g (3 oz) granulated sugar
3 tablespoons lemon juice
350 g (12 oz) fresh blueberries
large pinch of ground cinnamon
large pinch of salt
¾ teaspoon potato or cornflour
1 egg yolk

To make the pastry, beat together the softened butter, cheese and soured cream. Work in the flour and salt, form pastry into a ball, wrap, and chill for several hours.

Slice the quartered pear lengthwise – not too thinly – and toss, over a high heat, with the butter, 2 tablespoons sugar, and 1 tablespoon lemon juice until pears just barely resist a knife when pierced. Drain, save the juices and cool the fruit.

Put the blueberries into a saucepan with pears' liquid, the remaining sugar and lemon, cinnamon and salt. Cover pan and heat berries until just cooked and yielding their juice. Drain blueberries, add fruit to pears and cool. Take 150 ml (5 oz) of the fruits' liquid and thicken over a low heat by whisking with potato or cornflour dissolved in a teaspoon of water. Combine with berries and pears.

Halve the pastry, roll out half into a narrow rectangle, heap fruit and thickened juices along the centre. Paint the

Raft of pears and blueberries, Pumpkin brûlée

edges with a little cold water, roll out remaining pastry and place over first half. Trim the borders and press close to the fruit with the tines of a fork. Paint the top of the 'raft' with water, re-roll the pastry off-cuts and criss-cross three strips over the upper surface, pressing their ends into the border; turn this back on to itself and seal with a fork. Put a pastry knot into the centre of cross and pierce a steam hole on either side.

Refrigerate raft for several hours. Beat the egg yolk with a little water and just before baking, paint raft with two coats of this egg glaze; cross-hatch glaze with a fork. Place pastry on a heavy baking sheet. Bake in a preheated oven at 220°C, 425°F, Gas Mark 7 for 10 minutes. Reduce the oven temperature to 200°C, 400°F, Gas Mark 6 for 25 minutes further. Serve warm, with cream or vanilla ice cream. Serves 6.

A SENSE OF SERENDIPITY

Each of these recipes represents something I have tasted, heard described, or in one case, merely glimpsed, during my travels of the past few years. The common thread has been the pleasure of sudden, sometimes unexpected, discovery and the interest in comparison of diverse cuisines.

GYUVECH

This is a Bulgarian dish whose origins are Turkish. I first ate it, as *türlü güveç*, in a working man's restaurant at Van, eastern Turkey, where lamb appeared amid the many vegetables. In both Bulgaria and Turkey the list of ingredients can differ from place to place depending on regional and seasonal variations.

In Bulgaria, cubes of beef, lamb, or pork may accompany ten or twelve vegetables, or as here, the vegetables may be on their own. In rural districts, lard might be the cooking fat, though most often sunflower oil, or oil-and-butter is the usual medium. Sometimes mushrooms are added, 'for grandeur', and at the right season, unripe grapes will be put to sharpen the mixture; a dash of vinegar is an occasional substitute for this ingredient.

One or two chili peppers are an optional extra, but leave these out if you don't like the heat. Ingredients and quantities should be regarded as flexible, and though the cooked result – ideally made in an earthenware casserole, the *gyuvech* – looks rather dull, it is delicious and satisfying.

Accompanying this dish are jars of *sharena* or 'colourful' salt, also known as *chubritsa*, meaning 'savory', after the herb which is the chief ingredient of this pounded blend of red peppers, mint, dill and savory with salt and pepper. Bowls of *sharena* salt appear on Bulgarian tables as relish for the hot bread which begins the meal.

---

1 aubergine, cut into small cubes
2 large potatoes, peeled and cubed very small
3–4 courgettes, thickly sliced
1 green pepper, seeded and thinly sliced
100 g (4 oz) green cabbage, shredded
100 g (4 oz) slim green beans, topped and tailed and cut into short lengths
1 large onion, peeled and chopped
1–2 chili peppers, seeded and sliced into thin rounds (optional)
350 g (12 oz) canned Italian plum tomatoes, drained weight and coarsely chopped
100 g (4 oz) fresh okra, if available
handful of fresh parsley, flat-leafed if possible, finely chopped
1 teaspoon paprika
salt
50 ml (2 fl oz) corn or sunflower oil
good dash of wine vinegar
black pepper if not using chilis
3 eggs

Place the aubergine, potatoes, courgettes, pepper, cabbage, green beans, onion, chilis and tomatoes into a large, heavy casserole – earthenware, for purists. Cut the stems from the okra and peel their caps without piercing the pods (or the sap will be released). Add the pods to the casserole. Add about half the parsley, the paprika and 1 teaspoon of salt. Pour on the oil and vinegar. Mix thoroughly with your hands and cover with a piece of buttered, greaseproof paper. Bake in a preheated oven at 190°C, 375°F, Gas Mark 5 for 1½-2 hours, stirring two or three times and moistening the paper as you do so. When all the vegetables are cooked, taste and adjust the seasoning. Beat and season the eggs, add the remaining parsley and pour this over the vegetable mixture. Return to the oven for 5–10 minutes until the eggs are set. Present the *gyuvech* immediately, with hot bread. Serves 4–6.

PAPPA COL POMODORO

This is a Tuscan dish, a simple and agreeable peasant soup made of bread, tomatoes and water. The nicest I've eaten was actually in a restaurant, Le Cave di Maiano, near Fiesole, part of an immense and delicious meal, and this is more or less the recipe they gave me. Tuscan cooks use the local saltless bread which allows the flavour of their excellent tomatoes to predominate. Elsewhere, the *pappa* is worth making only with bread of good character, that won't become a gluey swamp when moistened.

---

first-pressing olive oil
6 large cloves garlic, slivered
1 kg (2 lb) canned Italian plum tomatoes, drained weight
275 g (10 oz) good quality bread, several days old
900 ml–1 litre (1½–1¾ pints) water
large bunch of fresh basil leaves, shredded
salt
black pepper

Run 2 tablespoons of oil round the base of a deep, heavy pan. Soften the garlic in the oil over low heat for about 5 minutes. Add the tomatoes, breaking them up with a wooden spoon, and simmer for

*Clockwise from top right: Tarte ovale, Pappa col pomodoro, Tarator, Tagine, Gyuvech,
Coeur de Camembert*

15–20 minutes until reasonably well cooked down.

Meanwhile, slice the bread with crusts on, and break it into small pieces. Add to the tomato and cover with 900 ml (1½ pints) of the water. Stir the mixture well and simmer for another 15 minutes, stirring occasionally, until the soup has become very thick. Add a little more water if you think necessary. Add the basil leaves towards the end of the cooking time and work them in. Season well.

I think the flavours and texture benefit when the *pappa* is made a day ahead, so cool and refrigerate. When required, reheat the soup, stirring and adding additional water only if necessary; the soup should not be thin. Ladle the soup into bowls, dribble olive oil over the surface of each bowl and eat very hot. Serves 4–5.

LAMB TAGINE WITH PRUNES

I seem to be in a minority of people who actually like Tangier, where I first ate this *tagine*, variously spiced and sweetened with honey and prunes. The recipe is slightly adapted from one of Paula Wolfert's, the American writer on Moroccan food.

---

1 shoulder of lamb
1½ large onions, peeled
25 g (1 oz) butter
good pinch of saffron threads
¼ teaspoon ground nutmeg
¼ teaspoon ground ginger
475 ml (16 fl oz) water
salt
1 tea bag
450 g (1 lb) prunes
½ teaspoon ground cinnamon
2 tablespoons honey
75 g (3 oz) whole blanched almonds
black pepper
small handful of fresh coriander leaves

Ask your butcher to cut the lamb, on the bone, into 2.5 cm (1 inch) cubes. Finely chop the half onion, thinly slice the whole one. Place the lamb in a deep, heavy pan or casserole with the butter, saffron (crumbled between index finger and thumb), nutmeg, ginger, and finely-chopped onion. Stir over a low heat to release the aroma of the spices, but do not brown the meat. Add the water, bring to the boil, lower the heat and skim the liquid. Add ½ teaspoon salt, cover and gently simmer for 1¼ hours, turning the lamb occasionally.

Meanwhile, use a tea bag to make a bowlful of strong tea and, while this is hot, immerse the prunes. Leave for 30 minutes or until the prunes have swelled just enough to cut out their stones, leaving each fruit whole.

When the meat has been simmering for 1¼ hours, add the cinnamon, honey and sliced onion. Cover and cook for about 30 minutes longer or until tender.

When the lamb is done, add the drained and stoned prunes and simmer the *tagine*, uncovered, for 5–10 minutes until the prunes are well-plumped. Meanwhile, toast the almonds under a preheated grill.

Drain the meat and transfer to a serving dish. Drain and distribute the prunes among the meat and keep hot. Degrease the sauce and reduce it, over a high heat, to a coating consistency. Adjust the seasoning, which should be well balanced between spicy and sweet, with pepper. Pour the sauce over the lamb and place on the upper shelf of a preheated oven at 230°C, 450°F, Gas Mark 8 for 2–3 minutes to glaze the meat and onions. Scatter with the almonds and the shredded coriander and serve. Serves 4–6.

TARATOR

During a week's trip to Bulgaria, I ate best in the staff restaurants of various state wineries. The Institute of Nutrition of the Bulgarian Medical Academy supervises the running of these, and the traditional Bulgarian cooking they serve is, in my experience, first-rate.

Since Bulgaria was part of the Ottoman Empire for nearly 500 years, some of the cooking, inevitably, derives from Turkey.

Such is the case with this cold yogurt soup which I've eaten both in Anatolia and at the Suhindol winery east of Sofia, the source of the recipe here. The name *tarator* is the same as for the Turkish sauce described earlier; a fact which I'm sure is attributable to the presence of walnuts and garlic.

---

850 g (30 oz) natural yogurt
450 g (1 lb) cucumber, peeled, seeded, finely chopped
50 g (2 oz) shelled walnuts, ground
2–4 large cloves garlic, peeled and crushed
2 tablespoons sunflower oil
300–400 ml (10–14 fl oz) water
salt
fresh dill, snipped, to taste

Put the yogurt into a large bowl and beat in the cucumber, walnuts, garlic and oil. Dilute with water to make a fairly liquid consistency. Add salt and dill to taste, beat well.

Refrigerate the soup for several hours to blend the flavours. Immediately before serving, float a few ice cubes on the surface. Serves 5–6.

COEUR DE CAMEMBERT AU CALVADOS

The idea for this graceful end to a meal was related to me by Philippe Olivier, *maître-fromager* of Boulogne, who says that formerly, in Normandy, it was not done to serve Camembert in its rind, in the same way as you would not pass round sardines in their tin. Instead the croûte was cut away and the cheese wrapped with breadcrumbs.

In this dish, warm apple sauce and Camembert touched with Calvados accompanied by Normandy cider to drink make a stirring combination.

APPLE SAUCE
750 g (1½ lb) apples, a mixture of tart cooking and sweet eating varieties, peeled, cored and chopped
15 g (½ oz) unsalted butter
about 40 g (1½ oz) light brown sugar

CHEESE
1 Camembert fermier, unpasteurized, creamy and ripe to the centre but not runny
Calvados
fine breadcrumbs, freshly-made from a granary or wholemeal loaf

TO SERVE
granary or wholemeal bread
naturally-fermented Normandy cider, chilled

Put the apples in a heavy saucepan with the butter, a little water and sugar to taste. The resulting sauce should not be too sweet. Cover and cook, stirring often to break down the apples, then beat into a smooth purée which holds its shape well. The sauce should retain an interesting texture and enough acidity to enhance the taste of Camembert. Keep the apple sauce warm while you prepare first the Camembert, then the toast.

Cut the entire rind from the Camembert. Pierce each side all over with a fork and pour on about 2 tablespoons Calvados. Press this into one surface with back of fork. Leave for 30 minutes, basting several times; turn the cheese over and repeat with more Calvados. After 30 minutes more, drain the cheese and cover completely with breadcrumbs. Shake away the excess and pour on a little more Calvados.

Cut the well soaked and breadcrumbed camembert into six wedges and serve with warmed apple sauce, hot toast and chilled cider. Serves 2–4.

Tarte ovale

TARTE OVALE

I first saw this glorified jam tart in the window of a pâtisserie at Vienne, in the Rhône valley in France, but never tasted it; I brought home the idea.

You need a firm pastry that requires no mould, and you may also find that quince jelly gives the perfect note of sweet, slightly exotic acidity.

PATE A CROUSTADE
275 g (10 oz) plain flour
large pinch of salt
150 g (5 oz) unsalted butter, chilled
1 egg, beaten with 2 teaspoons water

TO FINISH
225 g (8 oz) quince jelly or a thick, homemade, purée-like quince jam
icing sugar

Make the pastry by hand or in a food processor. Put the flour and salt into the bowl and blend briefly. Cut the butter into 25 g (1 oz) squares, add to the bowl and work for about 10 seconds until it reaches the consistency of coarse crumbs. Pour the egg and water through the feed opening with the machine on; the pastry will mass together after about 10 seconds. Turn it out on to a floured board and work deftly into a slightly moist ball.

Wrap in greaseproof paper and polythene and refrigerate for several hours or overnight.

Sieve the jelly or beat the jam until smooth, and reserve.

Bring the pastry to room temperature and roll out, between two sheets of floured greaseproof paper, to a thickness of about 3 mm (⅛ inch). Cut out a 23 × 25 cm (9 × 10 inch) oval. Transfer to a heavy baking sheet. Re-roll the trimmings to the same thickness and cut into thin strips. Spread the jelly over the oval to within 1.5 cm (⅝ inch) or so of the edge, all round. Lay the strips of pastry across from top to bottom, fanning them slightly, and press them against the unjellied border. Trim any excess dough. With your fingers, roll the edge to form a rim. Refrigerate the unbaked tart for about 2 hours.

Bake in a preheated oven at 180°C, 350°F, Gas Mark 4 for 30–40 minutes until the pastry is cooked and colouring. Turn round once during this time. The jelly will bubble up and out to some extent.

Remove the tart from the oven and allow to cool for about 10 minutes, then carefully loosen it from the baking sheet with a palette knife. When cold, transfer to a serving platter, cover half of the tart with a sheet of greaseproof paper and sift a good coating of icing sugar over the other half.

Present whole, and serve each person with a slice from both sugared and unsugared sections. Serves 4.

DELICACIES IN DISGUISE

Fresh chicken livers, a meal steamed in parchment, *polenta* with sausages, fresh figs and anything made with pig's ears are not commonplace, as far as I can tell, on today's dinner tables. I hope these recipes will encourage cooks to rectify this neglect.

We photographed the results, in late spring, in a beautifully-tended version of an eighteenth-century kitchen garden – this one a brick-walled half-acre in Warwickshire, looking from the greenhouse towards a fruit cage.

RADISH CANAPES, CROSTINI

Quickly-prepared mouthfuls served with drinks before dinner are not always considered worth the trouble, which is a great pity; radishes sliced on to buttered bread – a treasured snack of French children – and *crostini*, a hot Tuscan hors-d'oeuvre made with chicken livers, are two of my favourites. Try to persuade your butcher to get *fresh* livers. If you must use frozen ones, drain them very well after thawing.

RADISH CANAPES
1 narrow loaf of French bread
butter, unsalted if possible
radishes
salt
black pepper

CROSTINI
275 g (10 oz) chicken livers
salt
black pepper
olive oil
lemon juice

Cut French loaf into as many thin slices as you will want for the radish canapés, slice 14 or 15 further rounds for the *crostini* and put the latter to dry and lightly toast in a preheated oven at 140°C, 275°F, Gas Mark 1 for about 20 minutes.

Butter untoasted slices, top and tail radishes, and slice and fan them across bread. Season.

When the toasts are slightly coloured (finish them off under slow grill if this is taking too long), trim, wash and dry the livers. Season them, and sauté whole in a splash of olive oil over a high heat, tossing often, for about 3 minutes, until just cooked and still pink inside. Turn into a bowl, squeeze on lemon juice, and quickly mash with a fork. Spread the purée on to toasts, grind on pepper, and serve *crostini* hot, accompanied by radish canapés.

POLENTA WITH SAUSAGES

A meal-in-one, this time a big robust dish from northern Italy, as described in Marcella Hazan's *Classic Italian Cook Book*; I've adapted her recipe somewhat. This is a different use of *polenta* from the way it has been presented earlier, though the idea is the same.

175 g (3 oz) onion, peeled and chopped
1½ tablespoons olive oil
1 large carrot, peeled and chopped
2 medium celery sticks, chopped
75 g (3 oz) thinly-sliced pancetta
(cured belly pork in a sausage
shape), cut into 1 cm (½ inch) strips
450 g (1 lb) luganega or other slim,
sweet pork sausage
350 g (12 oz) canned Italian plum
tomatoes with their juices

1.5 litres (2½ pints) salted water
275 g (10 oz) medium or coarse-
grained polenta (maize meal)
salt
black pepper

Put the onion with olive oil in a large sauté pan and sweat, covered, until the onion is pale gold. Add the carrot, celery and *pancetta*, and sauté over medium heat for 3–4 minutes, stirring frequently.

Cut the sausage into 7.5 cm (3 inch) lengths, add to the pan and cook for 10 minutes, turning occasionally. Pour in the tomatoes and juice, and break up with a wooden spoon. Simmer for 25 minutes, stirring occasionally.

Meanwhile, bring the salted water to a brisk simmer and very slowly add the maize meal, whisking to prevent lumps. When all the maize is in, stir well with a wooden spoon and cook gently for 15–20 minutes, stirring frequently and thoroughly. The *polenta* is done when it comes away from sides of pan.

Season and pour into a large, round, heated dish. Make a depression in the centre, pour on the sausages and all their sauce. Serve immediately, with a large green salad to accompany or follow. Serves 6.

Clockwise from top right: Polenta with sausages, Silk purse salad, Radish canapés, crostini, La terrine de Jeanne, Fish with vegetables in parchment, Figs in fruit salad

SILK PURSE SALAD

The French know how good this can be, but most British and Americans look at me aghast when they learn the main ingredient here. They are usually converted, though, after tasting the dish. Pigs' ears in fact combine crunch and a slightly tongue-like quality which is excellent sharply-dressed with pickled gherkins and celery; they also lack the glueyness of pig's feet. While wooing your butcher for fresh chicken livers, ask him to order this inexpensive cut of pork at the same time.

---

4 pigs' ears
salt
1 carrot, peeled
1 onion, peeled
1 clove garlic, unpeeled
1 bouquet garni
3 tablespoons lemon juice
2 tablespoons Dijon mustard
1 celery stick, minced
4 pickled gherkins, minced
2 shallots, peeled and minced
fresh parsley, chopped
fresh chervil, chopped
fresh chives, chopped
2 eggs
4 tablespoons olive oil
black pepper
lettuce leaves

Clean the ears, singe off hair, and wash. Coat with salt and refrigerate overnight. The next day wash and drain the ears and put them into a large pot with the carrot, onion, garlic and bouquet garni. Cover with water, bring to boil, skim and simmer half-covered for 2–2½ hours until the ears test tender. Let them cool in the liquid.

Make the dressing by combining the lemon juice and mustard with celery, gherkins, and shallots. Add a lot of chopped herbs. Boil the eggs for 3 minutes, scoop yolks into dressing, chop and add whites. Beat in olive oil, add salt and pepper to taste.

Drain and dry cooled ears, cut away the very cartilaginous ends, slice ears in half lengthwise, cut the halves across and then into thin strips. Toss with the dressing, taste for seasoning, and present on a bed of lettuce. Serves 4–6.

LA TERRINE DE JEANNE

Chicken livers again, tasting almost like *foie gras* along the centre of a pork forcemeat. This is the recipe of Gisèle Mardon, a Frenchwoman who teaches cooking in London. Very easily made, this terrine is one for which fresh livers of firm texture and pale colour are absolutely essential.

---

225 g (8 oz) chicken livers, never
*   frozen*
1 tablespoon port
1 tablespoon cognac
about 500 g (1¼ lb) streaky fresh pork,
*   weighed after bones and rind have*
*   been removed*
1 shallot, peeled and chopped
1 clove garlic, peeled and chopped
¼ teaspoon quatre épices (sometimes
*   sold as Epices Marie or Epice*
*   Parisienne)*
2 tablespoons chopped fresh parsley
salt
black pepper
butter
enough streaky smoked bacon of good
*   regional cure if possible, to line a*
*   900 ml (1½ pint) terrine*
1 bay leaf
lard (optional)

TO SERVE
buttered toast

Trim livers and marinate in port and brandy, refrigerating overnight. The next day, trim the pork of excess nerve tissue, leaving you with about 450 g (1 lb) of streaky meat. Mince this with the shallot, garlic, *quatre épices*, parsley, and a little salt and pepper. Drain the

marinade from the livers and add it to the mixture. Test flavours by frying a small ball of this forcemeat in butter; add more seasoning if needed and test the flavours once again.

Cut away the bacon rinds if necessary and soak the rashers in tepid water to remove any excess salt. Rinse well, dry, and stretch the rashers with back of a knife. Line a 900 ml (1½ pint) terrine of attractive shape with overlapping slices of the bacon rashers.

Weigh forcemeat and press half into terrine; season livers and lay them on top in an even layer. Cover with rest of pork mixture, smooth and round with a damp hand, lay bay leaf in middle, fold over bacon from sides. Cover with foil and the lid, then place in a bain-marie. Bake in a preheated oven at 160°C, 325°F, Gas Mark 3 for 1½ hours, turning once. A trussing needle plunged into centre should test hot.

Remove the terrine from the oven and bain-marie with its foil intact, cover with 1 kg (2 lb) weight to compress the mixture. Cool, and chill the terrine still weighted, overnight; remove the weight in the morning, and leave uncut for 2–3 days to allow the various flavours to develop and mature.

To keep the terrine for longer, unmould it, scrape away and discard the jelly, wash and dry its container and carefully replace the contents, minus the bay leaf. Seal the surface completely with melted lard and refrigerate. Serves 4–6, with buttered toast.

FISH WITH VEGETABLES IN PARCHMENT

I like to combine fish or poultry with vegetables and herbs and bake them together in parchment or foil; the result is a meal-in-one whose aromas burst out as you tear apart the bag.

The quantities suggested are for amounts *per person*; multiply by any number up to four.

butter
three of the following fish: a few
mussels in closed shells, 2 scallops
with coral, 50 g (2 oz) each of
turbot, salmon, or halibut (without
skin)
a few mange-tout peas, topped and
tailed
salt
generous 25 g (1 oz) slim French
beans, topped and tailed
4–5 tiny new potatoes in skins
50 g (2 oz) courgette
fresh basil
fresh chervil
fresh chives
black pepper
beurre blanc

Fish in parchment

Figs in fruit salad

For each person cut a 35.5 cm (14 inch) round of baking parchment or grease-proof paper and butter one side. Scrub, beard and dry the mussels. Slice scallops into bite-sized pieces, leaving coral intact; slice any other fish into same size.

Blanch the mange-tout in boiling salted water until half-cooked. Blanch the beans until *al dente*, drain, refresh, and dry. Boil the potatoes until done, cut unblanched courgette into lengths.

Lay buttered side of the parchment on the work surface (greasing the exterior makes the paper less likely to tear accidentally) and arrange all the fish and vegetables over one half of the circle. Strew with shredded basil, snipped chervil and chives; grind on salt and pepper. Fold parchment across and roll edges tightly to make a sort of turnover. Staple edges at 2.5–5 cm (1–2 inch) intervals and just before closing the end of each turnover, insert a straw and blow to inflate the parchment. Staple the package shut. Place on a heavy baking sheet in a preheated oven at 190°C, 375°F, Gas Mark 5 for about 15 minutes; the bag will puff and colour.

Serve immediately in a hot soup plate. Tear open the bag and pour over a little *beurre blanc*, recipe is on page 46.

FIGS IN FRUIT SALAD

How to convince anyone that fruit salad has been neglected? I adore figs and their potential; like making their unskinned cross sections into patterns with other fruits, moistening everything with syrup and adding a herb or a few edible flowers. So I'll make this my last neglected dish and won't worry too much if the appellation has been stretched.

SUGAR SYRUP
100 g (4 oz) granulated sugar
250 ml (8 fl oz) water
dash of lemon juice
small piece of dried tamarind fruit

SALAD
2 ripe but firm peaches
2 small oranges
4 figs
12–16 fresh strawberries
8 cherries

First, prepare the sugar syrup by dissolving the granulated sugar in the water and boiling the liquid for 1 minute. Add the lemon juice to sharpen the taste and the dried tamarind fruit to give the syrup an agreeable tang. Cool and refrigerate

overnight and strain in the morning before use.

To make four individual salads, take the peaches, remove their skins in just-boiled water and gently poach in the strained syrup until a knife just pierces their flesh. Do not overcook or they will be mushy.

Let the peaches cool while cutting the peel and pith from the oranges. Cut the oranges into sections without their membrane and add their exuded juice to the sugar syrup.

Slice the figs across, and the strawberries from top to bottom. Pit and halve the cherries and slice the peaches.

Arrange all this fruit across four dinner plates. Spoon on a little syrup, cooled and strained once more (use the remainder elsewhere), surround fruits with edible flowers or herbs. Here I've added pansies, polyanthus, and the leaves and flowers of sweet cicely, an ethereal looking plant with a delicate sweet anise flavour.

These are some suggested combinations of various fruits with figs; figs and raspberries would be delectable on their own, or with sliced nectarines. Combinations of figs, plums and redcurrants are another possibility. Serves 4.

ANOTHER CULTURE

Yogurt is popular as never before, but buttermilk, its equally cultivated cousin, has become an undervalued relation. The family to which they both belong is that of the cultured milk products, which includes soured cream, smetana and various cheeses.

They are all formed by the introduction of benign bacteria which feed on lactose or milk sugar and produce lactic acid, which sours the milk and causes it to curdle. Different types of milk with various forms of bacteria, treated in differing ways, give individual results; the principle, however, is the same for all of them.

I love the silken-rich acidity of chilled buttermilk; to drink, to bake with, and to add focus to cool summer soups. Confusingly, little of what is sold in the shops as 'cultured buttermilk' is the by-product of churning cream into butter. It is, in fact, milk from which the cream has been skimmed, soured by the introduction of a bacteria or lactic culture, and often thickened by the addition of separated milk solids.

There is a strong case for the real thing. In my experience it tastes better with its sauve, satiny texture. The recipes which follow, however, are equally as good with true buttermilk or the cultured skim alternative and for practical purposes, I'll call both 'buttermilk'.

CHILLED CURRIED AUBERGINE SOUP

As I often demonstrate in these pages, the aubergine is a good vehicle for other flavours; here it is curry that adds an unexpected dimension. A flourish of buttermilk finishes it nicely.

scant 25 g (1 oz) butter
1 medium onion, peeled and sliced
1 teaspoon mild curry powder
500 g (1¼ lb) aubergines
1 litre (1¾ pints) chicken broth, made as on page 100
salt
350–450 ml (12–15 fl oz) buttermilk
juice of ½–1 lemon
black pepper
additional broth or buttermilk if necessary
fresh chervil
spring onions

Melt the butter in a medium saucepan and sweat the onion until soft. Add the curry powder and stir over a low heat for about 1 minute.

Meanwhile, grill the aubergines until skin is charred and flesh is soft. Cut away stems and peel off skin; rinse flesh under cold water and squeeze away bitter juices. Chop the flesh and add it to saucepan with broth and a dash of salt; half-cover, and simmer soup for 5–10 minutes, until the vegetables are tender. Half-cool and liquidize until very smooth. Add 350 g (12 oz) of buttermilk and strained juice of the half lemon. Season and decide whether to add remaining buttermilk and lemon, and more seasoning.

Chill soup overnight; its flavours will mellow if left until the next day. Remove from the refrigerator 30 minutes before serving, thin with more broth or buttermilk if need be, check seasoning, ladle into bowls and garnish each with a sprig of fresh chervil and a section through the base of a spring onion, its layers of skin curled by 30 minutes' immersion in cold water. Serves 4.

CHILLED SOUP OF YELLOW PEPPERS

Using almost exactly the same method, you can produce quite a different soup with sweet yellow peppers and without curry.

scant 25 g (1 oz) butter
1 medium carrot, peeled and sliced
1 medium onion, peeled and sliced
1 large clove garlic, peeled and crushed
500 g (1¼ lb) sweet yellow peppers
900 ml (1½ pints) home-made chicken broth, made as on page 100
salt
350–450 ml (12–15 fl oz) buttermilk
juice of ½–1 lemon
black pepper
additional stock or buttermilk, if necessary
slim strips of sweet red pepper

Proceed as for aubergine soup, sweating carrot and onion with garlic – but without curry powder. Grill peppers as aubergines, skin. Halve lengthwise, cut out stems, drain juices, remove ribs and seeds. Rinse flesh in cool water, cut into strips and continue preparation as with aubergines.

Thin if required, check seasoning, ladle into bowls, and garnish with strips of red pepper, prepared as for flesh of the yellow. Serves 4.

From the top: Curried aubergine soup, Soup of yellow peppers, Avocado and watercress salad

AVOCADO AND WATERCRESS SALAD, BUTTERMILK AND HERB DRESSING

I think that we don't often search for alternatives to the oil and vinegar sorts of dressings for salads. Buttermilk, enhanced with chives and the flair of mustard, sharpened with lemon juice and a touch of oil from toasted sesame seeds, does wonderful things for the long-familiar avocado. Add to this the pepper of watercress and you have a very striking salad.

1½ teaspoons sesame seeds
175 ml (6 fl oz) buttermilk, chilled
watercress
fresh chives
pinch of dry mustard
salt
black pepper
lemon juice
2–3 ripe avocados

Lightly toast the sesame seeds under a preheated grill set to a low temperature. Cool.

Put the buttermilk into a blender, add about 10 watercress leaves, some snipped chives, a good pinch of dry mustard, a grind each of salt and pepper. Blend until smooth and judge whether to add more of either herb, and/or mustard and seasoning. The dressing should be piquant without overpowering the subtlety of the buttermilk. Add a squeeze of lemon and blend the mixture again. Pour into a bowl and stir in the sesame seeds.

Halve the avocados, remove stones and skins, and slice each half into a fan across a small plate. Lay a few attractive sprigs of watercress into the spring of each fan, grind pepper over avocado and spoon a ribbon of dressing across centre of fan.

Serve without delay, with any additional dressing to accompany salad. Serves 4–6.

KAERENAELKS KOLDSKAAL

This is a cold Danish froth, to which I like to add a few cherries or raspberries when they are in season. The flavours should be fresh, so mix the various elements just before serving the drink.

950 ml (1 pint 12 fl oz) cold
*   buttermilk*
grated zest and juice of 1 lemon
2 eggs
2 tablespoons caster sugar
a small handful of fresh raspberries or
*   stoned cherries*

Whiz the buttermilk, lemon zest and strained juice in a blender. In a small bowl, beat the eggs and sugar until thick, add to the buttermilk with raspberries or cherries to taste, and purée. Makes 4 glassfuls.

BUTTERMILK ICE CREAM

100 g (4 oz) sultanas
120 ml (4 fl oz) dark rum
6 egg yolks
350 g (12 oz) caster sugar
¼ teaspoon salt
1 litre (1¾ pints) buttermilk
500 ml (18 fl oz) double cream
2 vanilla pods, split

Bring sultanas and rum to the boil, simmer briefly and leave fruit to cool.

With a hand-held electric beater, whisk the yolks, sugar, and salt until thick; combine the buttermilk, cream and vanilla pods in a heavy saucepan. Bring the liquid just to simmer and beat this into yolks. Return all to the pan and whisk over medium heat until mixture thickens and *just* comes to the boil. Immediately sieve into a bowl.

When custard has cooled, pour it into a deep plastic box, whisk well, cover, place in freezer and leave, stirring and beating every hour. When ice cream is about half-frozen, work in sultanas and rum, cover tightly and return to freezer; continue to stir about once every hour, until well on the way to setting.

Make 36 hours in advance as the alcohol in rum retards the freezing.

Serve scoops of the ice cream with a short biscuit, or in tandem with slices of buttermilk cake. Serves 6–8.

BUTTERMILK CAKE

This is a classic American recipe which I've adapted from Flo Braker's version in *The Simple Art of Perfect Baking*, published in 1985 in New York. Buttermilk gives the cake a tender crumb.

365 g (12½ oz) plain flour
1½ teaspoons baking powder
½ teaspoon baking soda
¼ teaspoon salt
1 teaspoon vanilla essence, not
*   'flavouring'*
generous 250 ml (8 fl oz) buttermilk,
*   at room temperature*
175 g (6 oz) unsalted butter, softened
265 g (9½ oz) caster sugar
3 egg yolks at room temperature
icing sugar

Butter the bases and sides of two loaf-shaped cake tins, each 1.5 litre (2½ pint) capacity. Line each base with a rectangle of buttered greaseproof paper cut to size. Dust sides and base with flour, and tap out excess.

Sift together the four dry ingredients, twice, and reserve. Stir vanilla into buttermilk and put aside.

In a large bowl, cream the butter until light, gradually beat in the sugar. Whisk together yolks, beat these slowly into butter base.

Spoon a quarter of the flour mixture over the creamed mixture, beat this in. Add a third of the buttermilk and vanilla and stir well. Continue alternating dry and wet ingredients until all are incorporated, finishing with flour.

Spoon the batter into loaf tins and spread, using a dampened palette knife and working from the centre outwards to create a slightly raised area around the rim; this will help to offset the eventual high rise in the cakes' centre.

Bake in the centre of a preheated oven at 180°C, 350°F, Gas Mark 4 for about 1¼ hours, turning the tins round half way through baking. Cakes are done when they have risen well, each centre bounces back when lightly pressed, and a fine metal skewer thrust into depths tests clean and hot.

Cool both cakes for 30 minutes before removing from loaf pans; peel away greaseproof paper, cool completely and store.

To serve, dust tops with icing sugar and slice. Good with buttermilk ice cream (see recipe on page 70), or a glass of chilled wine, white and medium-dry. These cakes keep very well if stored in air-tight containers.

Buttermilk cake, Buttermilk ice cream, Kaernaelks koldskaal

THE FOOD OF TURKEY

Turkey is almost entirely an Asian peninsula thrust west between the Black Sea rain which steeps thousands of acres of tea plantations, and Mediterranean semi-tropical heat where bananas and oranges prosper.

The Turks, who are self-sufficient in food, cook from the traditions of an empire which formerly stretched from North Africa to the Danube and the southern tip of Arabia. These are traditions that combine the epicurean customs of Byzantine and Ottoman court life with those of the nomad — a great variety of small items carefully prepared, very subtly flavoured and quickly transported.

The Turkish are discriminating, aware of nuance and the provenance of the best ingredients. They care greatly about the quality of drinking water, and will tell you without hesitation that there are fifty ways of preparing aubergines. As Turkish cooks are not given to experiment, many recipes have hardly changed for centuries, and regional dishes abound.

Ingredients for Turkish meals can be bought from supermarkets, Cypriot grocers, or other specialist grocers.

MEZE

Although meals in Turkey are a succession of individual dishes, various mouthfuls may be served all at once to start things off, olives, for example or nuts, *pastirma* (dried, spiced beef), smoked swordfish, and cold stuffed vine leaves. Or serve diced white cheese, diced melon, *sucuk* (sausage spiced with paprika and cumin) and the three meze which follow.

MIDYE DOLMASI (STUFFED MUSSELS)

1 medium onion, peeled and finely minced
¼ teaspoon crushed coriander seeds
2 tablespoons olive oil
75 g (3 oz) short-grain rice
generous 25 g (1 oz) pine-nuts
salt
50 g (2 oz) dried currants
3 tablespoons chopped fresh parsley
¼ teaspoon turmeric
black pepper
30 large fresh mussels in shells

Sweat the onion and coriander seeds in the oil in a medium saucepan for 5 minutes over low heat, stirring occasionally. Add the rice, nuts and a pinch of salt, then sweat, covered, for 5 minutes more, stirring several times to prevent the rice from sticking.

Add the currants, parsley, turmeric and water just to cover. Cover and simmer until the rice is tender and water is absorbed. Season well and cool on a plate. The turmeric colours the rice a warm yellow.

Beard, scrape and wash the mussels. Cutting from the point of each shell's straight edge, prise open the raw bivalves and spoon some stuffing between each pair of flesh-lined half-shells. Close the shells, scrape away excess stuffing, and tie each mussel tightly across with string. Pack the bivalves into a saucepan, add salt. Weight with a small inverted plate, pour on water just to cover, bring the water to the boil, cover and simmer for 30 minutes. Cool and drain the mussels, cut the strings and serve the shellfish cold each on its half shell.

ARNAVUT CIGERI (ALBANIAN LIVER)

225 g (8 oz) lamb's liver
2 teaspoons paprika
2 tablespoons seasoned flour
2½ tablespoons olive oil
salt
black pepper
1 medium onion, peeled and thinly sliced
chopped fresh parsley

Trim and dice the liver, wash and dry it. Coat with half the paprika and all the flour; toss in a sieve to be rid of the excess.

Heat 1½ tablespoons of oil until very hot and toss liver in this for a scant minute over a high heat. Drain, grind on salt and pepper. Warm the remaining 1 tablespoon of oil in a small saucepan, stir in the remaining paprika and pour this over the liver.

Sprinkle the onion with salt and let it stand for 30 minutes. Work the salt into the onion; squeeze out the moisture, rinse very well and dry. This process lessens the impact. Serve liver cold, strewn with onion and chopped parsley.

Clockwise from the top: Içli Köfte, Etli yaprak dolması, Envai khoshablar, Cılbır, Patlıcan ezme, Arnavut cigerı, Midye dolması

PATLICAN EZME (AUBERGINE AND CHILI PUREE)

1 aubergine, about 350 g (12 oz)
50 g (2 oz) onion, chopped
½–1 fresh chili pepper, split and seeded
small handful chopped fresh parsley
olive oil
2 tablespoons natural yogurt
salt

Grill the aubergine until its skin blackens and the flesh softens; cool, skin, wash the flesh and squeeze away all its bitter juice.

Combine the flesh in a food processor with the onion, chili (start with half, then add more to taste), parsley, 1 tablespoon oil, yogurt, and salt as needed. Purée the mixture, using a steel blade, until it is fairly smooth; the result should be hot but not overpowering.

Transfer to a small bowl, cover with a film of olive oil, and serve at room temperature with strips of split, buttered and toasted slices of *pide* or *pitta* bread. These *meze* serve 4–8 people depending on circumstances and appetites.

CILBIR

Another recipe using yogurt; the Turks eat a great deal of yogurt, mainly made of milk from the goat, sheep or buffalo. Yogurt is combined here with freshly-poached eggs and topped by paprika and butter to make a mixture of hot and cold which is again unusual and delicious. The recipe comes from Konya, south of Ankara.

225 g (8 oz) natural yogurt
2 small cloves garlic, crushed
salt
black pepper
2 eggs
25 g (1 oz) butter
¼ teaspoon paprika

Combine the well chilled yogurt, garlic and seasoning; beat until smooth; divide the mixture between two small bowls.

Gently poach eggs while melting the butter. Drain eggs, trim off straying white, and slide each, 'sunny side up', into the yogurt. Stir paprika into butter and spoon this in zig-zags across each egg. Eat without delay. This is one of the most satisfying 'fast foods' that I know. Serves 2 as a filling snack.

ETLI YAPRAK DOLMASI

This recipe for vine leaves stuffed with meat and rice and served hot, as a single course, with yogurt sauce was given to me by Mrs Semra Yasal of London and Ankara. Such *dolma* are a part of home cooking; restaurants usually confine themselves to rice, currant and pine-nut stuffed leaves served cold and in small quantities among the *meze*. The same meat mixture can be used to fill sweet peppers, aubergines or spinach leaves.

1½ × 225 g (8 oz) packets vine leaves in brine

STUFFING
450 g (1 lb) beef, minced
75 g (3 oz) short-grain rice
1 large onion, peeled and grated
100 g (4 oz) Italian plum tomatoes, drained and chopped
1½ tablespoons tomato purée
1 tablespoon chopped fresh parsley
large pinch of dried oregano
large pinch of fresh or dried chopped mint
salt
black pepper
15 g (½ oz) butter

SAUCE
275 g (10 oz) natural yogurt
3 cloves garlic, peeled
salt
black pepper

To make the stuffing, combine all but ½ tablespoon tomato purée of the first 10 ingredients; knead together well. Taste for seasoning; the mixture should be quite savoury. Drain the vine leaves, and if tough, boil in water for 15–20 minutes to soften. Drain and cool.

In a deep casserole, heat the butter, the remaining tomato purée and the water; mix to a paste and cool.

Spread out one vine leaf, underside up, pinch off the stem, put ½ dessert spoon of stuffing at stem end, and roll leaf tightly, folding in sides. Repeat with all remaining stuffing. Pack the rolls into rows – open-side down – across the casserole, closely wedged so as not to unroll, making two compact layers on top of the paste of tomato and butter. Weight with a small inverted plate, pour on water just to cover, add salt, bring water to boil, and simmer *dolma*, covered, for 30 minutes.

To make *sarmısaklı yoğurt*, the garlic-flavoured sauce; whisk the yogurt smooth with a fork, crush the garlic to a paste with the aid of salt and the blade of a heavy knife, add to the yogurt and season well. Drain *dolma*; serve hot, dribbled with cold sauce. Serves 4 as a main course.

ICLI KOFTE

These meatballs of lamb and cracked wheat, stuffed with lamb and walnuts and served in a stock, look unglamorous, but if made with care, they are tender and delectable. The recipe is reputed to be Armenian, from the eastern part of Turkey, near Malatya.

Cracked wheat, or bulgur, has been boiled, dried and 'cracked' into fine, medium or coarse grains; it is used throughout the Middle East for many different recipes; it is the chief ingredient of *tabbouleh*, from the Lebanon. Içli Köfte are time-consuming to prepare but have a delicacy which makes the effort worthwhile.

1 lamb shoulder
salt
bouquet garni
1 small carrot, peeled
1 small onion, quartered
175 g (6 oz) fine-grained bulgur
50 g (2 oz) onion, peeled and finely
   minced
black pepper

STUFFING

200 g (7 oz) fatty lamb from shoulder
1 medium onion, peeled and finely
   minced
25 g (1 oz) butter
salt
ground cumin, to taste
small handful fresh chopped parsley
50 g (2 oz) walnuts, finely minced
ground cinnamon, to taste
black pepper

Have your butcher bone the shoulder and give you both meat and bones, or if skilled enough, do this yourself.

Make a stock by simmering the bones for several hours with salt, bouquet garni and a small carrot and onion.

Cut up the shoulder and take 450 g (1 lb) of meat from it, free of all fat and connective tissue. Soak bulgur for 20 minutes in very hot water to cover. It will swell and soften. Grind the meat very, very fine and knead the minced onion into it by hand. Squeeze water from the bulgur; and when cool, knead with meat and a lot of seasoning. Work mixture on a board for 5 minutes.

To make stuffing, take the fatty meat from shoulder, without connective tissue and grind it finely (use any leftover lamb elsewhere). Sweat onion in butter for 5 minutes to soften. Add fatty lamb, break up with a fork, add salt and liberal sprinkling of cumin, and sauté, stirring, until lamb is just cooked. Drain, put in remaining ingredients; add more spices and seasoning if needed. The mixture should be highly flavoured.

Let the stuffing cool while rolling the lamb and bulgur into 2.5 cm (1 inch) balls, using wet hands. Turn each ball round the tip of the thumb to make a deep, cup-like hollow, spoon in about ¾ teaspoon stuffing and close up the surface, smoothing with wet fingers. Shape the ball into an oval. Continue until all the raw lamb is used, and rest the balls in the refrigerator for several hours.

Remove the fat from the strained stock, add water to make up to 1.5 litres (2½ pints), season, and when ready to go, heat stock to simmering in one or two large saucepans. Add the meatballs and poach gently for 5 minutes, or until they float to surface. Divide köfte and stock among warmed soup bowls. Serves 4–5 as a main course.

ENVAI KHOSHABLAR

Here are two recipes from the mysterious *Turkish Cookery Book*, published in London in 1884 by one Turabi Effendi. The book is rare, and the identity of its author unknown both to me and to the writer Alan Davidson, who owns a photocopy. The recipes are fascinating, clear and eminently usable. This pair of 'sherbets, or thin syrups with fruit in them', derive from a long tradition of cold, sweet drinks and fruit salads.

Orange and Sultana Sherbet

To serve 4, I make full quantity of the orange (without adding water or extra sugar) and half the sultana, using granulated sugar for both (50–70 g (2–3 oz) sugar for 225 g (8 oz) sultanas, and rose-water as a contrast to the first sherbet. Rose and orange-flower waters or essence can be bought from chemists.

PORTAKAL KHOSHABI (ORANGE SHERBET)

'Peel 5–6 oranges, and divide them in pieces; cut each clove or piece of orange in two, and remove the pips and the thin membranes from them; then put 100 g (4 oz) of powdered sugar in a stewpan, with the juice of 2 oranges: if they are not sufficiently sweet, add more sugar; put it on a slow fire, and stir with a wooden spoon until it begins to boil; then take it off. When cold, pour in a glass bowl, and mix it with water to form a nice sherbet; then add the pieces of orange, with a few drops of the essence of orange-flower, and a few small pieces of ice, and serve.'

CHEKIRDEKSIZ UZUM KHOSHABI (SULTANA SHERBET)

'Get 450 g (1 lb) of sultana raisins, take the stalks off and well wash them; put them in a stewpan with 600 ml (1 pint) of water, and set it to boil until they are swollen up; then take it off, and pass the liquor through a sieve into a saucepan, add sufficient loaf sugar, and boil until it becomes thickish, then remove it. When cold, pour it in a glass bowl, and moderate the sweetness with cold water, then put the boiled raisins in, with a few drops of the essence of orange-flower or rose, and a few small pieces of ice, and serve.

'All other raisins, currants, dried morella and other kinds of cherries, dried apricots, and dried plums of all kinds, may be done in the same way.'

THE SEASONS

Each year I look forward to the coming of a new season. While relishing the earthy spring freshness of new potatoes, I anticipate the sweet juice of mid-summer tomatoes. In September I think about wild mushrooms, while remembering that Christmas will bring on light, lemony fruitcakes and the fun of ornate pastries.

Spring is the time for these delicate new potatoes to be cooked simply, rolled in butter and seasoning and a chopping of fresh herbs; excellent in company with spring lamb or salmon steaks. Tiny courgettes or miniature turnips are delicious treated in the same way. By the summer, those tomatoes taste wonderful when eaten out of doors, strewn with pungent basil and served as an escort for cold braised meat or a crackling and succulent grilled fish.

In autumn, the mushrooms melt into sautés with spice and vegetables, following a soup that exploits the harvest produce. These are the weeks for grape-gathering, and wine adds interest to late-season dishes – a festive loin of pork, or a long-simmered stew in which the meat falls from the bone amidst wintery herbs and mellowed flavours. And then Christmas, with its fruitcakes and cranberries, is a time to relish the details of preparation that will fill your house with luscious scents of baking.

SPRING FEVER

What more need be said about spring; young vegetables, fresh tastes, early fruits, the clear pinks and greens that edge out lentil-brown? Let the food be witness for itself.

TOMATO AND COCONUT SOUP

This is an intriguingly delicate cold soup; the coconut flavour is elusive beneath the taste of uncooked tomatoes. This soup, however, must be only lightly chilled and should be eaten within a few hours of making. If refrigerated overnight, the various flavours of the soup wander disagreeably and results are not good.

8 tablespoons desiccated coconut
1.2 litres (2 pints) chicken broth; home-made is essential here, and for method, see page 100
1.25 kg (2½ lb) ripe tomatoes, skinned, halved and seeded
2 heaping tablespoons natural yogurt
salt
black pepper

Simmer the coconut in the broth for 5 minutes then leave the stock to cool thoroughly. Strain the resulting broth through a sieve lined with a double thickness of muslin then scoop 2 tablespoons of the simmered coconut back into the strained broth, gather up the muslin and squeeze its contents hard over the stock to extract as much flavour as possible.

Liquidize the broth with the tomatoes until smooth. Add the yogurt and blend once again. Season to taste. Serve, lightly-chilled, within the next few hours. Serves 6.

SALMON WITH RED WINE, IN PAPILLOTES

These salmon steaks are moistened with a light red wine then steamed in a paper envelope which captures the flavours of the fish and the wine, and releases them when the parchment is torn open. The technique is similar to that used for a mixture of fish and vegetable on page 66. Drink the same wine as accompaniment; a good Beaujolais Villages, briefly-chilled, is ideal.

butter
4 salmon steaks, about 175 g (6 oz) each
6 slim spring onions, trimmed and thinly sliced
salt
black pepper
Beaujolais Villages or similar light red wine, chilled

Cut four 30 cm (12 inch) circles from greaseproof paper or baking parchment, brush one side of each with oil.

Lay the sheets, oiled side down, on the work surface (oiling the exterior of the pouch supposedly makes it more difficult to tear accidentally). Put a small knob of butter off-centre on each piece of parchment and place a salmon steak on top. Strew over some spring onion and add a little more butter.

Season well, then spoon over each cutlet a tablespoon of the Beaujolais Villages. Fold over the *papillotes*, fold and roll edges together to a double thickness, stapling these all round. Just before closing the end of each envelope, insert a straw and blow to inflate the parcel — this creates greater space for moisture to develop and steam the salmon. Quickly staple the package shut to trap in the air. Place on heavy baking sheets. Bake in a preheated oven at 190°C, 365°F, Gas Mark 5 for 15 minutes until the *papillotes* are slightly browned and giving forth an alluring bouquet.

Serve immediately, each envelope on its own plate; slit and open the parcels at the table. Serve with boiled, buttered new potatoes and the chilled beaujolais. Serves 4.

NEW POTATO SALAD WITH SPINACH AND SORREL

New potatoes are turned into a salad and combined with the sharp tastes of lemon juice and sorrel. It is difficut to give exact quantities for this; I usually make it by 'eye'.

Take 175–225 g (6–8 oz) tiny new potatoes per person, scrub well but leave the skins intact. Boil the potatoes in salted water for 10–15 minutes until cooked. Meanwhile, trim the stalks of young spinach leaves, add a proportion of sorrel — you won't need very much, as sorrel is deliciously, teeth-strippingly acid and shouldn't be overdone here — wash, then spin the greens in a salad drier to remove all excess moisture.

When the potatoes are ready, drain well and slice while still hot. Toss with a vinaigrette made from 1 part lemon juice to 4 parts olive oil, a large helping of Dijon mustard, plus liberal salt and black pepper. Add the torn-up leaves of wide-leaf parsley, or the coarsely chopped leaves of the curly variety, plus chopped chervil. Toss further.

Taste, season again and serve the potatoes without much delay in a nest of spinach and sorrel. Eat this as a first course or as part of a light lunch.

BLANQUETTE D'AGNEAU PRINTANIERE

A few years ago I watched Rex Barker – at that time chef of La Petite Cuisine Cooking School – demonstrate a classic spring lamb stew, and this is my adaptation of the one Rex showed us.

---

1 boned shoulder of spring lamb
900 ml–1.5 litres (1½–2½ pints) light
*   stock, made from shoulder bones*
*   plus chicken pieces*
2 medium onions, peeled and each
*   stuck with a clove*
2 carrots, peeled and quartered
bouquet garni
salt
40 g (1½ oz) butter
25 g (1 oz) plain flour
200 g (7 oz) young carrots, peeled and
*   cut into thin sticks*
100 g (4 oz) haricots verts or mange-
*   tout or a mixture of both, trimmed*
200 g (7 oz) button mushrooms
1–1½ tablespoons lemon juice
3 egg yolks
85 ml (3 fl oz) double cream
black pepper
cayenne pepper

Trim lamb of skin, connective tissue and excess fat, then cut into 2 cm (¾ inch) cubes. Make the stock with the shoulder bones, etc; degrease thoroughly.

Put the meat into a large heavy saucepan or flameproof casserole, cover with cold water, bring to the boil and simmer for 1 minute. Drain and rinse the lamb thoroughly in cold water. Clean the pan or casserole, replace the meat and add the onions, carrots, bouquet garni, 900 ml (1½ pints) of the stock and a good pinch of salt. Half-cover the pan, bring the stock to the boil, skim and simmer over lowest heat for 1½–2 hours until the lamb is tender. Add more stock as necessary during the process.

When lamb is done, drain and reserve the stock; remove and discard the onions, carrots and bouquet garni. Clean the pan. Return the meat to the cleaned pan or casserole. In a medium saucepan, make a roux with 25 g (1 oz) butter and the flour. Cook gently, stirring, for 4 minutes. Add 900 ml (1½ pints) of the reserved stock, topped up with extra stock and whisk until it comes to the boil. Gently simmer the *velouté* for 20 minutes, skimming regularly.

Meanwhile, cook the carrots in boiling salted water until just tender. Drain, refresh and reserve. Cook the haricots verts or mange-tout in the same way. Simmer the mushrooms with a knob of butter, 1 tablespoon lemon juice and water to cover for 5 minutes. Drain (use the mushroom stock in a soup, or add some to the *velouté*). Put all the vegetables with the lamb.

Beat the egg yolks with the cream, whisk in a little of the hot *velouté* to warm the mixture. Sieve this back into the hot *velouté*, whisking smartly, and slowly heat, continuing to whisk, until the sauce simmers. The presence of flour will prevent yolks from congealing and the rich *velouté* should be of a smooth, medium consistency. Pour this enriched *velouté* on to the lamb and vegetables and reheat over a low heat on top of the stove, adding lemon juice, seasoning and cayenne pepper to taste.

Serve immediately with hot, buttered green noodles. Serves 4.

Potato salad, Tomato soup, Salmon in papillotes

SPAGHETTI WITH RED CAVIAR, LEMON AND CHIVES

A borrowed recipe, from a pair of gastronomic American pianists, Arthur Gold and Robert Fizdale, who published the ideas upon which I've based the version here about ten years ago in American *Vogue*.

This dish causes a sensation each time I serve it. No one quite believes that red caviar, which, as we know, is actually lumpfish roe, could be combined with lemon zest, chives and spaghetti! But the off-beat combination is always completely successful. Salt and fish meet lemon and the allium flavour of chives with conviction. Use wholewheat spaghetti for the interest of its colour and texture.

175 g (6 oz) unsalted butter
175 g (6 oz) red lumpfish roe
3 tablespoons double cream
3 tablespoons olive oil
salt
4 lemons
3 bunches very fresh chives
1 kg (2 lb) wholewheat spaghetti
black pepper

Allow the butter, roe and cream to come to room temperature. Bring a very large, deep pan of water to a brisk boil, add the olive oil and 1 tablespoon salt; put a large serving bowl to heat through in a low oven.

Meanwhile, grate the zest – without pith – from the 4 lemons. Scissor the chives into short lengths, combine the two and reserve.

Boil the spaghetti for 12 minutes or until *al dente*. Drain well. Add the butter and cream to the warmed bowl, swirl them round to melt the butter, and cover with the spaghetti. Toss well, liberally season with pepper, add a little salt and toss again. Place the zest, chives and roe on top, mix well and serve, eating without delay. Serves 8.

Blanquette d'agneau, Spaghetti with caviar

SPARKLING STRAWBERRY SORBET

This delightful sorbet can be made with pink champagne or, as I do, with a sparkling Saumur Rosé, vinified by the champagne method; the wine should always be brut, or extra-dry. The mixture of *pétillance* with strawberry is arresting. Make this 48 hours ahead of serving, as the wine will slow its freezing considerably. Serve this sparkling strawberry sorbet accompanied by ginger biscuits iced with a lemon glaze.

225 g (8 oz) granulated sugar
350 ml (12 fl oz) water
450 g (1 lb) strawberries
juice of 1½ small lemons
600 ml (1 pint) sparkling Saumur Rosé or Champagne Rosé brut well chilled
1 egg white

Dissolve the sugar in the water and boil for 10 minutes until a sugar thermometer registers 104°C, 220°F. Leave to cool completely.

Purée the strawberries in a blender or food processor and combine with the lemon juice. When the syrup is cold, mix with the puréed fruit and carefully whisk in the sparkling wine. Pour into a deep plastic box, stir again, cover and freeze. When the mixture has frozen to a slush, beat the egg white until soft peaks form and stir into the strawberry mixture. Freeze again, turning the sides into the middle several times during the process; this helps the distribution of the contents. The result, after 48 hours, will be a fairly loose sorbet of glittering paillettes, due to the quantity of wine. Serves 6–8.

GINGER BISCUITS

You could eat these tempting biscuits with the sparkling strawberry sorbet, with tea, coffee or a glass of milk, or wine. I like to spread half of them with a lemon glaze. Use vanilla essence, not 'flavouring' in this recipe.

175 g (6 oz) unsalted butter, softened
150 g (5 oz) caster sugar
1 tablespoon black treacle
3 tablespoons golden syrup
½ teaspoon vanilla essence
250 g (9 oz) plain flour, sifted
1 teaspoon baking soda
good pinch of salt
1½ teaspoons ground ginger
½ teaspoon ground cinnamon
¼ teaspoon ground nutmeg
50 g (2 oz) icing sugar
lemon juice

Strawberry sorbet, Ginger biscuits

Cream the butter with 75 g (3 oz) of the caster sugar. Beat in the treacle, golden syrup and vanilla essence. Sift together the flour, soda, salt and spices. Beat the dry ingredients into the butter mixture and, using one hand, work them into a dough. Cut the dough in half and wrap the halves in greaseproof paper. Refrigerate for about 30 minutes.

Take one piece of dough and cut into large dice. Roll the dice into balls the size of large marbles. Flatten each marble into a round about half its original height. Coat on all sides with some of the remaining caster sugar.

Place the rounds, well spaced, on heavy baking sheets. Bake in a preheated oven at 190°C, 375°F, Gas Mark 5 for about 12 minutes or until the biscuits are a pale golden-brown with a slightly crazed surface. Make sure they are not over-baked. Leave the biscuits on the sheets for a few minutes before removing to cool on wire racks.

Proceed in this way with all the dough, periodically sifting away the loose crumbs from the sugar meant for the coating.

When biscuits are cold, store half in an airtight tin, spread the other half with a glaze made from sifted icing sugar mixed with sufficient lemon juice until the consistency is fairly runny. When the glaze has dried, store these biscuits separately. They will become quite soft, due to the icing, while the plain ones will be firm but chewy; they should not be hard and dry, hence the importance of not over-baking. Makes about 48.

HIGH SUMMER

This is probably my favourite time of year for eating, particularly out of doors. With luck, the location will be close to the produce of a market, a fishmonger and a skilled butcher whose excellence allows cooks to do the minimum in the transformation of prime ingredients.

PORC A LA PERIGOURDINE

Elizabeth and Bill Kivlan, with whom we regularly stay in the South of France, are *fins becs*, and Elizabeth is an exceptionally good cook. If we're visiting them in July, she will sometimes make, for an outdoor evening meal, Elizabeth David's sumptuous recipe for cold loin of pork stuffed with truffles; accompanying this by haricots verts in a vinaigrette and tomatoes sliced and served with basil. This lovely *plat* is from *French Provincial Cooking*, and I've taken the liberty of adapting and rewriting it as I make it, using rosé wine as the cooking medium because I love the colour of the jelly which results. Ask your butcher to prepare a piece of rib end of pork loin by removing bones and rind, leaving fat on and giving you both rind and bones with the meat.

1.25 kg (2½ lb) boned weight rib end of pork
1 large clove garlic
2–3 black truffles
salt
black pepper
450 ml (¾ pint) dry rosé wine
150 ml (¼ pint) water

Lay the pork on a chopping board, boned side up; cut the garlic and truffles into long, thick pieces, incise the meat along its length, and tuck the truffles and garlic well into the incisions. Season. Turn the pork over and tuck tapering end of meat beneath eye of the loin to form a long rolled shape; tie this with soft white string at 2 cm (¾ inch) intervals.

Place the pork (fat upwards) with its bones in a deep, heavy casserole; cut rind into strips and add these. It is the rind which yields enough gelatine to set the cooled cooking liquid into a light jelly. Bake, uncovered, in the lower third of a preheated oven at 170°C, 325°F, Gas Mark 3 for 30 minutes until the exterior of meat has coloured.

Pour in wine and water, cover casserole – leaving lid ajar – lower oven to 150°C, 300°F, Gas Mark 2, and allow pork to cook, basting occasionally, until it reaches an internal temperature of just under 77°C, 170°F – test with a meat thermometer. This will probably take about 2 hours.

When ready remove pork from casserole, pour its liquid, twice, through a sieve freshly-lined each time with a double thickness of paper towels, and let stock drip through without squeezing paper. Let cool, cover, and refrigerate both pork and stock until the next day.

When ready to serve, lift fat from top of what is now the lightly-set jelly, carve pork into thin slices, removing string as you go. Haricots verts in a vinaigrette dressing, tomatoes thickly sliced with skins on, seasoned and served beneath leaves of basil make beautiful accompaniments.

Serve each person with appropriate pork, a small glass container holding jelly as garnish, and the beans, tomatoes and basil. Guests can remove and discard the fat from each slice as they eat. Serves 6, generously.

TOMATO QUICHE

When tomatoes are at their peak and have absorbed enough sun – preferably in a private English garden or somewhere along the Mediterranean – to give them their height of flavour, I abandon my usual devotion to the canned Italian version and make this quiche from the fresh ones.

The pastry incorporates cheese and the combination of well-reduced, highly-flavoured tomato with the rich taste of well-matured Cheddar is to be recommended.

CHEESE PASTRY
150 g (5 oz) plain flour
pinch of salt
75 g (3 oz) unsalted butter, chilled
75 g (3 oz) Cheddar or similar cheese, grated
1 egg, beaten

FILLING
1 tablespoon olive oil
1 small onion, peeled and finely chopped
2 large cloves garlic, minced
1.5 kg (3 lb) ripe tomatoes, peeled, seeded and chopped
1 bay leaf
sprig of thyme
sprigs of parsley
2 eggs
150 ml (¼ pint) double cream
a little milk
small handful of chopped fresh parsley
salt
black pepper
50 g (2 oz) Gruyère or Emmental cheese, grated

Tomato quiche, Porc à la périgourdine

Bake in a preheated oven at 180°C, 350°F, Gas Mark 4 until the pastry sets and starts to colour. Allow to cool completely.

Spread the tomato over the shell, strew on grated cheese, pour in the egg and cream and let the quiche bake at 190°C, 375°F, Gas Mark 5 for 20–30 minutes until filling has puffed and begun to colour. Cool the quiche for 10 minutes and slice. Serves 6–8 as a first course.

GRILLED SARDINES WITH GINGER BUTTER

Quickly made for a summer's lunch; only the butter, laced with grated ginger root and lemon juice, needs advance planning.

*75 g (3 oz) unsalted butter, very soft
but not melting
about 1½ teaspoons lemon juice
piece of fresh ginger root
salt
black pepper
8 fresh sardines, each 13–15 cm (6–7
inches), scaled, gutted, washed and
dried, heads and tails intact
olive oil*

In a small bowl, beat the butter with a wooden spoon until very light, gradually beat in lemon juice until the flavour is quite sharp. Peel the ginger root and grate in the flesh to taste; this should be assertive. Season the mixture well, shape the butter into a roll and chill until firm.

Season the sardines, brush them on both sides with oil and grill until the skin begins to char and the flesh has just ceased to be rosy at the bone. Serve with rounds of ginger butter that should melt over the fish. Serves 4.

To make the pastry, sift the flour with salt, cut the butter into small cubes and rub these in, add the grated cheese and bind with beaten egg, adding a drop of water if necessary to make the pastry adhere. Roll the mixture into a ball, wrap it well, and chill for several hours.

Meanwhile, run the oil round the base of a wide sauté pan, sweat the onion and garlic until soft and turning colour, add chopped tomatoes and herbs. Bring tomatoes to the simmer and let them cook over very low heat, stirring occasionally, until they are reduced to a purée which is almost dry. Be careful not to let it burn near the final stages. Stir con-

stantly at this point.

In the meantime, whisk together the eggs, cream plus milk to lighten the mixture, some chopped parsley and salt and pepper to taste.

When the tomatoes are ready, remove the pan from the heat, fish out parsley, thyme and bay leaf; season and let cool completely.

Take pastry from the refrigerator, allow it to lose its chill, and roll it out to line a 23 cm (9 inch) flan ring set on to a heavy baking sheet.

Refrigerate until the pastry is firm. Line the shell with greaseproof paper or foil held in place by coins or dried beans.

SWEETCORN AND MINT SOUP

I like corn best on the cob; it was one of the great treats of my American childhood summers.

Sweetcorn soup, with mint added right at the end, so that the heat releases its burst of flavour as you begin to eat, is a more sophisticated pleasure for which it's useful to have several pairs of hands willing to sever the kernels from cobs.

This is one of the rare times when I'm happy to use a frozen vegetable; if the best ripe, fresh sweetcorn is not available, frozen kernels give a very good result.

1 large onion, peeled and thinly sliced
15 g ($\frac{1}{2}$ oz) butter
1.75 litres (3 pints) home-made chicken broth; for method see page 100
450 g (1 lb) potatoes, peeled weight, cut into small chunks
750 g (1$\frac{3}{4}$ lb) sweetcorn kernels, either cut from corn ears with a small knife so as to leave about 3 mm ($\frac{1}{8}$ inch) depth of pulp still adhering to the cob, or added frozen
salt
black pepper
1 bunch fresh mint

Sweat the onion in butter in a deep, heavy pot. When softened and coloured, add broth, potatoes, 350 g (12 oz) of the corn, a dash of salt. Simmer, half-covered, until the potatoes have cooked, which will be about 5 minutes.

Cool the soup slightly and liquidize until smooth, seasoning to taste. Return soup to the pot, add the remaining corn and just heat mixture through until the whole kernels are done – usually a matter of about 1 minute. This is a soup which tastes best when freshly-made.

While the combination is reheating, rapidly cut up enough mint leaves to strew across the surface of eight bowls; ladle in the soup, stir in the mint, and serve immediately. Serves 8.

SALAD OF MILLET AND HERBS

Being fond of salads like *tabbouleh*, made from the cracked wheat called *burghul* or *bulgur*, I began to experiment with millet. This is an undervalued grain which, steamed until it cracks and then mixed with a liberal amount of enhancing ingredients, becomes delicious.

It's important to give plenty of acidity – in the form of lemon juice, yogurt, sorrel, and a sharp herb like Mediterranean rocket, plus crunch in the shape of cucumber, radish, and oven-toasted pine-nuts – or the millet will stick in your throat like heavy porridge.

1.2 litres (2 pints) salted water
225 g (8 oz) whole millet grains
2 or more tablespoons lemon juice
about 275–350 g (10–12 oz) natural yogurt
225 g (8 oz) piece of cucumber, peeled, seeded and finely chopped
100 g (4 oz) radishes, minced
50 g (2 oz) pine-nuts, lightly toasted
chopped fresh sorrel, rocket, chives, to taste
salad burnet or lemon balm (optional)
salt
black pepper
crisp lettuce leaves

Sweetcorn soup, Millet salad, Grilled sardines

Bring salted water to the boil, add grains, well rinsed and drained, and let simmer rapidly for about 12 minutes, until millet just cracks. Drain into a large metal sieve and rinse under a stream of cold water.

Steam this sieveful, covered, over boiling water for about 15 minutes – making sure that the steam reaches all parts of the sieve's contents – until grains are cracked and very fluffy. Spread them on to a board to dry and when cool, rake your fingers through the mass to make sure there are no lumps.

Transfer the millet to a bowl, beat in 2 tablespoons of lemon juice and the yogurt; leave the millet to absorb this. The consistency should be a bit like that of good rice pudding. Let everything stand, covered, in a cool place, until the following day.

When preparing to serve the salad, stir in the cucumber, radishes, pine-nuts, chopped sorrel, rocket, and chives to taste, the whole salad burnet leaves or the torn leaves of lemon balm if you like, plus salt and pepper. Judge whether to sharpen with more lemon juice or to let down with more yogurt. The final consistency should be fairly loose, without runniness.

Pile the millet into a pyramid on a large platter or plate and adorn with a few attractive herbs. Fill a bowl with lettuce leaves and encourage guests to roll a bit of salad on to a leaf, and to eat each roll in two bites. Serves 6–8 as a first course.

FRUIT TARTS WITHOUT PASTRY

These are fun to make. The ingredients are whatever fresh fruits you like and find appropriate, plus the edible leaves of flowers like nasturtiums or the variously-scented geraniums. For each tart, you place a leaf or two on the plate from which the tart will be eaten, and then construct whatever arrangement appeals.

Here, for instance, I've used the leaves of the lemon-scented geranium, which are strong, so shouldn't be overdone. I've built the tarts in various combinations of orange with the skin cut off, fig and star fruit, all thinly sliced across; sections of small ogen melon, sliced across, skin trimmed away, centre seeded; strawberries sliced from top to bottom, and whole raspberries.

The tarts should be assembled immediately before you expect to eat them, and served with a squeeze of orange or lemon juice, a sprinkling of sugar, and if you like, a spoonful of homemade *fromage blanc* which can be prepared as follows:

Warm 950 ml (32 fl oz) milk with 50 ml (2 fl oz) buttermilk to blood heat (37°C, 98°F), transfer to a bowl, and cool. Let stand at room temperature until milk sours and curdles, which can take up to 48 hours. When thickened, pour into a large sieve lined with muslin and let the whey drip from the curds for 5–6 hours. Strain this cheese and chill it until ready to serve. Makes about 175 g (6 oz).

Fruit tarts without pastry

A GARDEN'S YIELD

I regret having neither a herb, kitchen nor cottage garden, but perhaps I would spend too much time in whichever of these might be just outside the door. When gardening friends arrive with a basket of fresh parsley, potatoes and mint, with carrots that taste as though they've just been pulled from the ground and not moulded in plastic, or with an extravagant cabbage looking too good to eat, I find it hard not to drop everything and begin cooking.

LAMB CUTLETS WITH THREE PUREES

In this recipe you can either sauté the cutlets or roast them.

AUBERGINE PUREE
2 aubergines, each about 275 g (10 oz)
juice of 1 lemon
ground cumin
salt
black pepper
double cream

FENNEL AND APPLE PUREE
bulb fennel, with leaves
1 firm medium eating apple, cored and
*   peeled*
about 50 g (2 oz) butter
lemon juice
salt
black pepper

FRENCH BEAN PUREE
350 g (12 oz) young haricot verts
a small fistful of watercress
salt and black pepper
15 g ($\frac{1}{2}$ oz) butter
2–3 tablespoons double cream

TO FINISH
either 8 best end of neck of lamb cutlets,
*   trimmed of excess fat, rib bones*
*   shortened and pared of meat and fat;*
*   or 2 racks of best end, chined and*
*   prepared, with ribs exposed,*
*   trimmed, and cleaned*
vegetable oil
butter
salt
black pepper
watercress

All purées can be made in advance. Cut off tops of aubergines and roast them whole under a medium grill, turning as skin blisters and blackens and flesh softens. Allow to cool until the aubergine can be handled, lift off the skin and wash flesh. Squeeze out all the bitter juice. Put the aubergine into food processor fitted with a steel blade, add lemon juice and purée until smooth. Add cumin to taste and season with salt and pepper. Allow to cool, cover and refrigerate. The purée will be very strong; adding cream when heating will temper this.

Trim fennel of its upper stems and any damaged outer parts, reserve leaves. Cut both fennel and apple into large dice and put these, with 25 g (1 oz) butter, a tablespoon of lemon juice, a little water and some salt, into a heavy, covered saucepan and simmer over a low heat for 5–8 minutes or until tender. Drain away excess liquid, and purée, with some fennel leaves, until smooth but retaining a certain texture. Season, cool and refrigerate.

Top, tail and, if necessary, string the haricot verts. Wash and boil them in a large amount of well-salted water, uncovered, until just tender; about 3–10 minutes, depending on the beans. Im-mediately drain and refresh them in ice-cold water to stop cooking.

Remove stalks from the watercress, wash leaves and blanch them for 1 minute in boiling, salted water. Drain and refresh in icy water and squeeze away excess moisture. Purée beans and watercress together until smooth. Remove from food processor and freeze the mixture. Put green purée to thaw at room temperature 2–3 hours before needed.

If using lamb in racks, about 1 hour before they'll be carved rub them with oil and salt and roast them in an oven preheated to 230°C, 450°F, Gas Mark 8 for 15 minutes. Turn the heat down to 180°C, 350°F, Gas Mark 4 and roast them about 30 minutes more for rare meat. Let racks rest in a warm place for 15 minutes before carving.

Heat the three purées simultaneously in small heavy saucepans. Add several tablespoons of cream to the aubergine, enough to mellow it to your satisfaction. Correct the seasoning. Dry the fennel and apple over the heat if necessary. Season and add extra butter, and stir in more fennel leaves if you like. Dry haricot verts purée for 1 minute on the heat, season, add butter and a little cream. Meanwhile, if serving lamb sautéed instead of roasted, sear cutlets in oil and butter for about 3 minutes per side until pink in the middle. (The two-rack method will give you more meat per head and require less attention than keeping an eye on sautéing cutlets.

To serve, carve racks and arrange three roast cutlets per heated dinner plate – or put two sautéed pieces on each – give everyone an ample spoonful of each purée, and garnish plates with water-cress. Serves 4.

Lamb cutlets, Parsley custard, Cucumber and ginger sorbet

Cucumber and ginger sorbet

Mushroom and coriander soup

CUCUMBER AND GINGER SORBET

This is a sweet-sour ice to be eaten as a summer first course or as a palate-freshener between courses.

SORBET
2–3 cucumbers, 1.5 kg (3 lb)
5 tablespoons wine vinegar
2 teaspoons salt
¼ teaspoon sugar
2 small spring onions
1¼ teaspoons grated root ginger
100 g (4 oz) granulated sugar
175 ml (6 fl oz) water
2 leaves gelatine
150 ml (¼ pint) natural yogurt

SAUCE
65 g (2½ oz) peeled and chopped
  cucumber without seeds
350 g (12 oz) natural yogurt
about 3 tablespoons lemon juice
salt
black pepper

GARNISH
sliced cucumber
6 small spring onions

To make sorbet, peel, seed and roughly cut up cucumbers. You should then have 1 kg (2 lb) of flesh.

Put cucumber into a large flat glass dish with four tablespoons of the vinegar, plus the salt and sugar and leave for 3 hours, basting regularly. Salt draws out the water; sugar and vinegar add flavour.

After 3 hours drain cucumbers (don't wash) and pat dry. Put into food processor with two trimmed and sliced spring onions, ginger and remaining wine vinegar. Purée until smooth and chill.

Meanwhile make a syrup by dissolving sugar in water and boiling the liquid for 1 minute. Soak gelatine until soft, drain and dissolve it in hot syrup off the fire. Cool.

Whisk together cucumber and syrup, judge flavour and freeze this in a deep plastic box, covered. After several hours, when semi-frozen, turn into food processor and quickly re-purée; add the yogurt, whiz, combine and refreeze.

Prepare this 24 hours in advance of serving but no earlier than that or the sorbet becomes too crystalline.

Make the sauce by beating the finely-chopped cucumber into the yogurt, add lemon juice and seasoning. Chill.

Some hours before serving, wash and trim spring onions, cut their tops quite short and slash these several times above the bulb. Refrigerate in water to make tops curl. Put the sorbet into the refrigerator 1 hour before serving so that it's not rock-hard. Thinly slice unpeeled cucumber and wrap it in paper towels to preserve moisture. Scoop the sorbet into small dishes, spoon round sauce, add spring onion, and serve on dinner plates with sliced cucumber. Serves 6.

MUSHROOM AND CORIANDER SOUP

By mushrooms I mean wild ones – if at all possible – in combination with the ubiquitous cultivated flats or buttons. The silky richness of a wild species gives this soup its special quality. I've made it with ceps that I picked in a Surrey wood, and with imported oyster mushrooms – themselves cultivated, I suspect, but nonetheless distinguished – and have liked both versions.

I suggest finishing the soup with *crème fraîche*, the thick cultured cream of France for which I give a recipe below. Its soured tang works well here and, unlike 'soured cream', it can be boiled. If you don't want to do this, use ordinary double cream.

CREME FRAICHE
150 ml ($\frac{1}{4}$ pint) double cream
1 tablespoon buttermilk

SOUP
1$\frac{1}{2}$ large onions, peeled and thinly-
    sliced
1.25 litres (2$\frac{1}{4}$ pints) home-made
    chicken broth, as made on page 100
scant $\frac{1}{2}$ teaspoon coriander seeds,
    crushed
225 g (8 oz) flat or button mushrooms,
    sliced
225 g (8 oz) trimmed fresh wild
    mushrooms, such as morels, ceps,
    chanterelles or oyster mushrooms
salt
75 g (3 oz) pasta shells or other small
    macaroni
75 g (3 oz) of the crème fraîche *or*
    double cream
black pepper
fresh dill
fresh coriander

Prepare *crème fraîche* at least four days in advance of using, by heating the double cream to just less than 38°C (100°F). Transfer it to a bowl, add the buttermilk and mix well. Loosely cover the bowl and leave the cream at room temperature, undisturbed, to thicken and develop its acid tang. Depending on the weather, this will take from 1–3 days. Then chill the cream for another day until it becomes almost spreadable. The flavour is wonderful, and the cream will keep, refrigerated in a closed jar, for about 2 weeks.

To make the soup, add the onion to the broth and bring to the boil, then simmer for about 8 minutes, until the onions are cooked. Crush the coriander seeds in a mortar and add them to the slightly cooled broth, run it through the blender or food processor until the onions are puréed.

Slice and wash the cultivated mushrooms. Shake away excess moisture. Wipe the wild mushrooms well with a damp cloth unless they are very dirty and gritty, when they should be washed and well-shaken. Cut all types of wild mushrooms roughly.

If using chanterelles, which give off so much water when heated that it would dilute the soup, put them, salted, into a heavy, lidded saucepan over high heat. Hold the lid down and shake pan to prevent sticking. As mushrooms heat they will expel their juice. When this boils, drain mushrooms and continue recipe.

Put all the mushrooms into the oniony broth, add salt, and simmer for 5 minutes.

Stir in the pasta shells and simmer, stirring occasionally, for 8–10 minutes until the pasta is cooked. Cook the pasta only until it becomes al dente, otherwise it will lose its texture. Whisk in 75 g (3 oz) *crème fraîche* or double cream, simmer for 1 minute, taste the soup and then correct the seasoning.

I like to make this soup a day in advance and reheat it. The flavours pervade the pasta and make it seem like a third kind of mushroom. When serving, garnish each bowl with a sprig of fresh dill and a leaf or two of fresh coriander. Serves 4–5.

HARLEQUIN QUICHE

SHORTCRUST
225 g (8 oz) plain flour
1 tablespoon icing sugar
pinch of salt
150 g (5 oz) unsalted butter, softened
1 egg

FILLING
100 g (4 oz) red cabbage
salt
2 tablespoons vinegar
100 g (4 oz) courgettes
100 g (4 oz) carrots, peeled weight
3 shallots
25 g (1 oz) butter
black pepper
2 eggs
1 egg yolk
150 ml ($\frac{1}{4}$ pint) double cream
pinch of grated nutmeg
tablespoon chopped fresh chervil or
    chives
40 g (1$\frac{1}{2}$ oz) Gruyère cheese, grated

To prepare the shortcrust, sift the flour, sugar and salt on to a pastry board. Make a well in the centre and put the butter into it; make a trough in the butter and break egg into it. With the fingers of one hand, work the butter and egg into a sticky mass.

Use a spatula to toss and chop the flour into this until pastry starts to form. Bring the pastry together with both hands, adding water if necessary to make it adhere, knead briefly and form into a ball. Wrap in greaseproof paper and a plastic bag and refrigerate several hours or overnight.

Bring the pastry to room temperature, roll out about two-thirds of it to line a 23 cm (9 inch) flan ring set on to a heavy baking sheet. Chill for 30 minutes. Bake blind in a preheated oven at 180°C, 350°F, Gas Mark 4 for about 20 minutes or until the pastry has set and begins to colour. Cool.

To prepare the filling, shred the cabbage very fine and boil it for 3–4 minutes in salted, vinegared water (vinegar is to set the colour) until just tender. Drain and cool. Top and tail courgettes and, with the carrots, cut them into matchsticks 2.5 cm (1 inch) long. Peel and mince the shallots.

Melt the butter in a heavy saucepan, add the shallots and let them sweat, covered, for 3 minutes to soften; add the courgettes and carrots and let them cook gently, under buttered paper and a lid, stirring occasionally, for 6–7 minutes or until just tender. The three main vegetables should all retain a little crunch. Cool the three vegetables, combine with cabbage, and season.

Whisk together the eggs, yolk, cream, nutmeg, salt and pepper to taste, with about a tablespoon of chopped chervil or chives.

Fill quiche shell with the combined vegetables, scatter on the grated cheese, pour eggs and cream over the vegetables and bake at 190°C, 375°F, Gas Mark 5 for 20–25 minutes, until puffed and beginning to colour. Serve hot. This can be made a few hours in advance and reheated for 10 minutes in an oven of the same temperature. Harlequin quiche serves 8–10 as a starter, or 6 as a main course with salad.

BALLOTINE DE VOLAILLE, SAUCE SABAYON

When I was a chef at Ma Cuisine restaurant in London, we boned chicken legs, stuffed them with crab and served each with a lobster sauce. It taught me that boning and stuffing a chicken leg need not be viewed with terror. It is quite easy and can utilise a variety of forcemeats.

The one here involves a chicken breast, with tarragon and nuts. If you chill the leg, it can be thinly-sliced and eaten like a rather elegant, nut-studded terrine. The sauce, based on a reduction of wine and chicken stock, is made on the principle of a sweet sabayon.

Ballotine de volaille

BALLOTINE

1 fresh chicken, about 1.5 kg (3 lb)
1 carrot, peeled
1 onion, peeled and sliced
parsley stalks
pinch of dried tarragon
salt
25 g (1 oz) pine-nuts or shelled pistachios or mixture of the two
1 egg yolk
1 tablespoon fresh breadcrumbs
1 tablespoon chopped fresh tarragon or ⅓ teaspoon dried
4 shallots or spring onions, minced
large pinch cayenne pepper
black pepper

VEGETABLES

potatoes, carrots, small Belgian chicory, or whatever is in season
salt
butter
sugar
lemon juice
black pepper

SABAYON

3 tablespoons chicken stock
3 tablespoons dry white wine
3 egg yolks
salt and black pepper
fresh tarragon as garnish

Remove both chicken legs from the point at which they join the bird's carcass. Take up one leg and with a small, sharp knife, begin to work the flesh away from the bone of the thigh joint, keeping the knife's edge against bone and not the flesh. Work down to the ball joint at the knee and work flesh free, without piercing it, freeing it from cartilage and moving down to free the bone and tendons from the drumstick meat.

With a large, sharp knife, chop off the drumstick bone above the foot and remove any trace of splinters. Keeping the foot intact during poaching secures stuffing and keeps ballotines in shape. Turn the leg skin side out. You should now have 1 pouch without holes and ready to receive the forcemeat.

Repeat the process with the second leg. Remove 150 g (5 oz) skinless flesh from carcass (probably the value of 1 breast and wing) to make the stuffing. Detach second breast and wing as one piece and reserve.

Chop the remaining carcass into large pieces and with the leg bones, carrot, onion, parsley stalks, pinch of dried tarragon and salt, make a good stock. Simmer this for 3–4 hours and top up with water as necessary. Poach the reserved breast and wing in the stock and use the second piece for something else. Strain the stock when ready, reserving a few bones from the pot.

To make the stuffing, skin pistachios, if used, by blanching them for a minute in boiling water, draining, and rubbing away the skins in a towel. Toast the pistachios and pine-nuts for 5 minutes in an oven preheated to 180°C, 350°F, gas mark 4 until they begin to colour.

Purée the 150 g (5 oz) of raw chicken flesh, free of obvious nerve tissue, in a food processor, with the egg yolk. Remove to a bowl and add breadcrumbs, tarragon, nuts, the minced shallots or spring onions and liberal amounts of salt, cayenne and black pepper.

Open out each pouch, salt and

pepper it, divide stuffing in half and with wet hands, stuff forcemeat well into each pocket. It will expand on cooking and fill leg to the foot. Fold the flap of thigh flesh snugly over the stuffing, round each form to give it a good shape and refrigerate covered with moist paper towels until ready to poach. The legs can be prepared the day before needed.

If you have chosen vegetables like potatoes and thick carrots to be cut into olives, turn them a few hours before cooking. Cut about four small carrot olives and two small potato olives per person and hold them in cold water until ready to use. Core and trim one or two chicory plants per person and keep wrapped in dark paper in refrigerator. Combine three tablespoons of chicken stock and white wine, and reduce to two tablespoons for sabayon.

When ready to begin, put ballotines on to reserved bones in a medium saucepan, cover with stock that you've made from carcass and weight legs with a small, heavy saucepan lid. Bring the liquid gently to simmering point and poach legs in barely shuddering stock for 25 minutes.

Off the heat the ballotines can be kept hot in this broth, once poached, but try to have vegetables and sauce ready within 10 minutes of finishing chicken.

Cover the potatoes with fresh cold salted water, bring to the boil and simmer about 15 minutes, or until done. Hold in water if necessary. Cover the carrots with a little cold water, add a nut of butter, a little sugar and salt and simmer for 10–20 minutes, depending on age of carrots. The water should evaporate and the vegetables be glazed by the syrup formed with the sugar and butter. Drain away the excess water if necessary to achieve this. Toss carrots to coat them in glaze.

Poach the chicory, covered with some lemon juice, a little butter, salt and sugar, for some 15 minutes or so; glaze as for carrots at end of cooking. Pepper each vegetable when ready. If others are used instead – French beans, button onions, spring onions or whatever – prepare and glaze them as above.

When ballotines are ready, remove their saucepan from the heat and rapidly make sabayon. Bring a pan of water up to just below a simmer while whisking reduced wine and chicken stock with 3 yolks in a small heavy saucepan or heatproof bowl. Put this into hot water and whisk yolks into a thick, frothy mousse – a matter of about 3 minutes. Remove pan from water and whisk for a minute more. Season.

Lift ballotines from their stock, gently cut away each foot, lightly dry ballotines of excess moisture and place each on a heated plate (the stock makes an excellent basis for soup). Spoon on a pool of sauce, halve the chicory lengthwise and arrange vegetables. Garnish the ballotines with fresh tarragon if available and serve with extra sauce in a warmed boat. Serves 2.

Harlequin quiche, Mushroom soup,
Ballotine de Volaille, sauce sabayon

Harlequin quiche

Parsley custard

PARSLEY CUSTARD, TOMATO AND PEAR SAUCE

This is for those gardeners with a glut of parsley and mint.

CUSTARD
225 g (8 oz) very fresh parsley,
weighed with stalks
70 small and very fresh
mint leaves
salt
1 egg
3 egg yolks
2 tablespoons milk
black pepper
cayenne pepper

SAUCE
225 g (8 oz) can Italian plum
tomatoes, with their juices
1 large, ripe, aromatic pear
lemon juice
salt
black pepper

GARNISH
1 small ripe tomato
sprigs of mint
sprigs of parsley

Butter two ovenproof ramekins of 150 ml ($\frac{1}{4}$ pint) capacity each and line bases with buttered greaseproof paper cut to fit exactly.

Remove parsley stalks, wash leaves and blanch these for about a minute in boiling, salted water. Drain and plunge leaves into very cold water. Wash the mint leaves and boil in the parsley's water for about 30 seconds. Refresh. Squeeze from both as much water as possible and purée them very finely in food processor. Using a wooden spoon, force this purée through a coarse sieve.

Beat together the egg, yolks and milk and add puréed herbs. Season well with salt, pepper and cayenne. Divide the custard between the ramekins and put them into a pan filled with enough water to come halfway up sides, bring water to just below simmer and poach custards in this bain-marie in a preheated oven at 155°C, 310°F, Gas Mark 2 for about 40 minutes till risen slightly and cooked.

Meanwhile, open can of tomatoes and pour contents, including juice, into food processor or blender. Peel and core pear and add 90 g ($3\frac{1}{2}$ oz) of its flesh, blend thoroughly and add lemon juice to taste – probably about 2 teaspoons – along with salt and pepper. Sieve this into a small bowl. The pear gives just enough of its flavour to be intriguing.

Peel and seed tomato, finely chop half of it. When custards are ready, run the blunt edge of a knife round circumference of each, turn out into the middle of two small plates and peel off paper. Run sauce – unheated – round the outside and top each custard with a little chopped tomato and a sprig each of parsley and mint. Serves 2 as a first course.

THE HARVEST, THE VINTAGE

Wine, like apples or wheat, is a cultivated crop, though the transformation of the grape into a noble vintage requires perhaps more sophisticated knowledge than the baking of loaves or an apple pie. A debatable point, no doubt! But during the period of the vintage, I long to taste some harvest foods, including the produce of the grape, and to sample the sort of dish that satisfies appetites sharpened by the shorter, brisker days of autumn.

GRATIN OF MILLET

This is another use for millet, that unjustly neglected cereal, on which I have also based the Salad of Millet and Herbs (see page 84). I have layered it here with tomato sauce and cheese to make a warming lunch or supper dish.

I prefer to use canned Italian plum tomatoes when I cannot find good garden-grown varieties with a concentrated flavour. If you have the latter, however, do use them instead.

TOMATO SAUCE
100 g (4 oz) onion, peeled and finely chopped
2 large cloves garlic, peeled and minced
25 g (1 oz) celery sticks, chopped
25 g (1 oz) carrot, chopped
1 tablespoon olive oil
794 g (1 lb 12 oz) can Italian plum tomatoes and their juices
3 tablespoons dry white wine
2 teaspoons granulated sugar
1 bay leaf
pinch of thyme
a few parsley stalks
salt

MILLET
1.7 litres (3 pints) water
salt
350 g (12 oz) whole millet grains, rinsed and drained
½ teaspoon dry mustard
1 tablespoon olive oil
2 egg yolks
100 g (4 oz) Gruyère cheese, grated
grated Parmesan cheese
black pepper

TO FINISH
100 g (4 oz) Gruyère cheese, grated
grated Parmesan cheese
black pepper

To make the tomato sauce, sweat the onion, garlic, celery and carrot in the olive oil in a heavy medium sauté pan covered over low heat until the vegetables are soft but not coloured. Add the remaining sauce ingredients, including a little salt to taste, breaking up the tomatoes with a wooden spoon. Stir well, bring to the boil and simmer briskly, uncovered, for 15–20 minutes, stirring occasionally, until the sauce is reduced to a slightly thickened but still fairly liquid consistency. Leave to cool slightly, then remove the bay leaf and liquidize. Push the sauce through a coarse sieve to remove the seeds. Season to taste. The result is about 600 ml (1 pint) of sauce. Measure out 450 ml (¾ pint) sauce (using the remainder for other purposes).

Bring 1.75 litres (3 pints) water to the boil and add 1 teaspoon salt. Whisk the millet into the boiling water and simmer rapidly for about 12 minutes until the grains just crack. Drain into a large metal sieve and rinse under running cold water. Cover and steam the sieve of millet over a pan of boiling water for 15 minutes until the grains are cracked, fluffy and fairly dry.

Transfer the millet to a bowl and beat in the mustard, oil, egg yolks, Gruyère cheese and a liberal shaking of Parmesan. Season to taste and work the mixture well with your fingers.

With damp hands, rapidly spread this mixture evenly and about 5 mm (¼ inch) thick on to a large wooden board. Leave to cool completely.

Butter a 23 × 30 cm (9 × 12 inch) earthenware oval gratin dish.

Use a 4 cm (1½ inch) round cutter to cut the cooled millet into rounds; lightly moisten the cutter as you work for ease. Line the bottom of the dish with millet off-cuts, which will probably disintegrate as you transfer them, but no-one sees this so it doesn't matter! Spoon 3 tablespoons tomato sauce over the millet in the dish. Sprinkle over 25 g (1 oz) Gruyère, some Parmesan and a grinding of pepper.

Working down the long side of the dish, overlap the millet rounds in rows from top to bottom. You will probably make five rows across. Sprinkle with pepper, 75 g (3 oz) Gruyère and some more Parmesan. Pour the remaining sauce over the millet to cover. Sprinkle the surface with more of the Parmesan.

Bake in a preheated oven at 200°C, 400°F, Gas Mark 6 for about 30 minutes until the millet is completely heated through. Leave to rest for 5 minutes before slicing. Serve with a green salad. Serves 4–6.

PORC MIREVAL

I spent a week during one recent autumn observing the harvest of the muscat grape – near Mireval, west of Montpellier, in the South of France – and eating wonderful food prepared by our hostess Anne-Marie Cazalis. I particularly liked Anne-Marie's adaptation of *porc à la normande*, in which she substitutes for Calvados or cider, the Cazalis' own Muscat de Mireval, the sweet golden fortified wine made at the local cooperative from Cazalis and neighbouring grapes. This muscat is, as far as I can tell, not available outside France, but Muscat de Beaumes-de-Venise, from east of the River Rhône, is a graceful alternative that is readily obtainable. The sweetly fruity wine, with the acidity of apples, gives just the right note to pork. You'll see that this is the same cut of meat as in Porc à la Périgourdine, but prepared to give a different effect.

For this dish ask your butcher for a piece of rib end of pork loin, rind and bones removed, meat to be rolled and tied at 2 cm ($\frac{3}{4}$ inch) intervals. The finished, rolled weight should be a generous 1 kg ($2\frac{1}{4}$ lb), and the diameter about 7.5 cm (3 inches).

*75 g (3 oz) piece salted pig's belly,
   boned and rindless weight*
butter
vegetable oil
1 large onion, peeled and diced
*450 g (1 lb) tart cooking apples,
   peeled, cored and diced*
*generous 1 kg (2¼ lb) piece rolled rib
   end of pork loin*
juice of ½ lemon
salt
small handful of raisins
*4 tablespoons Muscat de Beaumes-de-
   Venise or Muscat de Mireval*
120 ml (4 fl oz) double cream
1 tablespoon milk
black pepper

Choose a heavy, flameproof casserole into which the loin will fit comfortably, with room on either side.

Soak the pork belly for several hours to remove excess salt. Dry well and slice into short lardons.

Melt a knob of butter with a little oil in the casserole and sauté the lardons until just beginning to colour. Add the onion and apple, cover and sweat until softened. Remove from the casserole, add more oil and butter if necessary, and brown the pork loin lightly all over. Wipe the casserole clean with paper towels, replace the meat, fat side upwards, and add the lardons, onion, apple, lemon juice and a little salt.

Warm the casserole over a low heat. Partially cover and cook in the lower third of a preheated oven at 150°C, 300°F, Gas Mark 2 for about $1\frac{1}{4}$–$1\frac{1}{2}$ hours, basting the meat occasionally with its own juices. Test pork with a meat thermometer; it should reach an internal temperature of 77°C, 170°F. Add the raisins during the last 15 minutes of cooking.

Remove the meat from the casserole and leave to rest in a warm place for 15 minutes. Shortly before carving, add the Muscat, cream and milk to the fruits and juices in the casserole. Simmer for several minutes until the alcohol evaporates and the sauce tastes sweetly piquant. Season.

Carve the pork thinly, removing the string as you go. Serve with the sauce on a bed of plain boiled rice. Serves 4–6.

PUMPKIN AND CHESTNUT SOUP

Earlier in this book I wrote with enthusiasm about a pumpkin *crème brûlée*; here the squash, to which pumpkins and courgettes are related, is back in a savoury role as part of an autumn soup. The unexpected ingredient is chestnuts; a little out of season now, but the canned French variety is fine for this purpose.

*450 g (1 lb) pumpkin or winter squash
   flesh, cubed*
*225 g (8 oz) canned, whole,
   unsweetened chestnuts, well drained*
*2 medium onions, peeled and thinly
   sliced*
*2 large cloves garlic, peeled and
   chopped*
3 long inner celery sticks, sliced
*1.6 litres (2¾ pints) well flavoured
   chicken broth; for method,
   see page 100*
salt
*4 small tomatoes, about 400 g (14 oz),
   skinned, seeded and sliced*
black pepper
50 ml (2 fl oz) milk
dash of double cream
fresh chervil leaves, if available
diced tomato flesh

Combine the pumpkin, chestnuts, onions, garlic, celery and broth in a large saucepan. Bring to the boil, add a pinch of salt and simmer, half-covered, for 10–15 minutes until the pumpkin and chestnut are almost cooked. Stir in the tomatoes and simmer for 5 minutes more.

Cool slightly, then liquidize until the soup is smooth, adding seasoning to taste. Dilute with the milk, and add the cream. Thin with more broth if necessary. Check the seasoning.

This soup is best reheated and eaten 24 hours after making. Serve in a tureen, garnished with chervil leaves and diced tomato flesh. Alternatively, use a hollowed-out, flat-bottomed pumpkin or winter squash; warm it first in a preheated oven at 180°C, 350°F, Gas Mark 4 for 20 minutes. Serves 6.

Clockwise from top right: Pumpkin and chestnut soup, Porc Mireval, A sauté of mushrooms with courgettes and spring onions, Cherry clafoutis

A SAUTE OF MUSHROOMS

This is a quick dish for lunch or supper, based on the field or the oyster mushroom or even the supermarket 'flat'. The ubiquitous courgette and spring onion give crunch; garlic, cumin and mint add interest.

butter
vegetable oil
225 g (8 oz) slim spring onions with
  bulbous base, trimmed
400 g (14 oz) small courgettes,
  trimmed
2 large cloves garlic, minced
ground cumin
juice of 1 small lemon
salt
275 g (10 oz) field, oyster or flat
  cultivated mushrooms, diced
fresh mint leaves, chopped
black pepper
whole mint leaves, to garnish
brown bread and butter

Melt a knob of butter with oil in two wide sauté pans.

Slash down into bulbs of the spring onions but leave whole.

Cut the courgettes across into thirds, slice each third lengthwise into quarters and set aside.

Put the onions into one pan with half the garlic, a good sprinkling of cumin to taste, and a little lemon juice and salt. Cover and sweat the onions until about half cooked.

Heat the butter and oil in the second sauté pan, add the remaining garlic, cumin to taste, the courgettes and salt. Put the mushrooms and remaining lemon juice in the first pan with the onions. Increase the heat and stir the mushrooms to cook rapidly, tossing the courgettes as you go. The mushrooms will expel a lot of liquid.

When courgettes are done but retain some bite, the mushrooms should also be tender; drain away their juices (use these, for instance, in a soup). Combine the contents of both pans, add the chopped mint leaves and season to taste. Stir and toss together for a minute longer over high heat.

Serve the sauté quickly, garnished with whole mint leaves and accompanied by bread and butter. Eat without delay. Serves 2–4.

CHERRY CLAFOUTIS

This is an absolutely classic French country dish from the Limousin region, in the south west – cherries in a thick batter, sugared and flavoured with cognac. Thinner batters do not rise as well and allow the cherry juices to flow unattractively.

Strictly speaking, this fruit is not part of the early autumn harvest. If there are late cherries around, however, or some imported ones available, or even if you have bottled your own in sugar syrup during July and August – as a Limousin cook might do – this is a lovely dessert to have right now.

450 g (1 lb) ripe cherries
75 g (3 oz) plain flour
1 tablespoon caster sugar
large pinch of salt
2 eggs
150 ml (¼ pint) milk
1–2 tablespoons cognac

TO SERVE
granulated sugar
double cream

Remove the stalks and stone the cherries; if using bottled fruit, drain well. Butter a shallow ovenproof dish, 24 cm (9½ inches) in diameter.

Sift the flour, caster sugar and salt into a bowl and break the eggs into the centre. Whisk the milk with 1 tablespoon cognac and slowly add half the liquid to the eggs, gradually whisking in the surrounding flour mixture. When half has been added, beat thoroughly until bubbles break on the surface. Whisk in the remaining milk and beat until absolutely smooth. Cover the batter and leave to relax in a cool place for about 1 hour.

Beat again lightly and pour enough of the batter into the dish to cover the base. Arrange the cherries in one closely packed layer, pour on the rest of the batter and dribble over some more cognac if desired.

Bake in a preheated oven at 180°C, 350°F, Gas Mark 4 until the batter has risen and browned at the edges.

Leave to cool for 15 minutes. Sprinkle with granulated sugar, then slice and serve with lightly whipped cream. Serves 4–6.

BASIL-FLAVOURED WINE JELLY

This is an old fashioned jelly, rarely seen now. I like it as an accompaniment to game birds, or with buttered toast at teatime. The basil leaves, infused while the juices and sugar are boiling, give it a subtle extra dimension.

1.5 kg (3 lb) ripe green grapes, weight
  without stems
350 ml (12 fl oz) dry white wine
750 g (1½ lb) tart cooking apples
1 lemon
450 g–1.5 kg (1–2 lb) preserving or
  granulated sugar
10–12 fresh basil leaves
2 tablespoons cognac

Put the grapes into a deep pan with the wine, then use both hands to squeeze and crush the grapes thoroughly. Bring the mixture to boil and simmer gently, uncovered, for about 30 minutes until the grapes are very soft.

Thinly slice the apples – unpeeled, cores and all – and the lemon and add to the wine and simmer for a further 30 minutes until the apples and lemon are thoroughly pulped.

Gratin of millet, Mushroom sauté

Clafoutis, Basil-wine jelly

Scald a jelly bag with boiling water, wring thoroughly when cool enough to handle and suspend above a large bowl. Pour in the mixture of wine and fruit, and leave the juices to drip overnight, without squeezing the bag.

Measure the juices into a preserving pan or stainless steel saucepan, and for every 600 ml (1 pint) juice, add 450 g (1 lb) sugar. Stir over a very low heat until the sugar is completely dissolved. Tie the basil leaves into a muslin bag, add to the pan, raise the heat and let syrup boil, without stirring.

Start testing for a set after 10 minutes. Chill a saucer, spoon on a little syrup, cool in the freezer, then run a finger over the surface; if a skin has formed wrinkles when you push it, the setting point has been reached.

When the setting point arrives, take the pan from heat, remove the bag of basil, dip a large spoon into hot water and skim the surface of the jelly thoroughly. Add the cognac and boil for 1 minute longer. Pot the jelly immediately in hot, dry, sterilized jam jars. Cover without delay.

Makes two 450 g (1 lb) jars and one 225 g (8 oz) jar using 3 lb of grapes and 1½ of cooking apples. The amount of sugar may vary depending on the pectin content of the fruits. Keep testing for set.

AUTUMN SOUPS

The weather of September and October can move unpredictably along the thermometer from hot to cold and back, so it is good to have a repertoire of soups which take heed of the temperature and the variety of available ingredients. For example, a cold purée of the last asparagus and basil, with spinach, for early in the season and a thick lentil, onion and sausage soup for the cold nights of October.

Six of these soups are based on one of three good, home-made stocks, for which there is no instant substitute. The seventh is a hot tomato surprise beneath a dome of puff pastry called, in a loose reference to an old-fashioned cooking method, a 'huff'.

THREE-LENTIL SOUP

A nourishing meal of a soup, made colourful in the initial stages by three different kinds of lentil. The trick is not to cook the soup too much, so as to preserve the variety of its texture. The garnish of fried onion adds an interesting, slightly charred and caramelized sweetness.

50 g (2 oz) brown lentils
50 g (2 oz) dark green (Puy) lentils
50 g (2 oz) red lentils
2 rashers green streaky bacon, rinded
1 thick carrot, peeled
200 g (7 oz) onion, peeled
3 large cloves garlic, peeled
1 celery stick
90 g (3½ oz) butter
vegetable oil
900 ml (1½ pints) basic meat broth, as described for Cold Asparagus, Spinach and Basil Soup, page 102

2 medium tomatoes, peeled, seeded and chopped
2 small beef sausages
salt
black pepper
lemon juice
1 large onion, peeled and sliced

Rinse and drain all lentils; soak brown lentils in water to cover for 2 hours, green ones for 1½ hours, but red ones should not be soaked at all.

Finely chop rashers of bacon, carrot, onion, garlic cloves and celery and sweat all of the vegetables, covered, for 10 minutes in 40 g (1½ oz) butter and a little oil in a large covered saucepan.

Drain the lentils, add all three kinds to the saucepan and stir well. Add the broth, tomatoes and sausages. Do not salt. Half cover, bring them up to the simmering point and simmer for 20 minutes or until the lentils are cooked but have not started to disintegrate. Add salt and pepper to taste and a liberal squeeze of lemon juice.

Slice the sausages and serve soup garnished generously with fried onion slices, which you have prepared as follows:

First clarify the remaining butter. Clarified butter is less likely to burn at reasonably high temperatures. Melt the remaining butter, allow to stand, then spoon clear, yellow liquid away from milk residue. Heat the clear liquid in a heavy, medium-sized sauté pan and toss the onion in this clarified butter until brown and crisp. This takes quite a while to do properly. The onions should first be softened, then gradually coloured until their flavour is highly concentrated. Season and drain on paper towels. Serves 4.

TOMATO SOUP-IN-A-HUFF

When the puff pastry dome is tapped open with a soup spoon, wonderful aromas fly up.

SOUP
2 large onions, peeled and finely chopped
6 cloves garlic, peeled and finely chopped
25 g (1 oz) butter
vegetable oil
50 ml (2 fl oz) dry white wine
1.25 kg (2½ lb) ripe tomatoes
1 tablespoon granulated sugar
pinch of thyme
salt
1 tablespoon tomato purée
50 ml (2 fl oz) double cream
black pepper
1 thick carrot, peeled
1 celery stick
fresh chives

PASTRY
450 g (1 lb) puff pastry, made with unsalted butter; see page 47 for method
1 egg
single cream

Sweat the chopped onion and garlic with butter and a splash of oil in a medium-sized sauté pan, covered, for 8–10 minutes, or until soft. Pour in white wine and reduce to about 1 tablespoon.

Seed and chop tomatoes, add to sauté pan with sugar, thyme and a little salt. Simmer for 20–30 minutes. The mixture should not reduce too much. Add the tomato purée and cook 1 minute longer.

Cool slightly, then pour into a blender or food processor, purée and season. Rub soup through a sieve; it will be quite thick. Boil the double cream to reduce it to $1\frac{1}{2}$ tablespoons, add to soup. Correct seasoning, divide the soup among four tureens and allow to cool.

Meanwhile, slice the carrot and celery into thin strips, cut the strips into tiny dice and put a tablespoon of each into each tureen. Scissor on the chives and stir vegetables partly into soup.

When the soup is completely cold, divide puff pastry into four equal pieces. Roll out each piece 5 mm ($\frac{1}{4}$ inch) thick, and, using a plate 5 cm (2 inches) wider than tops of tureens, cut out four pastry circles. Brush one side of each circle liberally with a wash made from an egg well-beaten with a dash of cream. Place the pastry egg-side-down on each tureen, and carefully but firmly press the pastry against china. Refrigerate for 1 hour.

Brush the pastry all over, including the sides, with the remaining egg wash. Bake in a preheated oven at 230°C, 450°F, Gas Mark 8 for 15–20 minutes or until the pastry has puffed into a dome and is golden brown.

Serve immediately, encouraging people to break the crust into the soup as they eat. Serves 4.

Clockwise from top right: Carrot and tarragon soup, Tomato soup-in-a-huff, Fennel, bacon and haddock soup

FENNEL, BACON AND HADDOCK SOUP

Three flavours which marry unexpectedly well.

BASIC FISH BROTH
*1 kg (2 lb) bones and heads from lean
    fish such as Dover sole, plaice or
    lemon sole*
1 large leek, cleaned and sliced
1 large onion, peeled and sliced
6 parsley stalks
3 tablespoons lemon juice
1 large glass dry white wine
¼ teaspoon salt

SOUP
*475 g (1 lb 2 oz) bulb fennel, with
    leaves*
275 g (10 oz) onion
*4 rashers green streaky bacon, with
    rinds*
100 g (4 oz) butter
vegetable oil
*1.5 litres (2½ pints) basic fish broth,
    (as above)*
salt
275 g (10 oz) haddock fillet
300 ml (½ pint) milk
175 ml (6 fl oz) dry white wine
black pepper

TO GARNISH
*small croûtons made from firm-
    textured, slightly stale bread*
*4 rashers green streaky bacon, with
    rinds removed*

Make a fish broth as for the Scallop Broth with Julienned Vegetables (see page 101) using the above quantities but less water. There is no need, here, to line the colander with muslin for straining, and don't worry about separating clear broth from sediment.

Reserving the fennel leaves, finely chop the fennel bulb, onion and bacon. Sweat in 50 g (2 oz) butter and a little oil in a large, heavy saucepan, covered, until soft, for about 8–10 minutes. Add 1.5 litres (2½ pints) broth, sediment and all, very little salt, and simmer for 10 minutes.

Meanwhile, poach the haddock in milk, covered, for 5 minutes. Cool.

Add the glass of white wine to soup base and simmer away alcohol for 2–3 minutes. Allow soup base to cool a little. Purée and correct seasoning, being careful with the salt.

Make croûtons by slicing the bread thinly, cutting the slices into slim fingers, and then the fingers into tiny cubes; you will need about 50 of these. Over low heat melt the remaining butter with a little oil in a wide sauté pan, add cubes and fry gently, tossing often, until croûtons turn pale golden brown. Remove from the pan and allow to cool on paper towels.

Fry the rashers of rindless bacon until crisp; chop and crumble finely. Remove haddock from milk and flake it.

To serve soup, reheat with haddock and 250 ml (8 fl oz) of the strained milk in which the fish was cooked. Do not allow this to boil or simmer, as the acid in the soup may curdle the milk and cause it to separate.

Ladle into bowls and garnish with croûtons, bacon and a few fennel leaves. Serves 6.

COLD PUMPKIN AND GINGER SOUP

An unusual and complementary mixture of flavours.

BASIC CHICKEN BROTH
*750 g (1½ lb) fresh chicken pieces, or
    half a boiling fowl, with excess fat
    removed*
2 carrots, peeled
1 onion, peeled and sliced
1 celery stick
6 parsley stalks
1 bay leaf
pinch of dried thyme
½ teaspoon salt

SOUP
225 g (8 oz) onion, chopped
*500 g (1¼ lb) pumpkin or winter
    squash flesh, cubed*
1.5 litres (2½ pints) basic chicken broth
salt
*2 pieces fresh ginger root, each about
    the size of a thumb*
black pepper
3–4 tablespoons double cream
*pistachio nuts, shelled, skinned and
    finely chopped*

Make the broth by placing the chicken pieces or boiling fowl, cut into manageable sizes, into a large, heavy saucepan or stockpot of 3.4–4.5 litres (6–8 pints) capacity.

Cover well with water, bring the water slowly to the boil and skim thoroughly. Add the carrots, onion, celery, parsley, bay leaf, thyme, and skim again as the water returns to boil. Add a little salt, lower the heat and half cover the pot with a lid. Barely simmer for 3–4 hours, topping up with water as necessary.

Strain the broth through a colander lined with a double thickness of muslin, degrease with paper towels, or cool and refrigerate, removing solidified layer of fat when ready to use.

For the soup, simmer the onion, pumpkin, strained broth and a little salt for about 10 minutes, until the vegetables are just cooked.

Cut away the skin of one ginger root with a small, sharp knife, and finely grate 1 teaspoon's worth; add some of this to the soup and purée, in two batches if necessary, in a blender or food processor, adding salt and pepper to taste. Add the double cream, and more ginger to taste. Its flavour should be evident but not overpowering.

Chill the soup for 2–3 hours. Stir well to reintegrate the cream, before ladling into cups or bowls.

Garnish each serving with more fresh grated ginger and pistachio nuts. Serves 5–6.

SCALLOP BROTH WITH JULIENNED VEGETABLES

This is an elegant, subtle soup and an effective means of making the most of an expensive shellfish.

BASIC FISH BROTH

1.5 kg (3 lb) bones and heads from lean fish such as Dover sole, plaice or lemon sole
2 leeks, cleaned and sliced
1 onion, peeled and sliced
8 parsley stalks
4 tablespoons lemon juice
2 large glasses dry white wine
½ teaspoon salt

SCALLOP BROTH

1 small sweet red pepper
1.5 litres (2½ pints) basic fish broth
1 thick carrot, peeled
a few button mushrooms
1 small leek
8 or 9 scallops (depending on size of muscle), with coral, bought in shell if possible; ask your fishmonger to clean them
120 ml (4 fl oz) dry white wine
salt
black pepper
gin

Make the basic broth by washing bones and heads thoroughly of blood and removing gills. Chop them into convenient sizes. Put them into a large saucepan or stockpot of 3.4–4.5 litres (6–8 pints) capacity with the leeks, the onion, parsley and lemon juice. Cover well with water. Bring to a simmer over a low heat, skim thoroughly, add wine and salt and simmer, uncovered, for 30 minutes. Strain the broth through a colander lined with a double thickness of muslin. Add a few more drops of white wine, let cool and refrigerate for 1–2 hours. The fine particles suspended in the broth will settle to the bottom of bowl. Disturb as little as possible.

Meanwhile, roast the red pepper under a preheated medium grill, turning as skin blisters and blackens all over. Cool under wet paper towels which will help loosen skin. Peel off all the skin, cut pepper open and remove core and seeds. Slice the pepper into very thin strips of about 4 cm (1½ inches) long then set aside as garnish.

When ready to proceed, carefully ladle 1.5 litres (2½ pints) clear broth away from its sediment and pour into a large saucepan. Make a very, very fine julienne from thin slices of carrot, mushroom tops, and inner part of the leek – you should have about 25 g (1 oz) of each type of julienne – and add to the broth. Place this over low heat.

Take cleaned and washed white muscle and coral of scallops (it is not worth making this from frozen scallops; buying them in shells is a guarantee that freezing has not occurred). Keep the corals whole and slice the muscles diagonally into thirds or quarters, depending on size.

Put into another saucepan, heavy and of medium capacity, with the white wine and grindings of salt and pepper. Cover the pan, set over a very low heat and poach scallops in the wine for 2–3 minutes or until just cooked. They must not boil or cook too long or they will toughen and lose all appeal. When done, carefully transfer the fish with a slotted spoon to the saucepan containing the broth, which should be heating without simmering.

Add a splash of gin to the wine in which scallops were poached, and rapidly boil this down to 1½ tablespoons. When the broth has been heated through and is just about to simmer, strain in the reduced liquid. Correct seasoning and ladle broth with its vegetables and fish into cups or bowls. Garnish with strips of red pepper.

This broth is also very good if cooled and refrigerated for several hours, garnish and all. The broth jells slightly and the result is delicate. Serves 5.

Asparagus soup, Three lentil soup, Scallop broth with julienned vegetables, Pumpkin soup

CARROT AND TARRAGON SOUP

BASIC CHICKEN BROTH
750 g (1½ lb) fresh chicken
2 carrots, peeled
1 onion, peeled and sliced
1 celery stick
6 parsley stalks
½ teaspoon dried tarragon
½ teaspoon salt

SOUP
225 g (8 oz) onion, peeled weight,
thinly sliced
625 g (1 lb 6 oz) carrots, peeled
weight, chopped
75 g (3 oz) butter
vegetable oil
1.75 litres (3 pints) chicken broth (as
above)
2 tablespoons long-grain rice
bunch of fresh tarragon
1 teaspoon granulated sugar
salt
black pepper
25 g (1 oz) butter

Make the chicken broth as described in Pumpkin and Ginger Soup (see page 100) but substituting tarragon for bay leaf and thyme.

To make the soup, sweat the onion and carrots in 50 g (2 oz) butter and a little oil in a large heavy saucepan, covered, for 8–10 minutes or until the onion softens. Add the chicken broth, rice, fresh tarragon, sugar and a pinch of salt. Bring to boil and simmer for 15–20 minutes, or until rice and carrots are cooked.

Cool slightly, purée in a blender or food processor, adding salt, pepper and two or more tablespoons of fresh tarragon leaves, to taste. Blend well. If the resulting purée is too thick, add a bit more broth to thin.

Reheat soup with 25 g (1 oz) butter, garnish bowls with fresh tarragon, and present. Serves 6.

COLD ASPARAGUS, SPINACH AND BASIL SOUP

BASIC MEAT BROTH
350 g (12 oz) shin of beef
100 g (4 oz) veal trimmings, if
available
450 g (1 lb) veal bones, cut into
manageable pieces (if veal bones are
unavailable, substitute a chicken
carcass)
2 carrots, peeled
1 onion, peeled and sliced
1 large clove garlic, unpeeled
1 celery stick
6 parsley stalks
1 bay leaf
pinch of dried thyme
½ teaspoon salt

SOUP
15 g (½ oz) butter
1 tablespoon flour
1.2 litres (2 pints) basic meat broth,
heated
1 celery stick, chopped
salt
500 g (1¼ lb) green asparagus
50 g (2 oz) fresh spinach leaves, well
washed
6 large basil leaves
black pepper
3–4 teaspoons lemon juice
seasoned whipped cream
about 15 small basil leaves

To make the broth, place the beef, veal and bones in a large, heavy saucepan or stockpot of 3.4–4.5 litres (6–8 pints) capacity. Cover well with water, bring water slowly to the boiling point, and skim thoroughly. Add the carrots, onion, garlic, celery, parsley, bay leaf, thyme, and skim again as water returns to boil. Add a little salt. Lower heat, half-cover pot with a lid and barely simmer for 4–5 hours, topping up with water as necessary. This should give a full-flavoured broth of good body.

Strain broth through a colander lined with a double thickness of muslin. Degrease with paper towels, or alternatively cool and refrigerate, then remove the layer of fat which has solidified at the top.

To make the soup, melt butter over a low heat in a heavy saucepan, blend in flour, whisk for 1 minute and, off heat, pour in hot broth all at once, whisk vigorously and bring to boil, stirring. Add celery and a pinch of salt. Lower heat and let liquid barely simmer on side of burner for 30 minutes, skimming off the skin which will form regularly.

Meanwhile, peel and trim the hard stems of the asparagus stalks. Remove the tips and blanch these for 1 minute in boiling, salted water; drain and refresh them under cold water to halt cooking. Add stalks to soup base and simmer for 15 minutes. Add the asparagus tips and spinach leaves (minus stalks), simmer for 3–4 minutes or until both are just cooked, add large basil leaves and simmer 1 minute longer.

Cool the soup slightly, then pour it into a blender or food processor fitted with a steel blade and purée, adding salt and pepper. Rub the soup through a sieve, correct the seasoning and add lemon juice; just enough to sharpen flavour slightly. Allow to cool, then chill for about 2 hours; if chilled for too long soup based on broth, which contains a lot of natural gelatine, will set like a mousse.

Garnish each serving with a swirl of seasoned whipped cream and 2 or 3 small basil leaves. Serves 4–5.

CHRISTMAS FESTIVITIES

Winter brings the dazzle of Christmas, with its dinner parties, children's beanos, and specially sumptuous teas. Here are some ornaments, enhancing details like Picasso's cookies, the Earl Grey's truffles and jam tarts in miniature, that will add their sparkle to your entertainments.

MARBLE CAKE

A classic mixture of chocolate and lemony swirls.

225 g (8 oz) unsalted butter, softened
grated zest of 1 large lemon
225 g (8 oz) caster sugar
3 eggs
225 g (8 oz) plain flour
large pinch of salt
2 teaspoons baking powder
about 2 teaspoons milk
2 tablespoons unsweetened cocoa

Butter two loaf tins of about 18.5 × 8 × 5.5 cm ($7\frac{1}{4}$ × $3\frac{1}{4}$ × $2\frac{1}{2}$ inches) and line the bottom of each with a strip of buttered greaseproof paper.

Cream the butter with lemon zest, gradually add caster sugar; whisk eggs and beat by tablespoons into base until really light and fluffy.

Sift together the flour, salt and baking powder; sift them again over the creamed ingredients and fold all together lightly and deftly; add a drop or two of milk if necessary to make the batter a heavy dropping consistency.

Portion off one-third of this mixture and combine well with sifted cocoa. Spoon a layer of the lemony base evenly over the bottom of each tin, followed by a layer of chocolate, then lemon, then chocolate. Run a butter knife back and forth through the length of each tin to marblize the batter, than cover the marblized batter completely with the remaining lemon base.

Bake in a preheated oven at 180°C, 350°F, Gas Mark 4 for 45–50 minutes or until they test done. They will rise high and crack down the centre. Cool on wire racks for 10 minutes. Remove from tins, peel off the paper and allow to cool. These cakes will keep for about a week stored in an airtight container. Makes 2 small loaves.

CROSS TARTS

These are miniature versions of an old-fashioned type of jam tart, once very popular and, in the north of England, quite complex.

Strips of pastry divide each tart into sections, each ready for a different jam, or as here, two contrasting ones. Some cooks devised star patterns and, showing off, put in thirteen different flavours, others stuck to simple crosses or ran a whirl of pastry round the middle. A cunning way of turning remnants of jam to advantage.

SHORTCRUST PASTRY
275 g (10 oz) plain flour
3 tablespoons icing sugar
large pinch of salt
pinch of ground nutmeg
1 teaspoon baking powder
175 g (6 oz) unsalted butter, softened
yolks of 2 hard-boiled eggs, sieved
1 egg

TO FINISH
jams, in contrasting colours

To make the shortcrust, sift the flour, sugar, salt, nutmeg and baking powder on to a pastry board, make a centre well and place butter in the well. Form a trough in the butter, add the sieved yolks and break the egg into this.

With one hand, deftly work the butter, yolks and egg into a sticky mass, then use a spatula to toss and chop flour gradually into butter and egg until it begins to resemble pastry.

Use both hands to bring the pastry into shape, add a few drops of water if necessary to bind. Knead briefly handling as little as possible and form into a ball. Wrap in greaseproof paper and plastic and refrigerate for several hours or, better still, overnight.

Bring the shortcrust pastry to room temperature, roll out and line small circular tins of about 5.5 cm ($2\frac{1}{4}$ inches) in diameter. With a sharp knife or a pastry cutter, cut narrow strips of dough and fit them across each other on top of the pastry linings, pressing strips gently into place.

Chill the tarts for at least 30 minutes, then bake on baking sheets at 180°C, 350°F, Gas Mark 4 for 15–20 minutes, or until golden, with browning edges. Cool the tarts and remove them from tins.

I filled these tarts, when cold, with redcurrant jelly and orange marmalade. I think that for this size it is more attractive to use two contrasting colours rather than a mixture of four. But there is no reason not to make up different combinations of two; blackcurrant with strawberry, plum with raspberry and so on, thereby creating a decorative and colourful array.

These tarts are best if made within a few hours of serving. Makes about 20.

TWIST-OF-GRAPE TARTS

A simple technique gives unusual results.

---

750 g (1½ lb) puff pastry made with
unsalted butter, see page 47 for
method
1 egg
small bunch of black or green grapes
lemon juice (optional)
175 g (6 oz) apricot jam

Roll the puff pastry to a thickness of about 3 mm (⅛ inch), and with the aid of a pastry cutter, cut out 10 cm (4 inch) squares (use off-cuts to make something else such as palmiers). Fold each square into a triangle and make a sharp cut 9 mm (⅜ inch) in from edge of each short side to within 9 mm (⅜ inch) of the point where the two halves of pastry meet. Unfold the entire triangle, and fold each pointed strip of thin pastry across the centre to the opposite side.

Make an egg wash with the egg beaten with a little water and use it to anchor each strip. The twist is now formed and should be symmetrical – if not, trim as necessary. Prick the centre of each twist with a fork and chill, on baking sheets, for at least 30 minutes.

Paint the angled strips with a little egg wash. Bake in a preheated oven at 190°C, 375°F, Gas Mark 5 for about 25 minutes until well risen, cooked through and browning. Cool completely.

While the tarts are baking, peel the grapes with a small, sharp knife, halve them and remove the pips. If preparing

Clockwise from the top: Twist-of-grape tarts, Cross tarts, Pumpkin mousse, Earl Grey's truffles, Fruit and nut cake, Picasso's cookies, Marble cake

in advance, sprinkle with lemon juice and refrigerate.

When the tarts are cold, scoop some of the pastry from each centre if you think there are too many layers. Simmer the apricot jam with a little water, sieve, and paint inside of each tart with this glaze.

Fill with well-dried grape halves. Brush grapes and surrounding pastry with glaze and serve as quickly as possible – within at least 2 hours of assembling, as the fruit and apricot will soften the pastry. Makes 10–12 tarts.

PICASSO'S COOKIES

A treat for children to make and paint, these are shortbreads cut into all sorts of shapes, then painted and piped with various brightly-coloured icings. Time-consuming but absorbing work.

COOKIES
100 g (4 oz) unsalted butter, softened
150 g (5 oz) caster sugar
1 egg
about 2 tablespoons milk
350 g (12 oz) plain flour
large pinch of salt
1 teaspoon baking powder

ICING
2 egg whites
a few drops of lemon juice
300 g (11 oz) icing sugar
yellow, red, blue and green food
colouring

For the cookies, cream the butter until light, gradually adding caster sugar until well integrated. Whisk egg and add to butter in two pours, beat in 2 tablespoons milk. Sift the dry ingredients and beat thoroughly into the creamed base. The dough should be moist but not damp – if necessary add a few more drops of milk. Roll the dough into a ball, wrap in greaseproof paper and refrigerate until firm but not hard.

Break off pieces of dough, roll out on a floured board to slightly more than 3 mm (⅛ inch) thick and with various shaped cutters, stamp out stars, fish, birds, half-moons, mushrooms, pigs; whatever appeals.

Place the cookies on heavy baking sheets. Bake in a preheated oven at 180°C, 350°F, Gas Mark 4 for about 10 minutes until the edges are golden brown. Cool for 1 minute before removing from sheets with a spatula and placing on wire racks to cool. They can be stored in airtight containers for weeks, if necessary.

To make the icing, put the egg whites into a very clean bowl with lemon juice, and beat whites, electrically if possible, at a high speed until frothy. Gradually sift in the icing sugar and beat until whites are thick, smooth, and standing in peaks when beater is removed. This will take 5–6 minutes. Put aside, covered with a damp cloth, until ready to use.

Make up 10 or so small piping bags from greaseproof paper, keeping the tips tiny. Have ready some small paintbrushes and some cups of water.

Put quantities of icing into little bowls or teacups. Keep one part white and mix drops of various food colourings into others until desired primary colours have been reached. Experiment!

To paint, thin some of icings with water so that various glazes, including white, can be brushed on to cookies. To pipe, fill bags two thirds full of unthinned colour, fold the tops down, cut tips slightly (keeping openings small), and use, renewing bags when necessary. There are no rules here, except to let various layers and adjoining colours dry sufficiently before painting or piping over them, and to rinse brushes thoroughly when changing colours. When finished, allow the cookies to dry for several hours before serving or storing in an airtight container. Makes 48–60.

THE EARL GREY'S TRUFFLES

Made with a *ganache* of chocolate, cream and egg yolk, these have the haunting aftertaste of Earl Grey tea.

---

175 ml (6 fl oz) double cream, very
fresh
25 g (1 oz) unsalted butter
1½ teaspoons Earl Grey tea
275 g (10 oz) semi-sweet dark
chocolate
1 egg yolk
cocoa powder (optional)
icing sugar (optional)

In a small, heavy-bottomed saucepan, bring the cream to the boil with the butter; add tea, stir, cover, and leave to infuse, off the heat, for 10 minutes.

With a large knife, thoroughly chop chocolate. Strain the cream through a fine sieve and discard the tea; wash and dry the pan, return cream to it and bring it again to the boil. Off the heat, add chocolate, stir, cover pan, and leave the chocolate to melt for 4–5 minutes. Add the egg yolk and, with a wooden spoon, beat the mixture smooth. Pour into a wide, medium-sized bowl and leave this *ganache* to cool, about 30 minutes.

Prepare about 30 paper cases – chocolate brown are the most appropriate in colour – to receive the truffles, and fit a nylon piping bag with a plain 1 cm (½ inch) tip.

Using a hand-held electric beater, whisk cooled *ganache* at high speed for 3–5 minutes. It will lighten. When it forms very, very soft peaks, stop beating and immediately pile into prepared bag; pipe the chocolate into paper cases.

If you find the *ganache* too liquid to pipe, remove from the bag and beat it further. If, on the other hand, you have beaten it too much to achieve a stylish result, simply stir the mixture in a small, heavy saucepan over a very low heat until it returns to liquid form, turn into a clean bowl, beat, and try again.

If, however, your *ganache* should

Earl Grey's truffles

prove to be totally uncooperative, which can happen with this temperamental substance, all can be salvaged by letting it stand until firm enough to shape with the hand. Then spoon small, compact nuggets of *ganache* on to a plate or tray covered with unsweetened cocoa sifted with a little icing sugar. Dust your fingertips with cocoa-sugar mixture and deftly roll each nugget into a ball, roll again in cocoa, and place in prepared paper cases.

These truffles can be stored in an airtight tin for up to a week if refrigerated. Eat about 30 minutes after removing from the refrigerator, because they soften quickly. Makes 20–30 chocolates.

FRUIT AND NUT CAKES

These are loaves of a Christmas cake-like nature, the batter a mixture of equal weights of butter, sugar, eggs and flour, just enough to bind the abundance of fruit and nuts. It is worth using the very best ingredients: Smyrna raisins if you can get them; slices of candied citron (not the cheap 'mixed peel' sold in supermarkets); a combination of red, green and white candied cherries if available. This quantity makes 4 small loaves, but you can use a 20 cm (8–9 inch) high-sided round tin instead if you prefer.

---

225 g (8 oz) Smyrna raisins, weighed
after stoning (or best available
stoned or seedless raisins)
175 g (6 oz) candied pineapple rings
100 g (4 oz) candied citron slices
50 g (2 oz) crystallized ginger
225 g (8 oz) whole candied cherries –
ideally, a combination of colours
50 g (2 oz) walnuts, very coarsely
chopped
50 g (2 oz) pistachio nuts
225 g (8 oz) plain flour
large pinch of salt
225 g (8 oz) unsalted butter, softened
grated zest and juice of 1 lemon
225 g (8 oz) caster sugar
4 eggs, weighing 50 g (2 oz) each in
the shell
4 tablespoons cognac and more for
ripening (optional)

Butter four loaf tins measuring approximately 18.5 × 8 × 5.5 cm (7¼ × 3¼ × 2¼ inches), or a larger round tin if you wish, line with a double thickness of buttered greaseproof paper or baking parchment. Cut this to extend at least 5 cm (2 inches) above rims to protect the tops of cakes from excessive browning.

Stone raisins if need be, and coarsely sliver the pineapple, citron and ginger. Combine in a bowl with the cherries and nuts. Sieve the flour with salt, and sift some of this over the fruits and nuts, turning them in the flour to separate the elements of this sticky mixture.

Cream the butter with the grated lemon zest, gradually adding all the sugar until butter is well aerated. With an electric whisk, beat the eggs for 10 minutes, until thick and light, and then with a wooden spoon beat eggs gradually into the base. Beat the remaining flour into base alternately with cognac and lemon juice, until the batter is of firm dropping consistency. Stir in the fruit and nuts.

Divide the batter among the four tins, and with the back of a damp spoon, make a smooth hollow down the centre

Fruit and nut cake

of each so that cakes rise evenly. Put the tins into an oven preheated to 140°C, 275°F, Gas Mark 1, with a water-filled roasting tin on lowest shelf to keep them moist. They will bake in 1¾–2 hours (a single 20–23 cm (8–9 inch) circular tin will take just under 3 hours) and are done when the tops turn a pale golden brown and a trussing needle thrust into centre tests clean and hot.

Cool the cakes on wire racks, in tins, for about 30 minutes, then turn out, and remove greaseproof paper. If not to be ripened, the cakes can be eaten straightaway, or kept for about one week in an airtight tin. But these cakes are lovely when soaked well with cognac top and bottom, wrapped snugly in greaseproof paper and then with foil, stored for a week in a sellotape-sealed tin, then rebrandied and rewrapped once a week for about a month. They can then be kept for a long time in a closed and sealed container. Makes 4 small loaves or 1 large fruit and nut cake.

PUMPKIN MOUSSE WITH CANDIED PEEL OF LIME

A frothy mixture of eggs, pumpkin, cream and spices. The mousse contrasts well with the snap and tang of its lime garnish. Although the ingredients are almost identical to those of the Pumpkin Brûlée on page 58 the effect when eating is interestingly different.

MOUSSE
4 leaves gelatine
120 ml (4 fl oz) dark rum
4 eggs
100 g (4 oz) caster sugar
225 g (8 oz) fresh pumpkin, cooked and smoothly puréed, or canned pumpkin
scant ½ teaspoon ground cinnamon
scant ½ teaspoon ground ginger
¼ teaspoon ground cloves
¼ teaspoon nutmeg
175 ml (6 fl oz) double cream

CANDIED PEEL
225 g (8 oz) granulated sugar
450 ml (¾ pint) water
2 limes with very green skins (if limes unavailable, use lemons)
caster sugar

To make mousse, soften the gelatine in a jug of water, drain and dissolve in rum that is gently warmed in a small heavy saucepan on top of a low heat.

Place the eggs in a medium-sized heat-proof mixing bowl set over a small saucepan of simmering water. Using a hand-held electric beater if possible, whisk eggs at high speed, gradually adding sugar. Whisk for 5–6 minutes or until eggs grow very light, thick, voluminous and rather warm. Take the bowl from the heat and whisk contents until almost cool.

Beat the pumpkin briefly to loosen its texture and fold, with the spices, into the egg base. Ensure that the gelatine-rum mixture is liquid, and strain this into the egg and pumpkin. Fold everything together thoroughly but with a light hand so as not to break down the volume. The base will probably now have cooled completely, but if not, let it stand the few minutes necessary to achieve this.

Whip the cream into very soft peaks (it should have the same consistency as the eggs and pumpkin) and fold into base. Spoon or pour the mousse into pots or ramekins and chill for 3–4 hours. Serve on the day made.

While mousse is chilling, prepare candied peel. Make a syrup by dissolving the granulated sugar with water in a heavy saucepan over a low heat. When the sugar has become completely liquid, boil the syrup for 1 minute.

Wash and dry the limes, and with a small, sharp knife, peel off the zest, without its bitter white pith, and cut into matchstick slivers; boil these in the syrup for 5 minutes. Lift out with a fork or slotted spoon and allow the candied peel to cool, scattered on a plate and free of excess syrup.

When the peel is cold, sprinkle caster sugar on another plate and roll half the peel in this, shaking away the excess crystals. If you like, prepare peels the day before they are needed. The syrup, well-diluted with lime or lemon juice and water, can then be made into a refreshing cool drink.

Remove the mousse from the refrigerator about 30 minutes in advance of serving, and at the last minute, garnish each pot with a combination of both peels. Makes enough for 16–20 small porcelain pots or ramekins.

Pumpkin mousse

WINTER WARMTH

An increasing number of people in English-speaking countries are renouncing meat and poultry, for a variety of reasons. I have never eaten these daily, but would hate to forgo the pleasure of them completely.

Recently I have begun to revive and diversify some old favourites like stewed oxtail and poached chicken. I've also been experimenting with grains and pulses, rediscovering the comfort of a good barley soup and the savour of kidney beans. For me, the prospects for cooking with meats look more interesting all the time.

BARLEY AND BLACK BEAN SOUP

This is a robust mixture, not without finesse, which can be served as a meal-in-one if escorted by toast, cheese and possibly a green salad.

1.25 litres (2 pints) basic meat broth,
  see page 102
75 g (3 oz) black beans
75 g (3 oz) barley groats (not pearl
  barley)
butter
50 g (2 oz) rindless, boneless, salted
  belly pork
100 g (4 oz) onion, peeled and finely
  chopped
salt
black pepper
175 g (6 oz) mushrooms,
  finely sliced
3 egg yolks
150 ml ($\frac{1}{4}$ pint) double cream
2–4 tablespoons milk
fresh parsley, chopped

Make the broth as described on page 102, browning the beef, veal trimmings and bones, carrot and onion first in a little oil in the saucepan to give a good colour.

Rinse black beans and soak them overnight. Rinse barley and soak for 2 hours. Soak pork for 1 hour to remove excess salt. Drain and mince.

To make the soup, melt a little butter in a heavy saucepan, add the pork and onion. Sweat these over a low heat until onion is translucent. Drain the beans and barley, add to pan with broth. Bring this to the simmer and skim. Boil the soup briskly for at least 25–30 minutes, stirring occasionally, until the beans and barley are tender. Taste for salt near the end of cooking; if pork is still quite salty, you may not need this.

Meanwhile, season and sauté the mushrooms in a little butter over a high heat for several minutes until cooked. Drain their expelled liquid into the soup.

Whisk together the egg yolks, cream and 2 tablespoons milk. When barley and beans are ready, add mushrooms to soup and beat a little of the hot liquid slowly into egg and cream to warm them. Beat this back into soup and stir constantly over a low heat until yolks have thickened the mixture; don't let it boil. Thin a little with milk if necessary, taste and season. Ladle into bowls and garnish with parsley. Serves 4–5.

OXTAIL STEW

This is my husband's recipe and I must admit he always makes it better than I do! The secret, he says, is to use up bottles of oxidised wine in the preparation, but I doubt that's all there is to it. The results are wickedly delicious.

---

6 large pieces oxtail, weighing about
  1.5 kg (3 lb) in total
1 bottle full-bodied red wine
1 large carrot, peeled and halved
1 bay leaf
2 large pinches dried
  mixed herbs
flour
salt
black pepper
vegetable oil
1 large onion, peeled and finely
  chopped
100 g (4 oz) red kidney beans
2 tablespoons brandy
tomato ketchup
50 g (2 oz) chorizo or other dried,
  spiced sausage
parsley sprigs

Marinate the oxtail overnight in wine with the carrot, bay leaf and herbs, turning the meat periodically to allow the flavour of the marinade to fully penetrate the meat, tenderizing as it marinates.

Remove the pieces from the marinade, dry them and roll in flour seasoned with salt and pepper. Brown the oxtail all over, with a little oil, in a sauté pan.

Take the meat from the pan and sweat the onion in the oil left behind until the onion turns golden. Deglaze the pan with a little marinade, and put the onion, all of the marinade and the oxtail into a heavy casserole. Add a dash of salt. Bring the liquid to simmering point on top of the stove. Partially cover and poach in a preheated oven at 150°C, 300°F, Gas Mark 2 for 3–4 hours, turning the meat occasionally until the flesh is tender and falling from the bones. Cool the meat slightly in its winy stock, drain and cool

Clockwise from top: Fettuccine, Chicken with ginger, Oxtail stew, Veal cutlets,
Barley and black bean soup

completely. Strain the stock. Cover and refrigerate both overnight.

Rinse and drain the kidney beans and soak them in water overnight. Bring the beans to the boil and boil hard for 15 minutes, then simmer for 20–30 minutes further, or until tender. Cool.

Remove the meat from the refrig-erator, wipe away excess fat and slice the flesh into bite-size pieces. Put these into a saucepan with the oxtail's stock and heat. Add the brandy, a little ketchup, and a few spoonfuls of water if the sauce is very concentrated. Thinly slice *chorizo*, add with the drained beans and heat all thoroughly, seasoning with salt and pepper. Check flavours, which should be rich and dark. Add a drop more brandy and extra ketchup – and even more water – if necessary.

Simmer for several minutes and serve garnished with parsley and accom-panied by boiled, buttered rice, potatoes or noodles. Serves 4.

FETTUCCINE WITH GAMMON AND AN EGG SAUCE

This dish is a herby pasta with ham, eaten at room temperature, its sabayon sauce flavoured with gammon poaching liquid. If fresh fettuccine are unavailable, do of course substitute the best dried noodles you can find.

---

150 g (5 oz) thinly sliced smoked
    gammon
600 ml (1 pint) water
150 ml ($\frac{1}{4}$ pint) dry white wine
2 large cloves garlic, crushed
1 long strip lemon zest, pith removed
2 large parsley sprigs
50 g (2 oz) whole blanched almonds
salt
olive oil
6 egg yolks
black pepper
350 g (12 oz) fresh green and red
    fettuccine or dried of whatever shade
fresh dill and chervil, or 2 other
    complementary herbs, coarsely
    chopped

Trim the gammon of fat and place in a small saucepan with water, wine, garlic, lemon zest and parsley. Bring to the simmer and poach gammon for about 7 minutes. Remove the meat, cool and cut into short, thin strips. Raise heat under liquid and reduce it, aromatics in place, to 150 ml ($\frac{1}{4}$ pint). Drain and reserve.

Meanwhile, cut the almonds into pine-nut-like nibs. Toast for 5–10 minutes until pale brown in a preheated oven at 180°C, 350°F, Gas Mark 4.

Bring a large saucepan of salted water to the boil, add a dash of olive oil and simultaneously heat a smaller saucepan of water. Take a heavy, heat-proof bowl, add the egg yolks and gammon-poaching liquid and whisk together well. Place bowl over the small pan of water (keeping it just at the simmer) and whisk yolks to a thick frothy mousse; a matter of 3–5 minutes.

Remove from the water and whisk sauce for 1–2 minutes more. Taste for seasoning.

Set the bowl aside in a warm place, and plunge pasta into boiling salted water. Boil uncovered until al dente – anywhere from 1–12 minutes, depending on the noodles – drain, season, toss for several minutes in another bowl to cool. Give sabayon another whisk and pour on most of it, tossing noodles with ham, nuts and herbs. Season again, and present pasta with extra sauce in a warmed boat. Serves 3–4.

VEAL CUTLETS BAKED IN FOIL

I usually find veal dry and uninteresting, but a cutlet baked with good condiments in a sealed bag of aluminium foil retains moisture and makes its own piquant sauce. Serve this when you're feeling rich and very hungry.

---

2 veal cutlets, on bone, from wing end
    of loin, each weighing about 450 g
    (1 lb) and measuring 2.5–3 cm
    (1–1$\frac{1}{4}$ inches) thick
vegetable oil
butter
1 small onion, peeled
2 large cloves garlic, peeled
4 rashers green streaky bacon
4 anchovy fillets
black pepper
2 tablespoons dry white vermouth

Sauté cutlets in a little oil and butter for 5 minutes on each side, just to colour. Remove from the pan and cool. Mince the onion and garlic and sauté in the cutlets' oil and butter until golden and browning. Cut rinds from bacon (if present), and divide each rasher in half lengthwise.

Take two large sheets of foil, fold each in half and lay an X of bacon across each centre. Place a cutlet on top, cover both cutlets with another X of bacon and

wrap all bacon ends around veal. Halve the anchovy fillets lengthwise and lay the fillets across each cutlet. Grind on pepper, spread onion and garlic on top of the meat and sprinkle on vermouth.

Bring the edges of the foil up around each set of contents and fold into two loose but airtight bags. Bake in a preheated oven at 190°C, 375°F, Gas Mark 5 for 25 minutes.

Present each bag, intact, on a hot plate; open foil at the table and the burst of aromas will rise to greet you. Have an extra plate to hand for discarding wrapping and accompany the cutlets with mashed potatoes. Serves 2.

POACHED CHICKEN WITH GINGER AND ORANGE

The sliced ginger under the skin and the zest of orange in its poaching liquid give this bird an unexpected and delicate flavour.

1.5 kg (3$\frac{1}{2}$ lb) roasting chicken, dressed
    weight
50 g (2 oz) piece fresh root ginger,
    peeled and finely sliced
1 carrot, peeled and sliced
1 onion, peeled and sliced
3 long strips orange zest, pith removed
2 parsley stalks
4 black peppercorns
250 ml (8 fl oz) dry white wine
salt
6 tablespoons double cream
2 teaspoons arrowroot
350 g (12 oz) carrots, peeled and sliced
350 g (12 oz) broccoli, trimmed and
    sliced
black pepper
butter

Remove any fat from the chicken cavity; wash and wipe inside and out. Peel a third of the ginger, slice this into very thin rounds; carefully loosen skin from chicken breasts and legs by working fingers beneath skin and push the slices

Fettuccine with gammon

Chicken with ginger

into place all over the area. Truss the chicken with soft white string.

Place it in a heavy, deep flameproof casserole that holds it snugly. Add half the remaining ginger, cut up, the carrot and onion, 2 strips of orange rind, parsley, peppercorns and wine. Pour in water to come halfway up the chicken and hold casserole, covered, in bottom of refrigerator overnight; this gives the flavours time to blend.

Next day, bring the casserole to room temperature and place on top of the stove, bringing the liquid to the simmer. Skim thoroughly, add salt and cover chicken breasts with a double thickness of washed and wrung out muslin, the ends of which should fall into the potential broth to draw this over the bird, keeping the breasts moist and basted during cooking.

Lower heat until the liquid simmers slowly, cover casserole with a close-fitting lid and poach for 1 hour. Test the bird by pressing its flesh and seeing if you

can move the legs in their sockets. If in doubt, poach for 5 minutes more.

Carefully strain off 600 ml (1 pint) of stock and keep chicken hot at the bottom of a very low oven. Keep the chicken in its casserole with a little stock, and with the muslin in place, while you make the sauce.

Let the fat rise to top of the stock as you beat the cream with the arrowroot in a small bowl. A sauce thickened with arrowroot is much subtler than the roux-based variety, which needs long, slow cooking to eliminate its taste of flour.

Thoroughly degrease the stock, whisk some of this into the cream and arrowroot to warm them, and whisk all together in a saucepan. Set this over a low heat, beating constantly until the sauce comes to the simmer. Add the remaining peeled and sliced ginger and orange zest to refresh these flavours, and let sauce simmer very gently, whisking occasionally, for several minutes to reduce and thicken.

Meanwhile, simmer the carrots and broccoli in pans of salted water until tender. Drain and season, add a little butter, and hold.

When the sauce is ready – it should coat the back of a spoon – season and strain it into a heated boat. Drain, de-truss, and carve the chicken, removing ginger from under its skin. Serve with vegetables and sauce. Serves 4.

CELEBRATIONS

Celebration calls for special food – dishes which the cook loves to prepare, which friends will find hard to resist, or which anyone would recognize as a luxury.

Celebrations demand, too, a sense of occasion. At an indoor picnic, for instance, rain will scarcely dampen the whoosh of champagne or the elegant pleasures of a rolled soufflé, a wine-drenched Camembert, or a sparkling sweet jelly, while a springtime birthday that is centred around smoked salmon lasagne has a note of unusual exuberance. But self-indulgent pastimes can be truly simple: a slice of wholemeal toast spread with runny, peppery Brie, or a robust lamb stew that is easy to make and amiably adaptable once prepared.

Cooking with wine has always, for me, the atmosphere of celebration, particularly when the result looks as striking as a slim glass of strawberry cream surrounded by perfect fruits. But, for some of us, nothing else has the allure of a plate of miniature cakes and pastries, or chocolate in as many glorious forms as possible.

AN INDOOR PICNIC

I love picnics, and have given many – sometimes indoors, faced with last-minute showers or an out-and-out downpour. So I like to plan alternatives to the lawn and field; one way of having your spread and eating it without showers is to borrow a conservatory, which gives the illusion of outdoors without its changeability.

CAMEMBERT AU MUSCADET

A smooth and surprising alternative to the cheese itself.

$1\frac{1}{2} \times 225\,g$ *(8 oz) Camembert cheeses,*
  soft and fairly ripe
Muscadet or other dry and fruity white
  wine
175 g (6 oz) unsalted butter, softened
black pepper
150 g (5 oz) blanched almonds
Bath Olivers or water biscuits

Pierce the Camemberts all over with a fork, place in a wide bowl, and barely cover the cheese with wine. Leave to marinate for about 12 hours, turning periodically.

Drain off the wine, break up the cheese, and put, with butter, into a blender or the bowl of a food processor fitted with a steel blade. Add a tablespoon or two of the marinading wine (the rest can be added to stock or soup) and a few turns of the pepper mill. Blend until smooth. Taste and add pepper if necessary.

Turn the cheese out into a bowl – it will be a sticky mass – and refrigerate for about 30 minutes, or until firm enough to shape.

Meanwhile, chop the almonds fairly finely and place on a baking sheet. Toast in a preheated oven at 180°C, 350°F, Gas Mark 4 for 5 or 6 minutes or until pale golden brown. Remove from the baking sheet and cool.

When the cheese has firmed, shape it with your hands to re-form a Camembert, cover it all over with the cooled nuts, and lower, on a piece of foil, into a plastic box. Put a lid on the box and refrigerate for several hours or overnight. Remove from the refrigerator and box in good time before eating, to allow cheese to develop its bouquet; on a hot day, try to keep cheese fairly cool once it has been out of the fridge for more than 20 minutes, so that the butter does not melt. Serve with Bath Olivers or water biscuits. Serves 6.

LETTUCE AND VINAIGRETTE

To me, the best salad is simply a crisp, green lettuce and a very pungent vinaigrette; the kind that makes you want to wipe up every drop with good bread.

1–2 heads round-heart, garden, or
  long-leafed lettuce, depending on
  size of lettuce and appetites
red wine vinegar
Dijon mustard
2–3 cloves garlic
salt, preferably freshly-ground sea salt
black pepper
caster sugar
5–6 tablespoons olive oil

Wash and thoroughly dry the lettuce; tear large leaves into smaller pieces and place in a large salad bowl, or hold in a damp cloth until ready to use.

Put about 1 tablespoon of vinegar into a small bowl. Add a generous 1 tablespoon of Dijon mustard. Bruise 2 garlic cloves with the handle of a heavy knife, peel, sprinkle with $\frac{1}{2}$ teaspoon of salt, and with the blade of a small knife, work garlic and salt on the chopping board into a smooth paste. Add to the bowl.

Grind on a liberal amount of salt and pepper, add a teaspoon of caster sugar, whisk all together with a fork and slowly pour on the olive oil. The mustard will cause oil, vinegar, and seasonings to form a thick, creamy emulsion. After adding about 5 tablespoons oil, stop and taste. At this point I usually add more mustard and seasonings and sometimes more garlic! The ideal is very well-seasoned but not too acid; the sugar gives an interesting dimension to the flavour.

When you like the result, whisk vigorously. The vinaigrette is ready to use, or can be stored, tightly covered, for weeks in the fridge. Bring to room temperature and whisk well before pouring.

To serve salad, add a small amount of vinaigrette to a bowl of leaves and toss with your hands, if possible. In this way you can ensure that the leaves are just covered with dressing, without excess. Store the remainder for another time. Serves 6.

Clockwise from top: Lettuce and vinaigrette, Rice flour shortbreads, Cava jellies with soft fruits, Marinated vegetables, Mackerel, fennel and anisette, Camembert au Muscadet, Rolled tomato soufflé

ROLLED TOMATO SOUFFLE WITH TOMATO AND PESTO SAUCES

A rolled soufflé is impressive and not difficult to make. A picnic encourages appetites, and you will probably be happier with a pair of soufflés. If so, make 1½ quantities of tomato sauce, double quantities of *pesto* and of soufflé filling, but make and bake each soufflé separately.

TOMATO SAUCE

1 medium onion, finely chopped
2 large cloves garlic, finely chopped
1 carrot, peeled and finely chopped
1 celery stick, finely chopped
25 g (1 oz) butter
olive oil
794 g (1 lb 12 oz) can Italian plum
 tomatoes, with their juices
3 tablespoons dry white wine
2 teaspoons granulated sugar
salt
1 bay leaf
pinch of thyme
fresh parsley stalks
black pepper

TOMATO SOUFFLE

40 g (1½ oz) plain flour
350 ml (12 fl oz) milk
175 ml (6 oz) of the tomato sauce
3 egg yolks
salt
black pepper
75 g (3 oz) Gruyère cheese, grated
5 egg whites

FILLING

2 shallots or white part of 2 spring
 onions, finely chopped
2 small cloves garlic, peeled and finely
 chopped
15 g (½ oz) butter
100 g (4 oz) ham, chopped
50 g (2 oz) walnuts, coarsely chopped
85 ml (3 fl oz) double cream
salt, black pepper
25 g (1 oz) Gruyère cheese, grated

PESTO SAUCE

2 large bunches fresh basil, or all the
 leaves from one large basil plant
25 g (1 oz) pine-nuts
2 large cloves garlic, peeled and sliced
85–120 ml (3–4 fl oz) olive oil
salt
50 g (2 oz) grated Parmesan cheese
1–2 tablespoons freshly grated
 pecorino cheese (a hard, sharp,
 sheeps' milk cheese sold by the piece
 in Italian delicatessens), to taste
40 g (1½ oz) butter

To make the tomato sauce, sweat the onion, garlic, carrot and celery stick in butter and a splash of olive oil in a large sauté pan, covered, for about 10 minutes, until onion becomes soft and golden.

Add the tomatoes and their liquid, the wine and sugar, about a 1¼ teaspoon of salt and the herbs. Bring to the boil and simmer uncovered for 20–30 minutes, stirring occasionally. Don't allow the liquid to reduce too much.

Remove the bay and parsley, cool sauce slightly and liquidize. Put through a coarse sieve, add freshly-ground pepper and more salt if necessary. Yields about 600 ml (1 pint).

To make the soufflé, line a Swiss roll tin measuring 23 × 32 cm (8½ × 12½ inches) with unbuttered greaseproof paper in a sheet large enough to extend above sides of tin.

Sift the flour into a small, heavy saucepan. Gradually whisk in half the milk, beating absolutely smooth before adding the rest of the milk and whisking well. Place the pan over a low heat and beat mixture until thick; let it boil for 30 seconds, beating constantly. Remove from heat and beat until smooth.

Whisk in the tomato sauce, followed by the egg yolks. Season liberally with salt and pepper; more than you think necessary at this stage, to compensate for the bland egg whites.

Have the grated Gruyère to hand and make sure it is not stuck together in clumps.

Whisk the egg whites to peaks. Beat a quarter of the whites into the soufflé base to lighten it, then fold the lightened base quickly and deftly into the rest of the whites, adding the cheese as you go.

Pour the tomato soufflé mixture into the Swiss roll tin and lightly spread to level it. Bake in a preheated oven at 190°C, 375°F, Gas Mark 5 for about 40–45 minutes. The soufflé will rise and turn brown.

Meanwhile, prepare the filling. Sweat the finely-chopped shallots or spring onions and garlic in butter, in a small saucepan, covered, for about 5 minutes until golden. Add the chopped ham, walnuts and cream. Let the cream reduce to form a sauce with the rest, then remove from heat and season to taste. Set aside to cool until you have completed the pesto sauce.

Moisten and wring out a tea-towel and spread it on to a work surface.

Test the soufflé with a skewer plunged into the centre; if the skewer is piping hot and dry to touch when applied to the back of your hand, the soufflé is ready.

Remove the soufflé from the oven and invert smartly on to a tea-towel. Carefully peel off greaseproof paper with the aid of a palette knife; the soufflé will probably stick round the edges but don't worry, just remove any particles which come away with the paper and patch the soufflé as needed; no one will suspect.

Spread with filling, sprinkle on the grated Gruyère cheese and, using the damp cloth to help you, gently roll up the soufflé – *not* incorporating the towel into the roll. Carefully transfer the soufflé to a large piece of foil in which to store or transport it.

Serve the remaining tomato sauce with this, plus the *pesto* which you have made as follows.

Tear all of the basil leaves into two or three pieces, put into a blender or food processor along with pine-nuts, garlic, 85 ml (3 fl oz) olive oil and a large pinch

Cava jellies

Marinated vegetables

of salt. Purée, add more olive oil if the mixture looks too stiff. The purée should retain a certain amount of texture.

Remove to a bowl and beat in the Parmesan. Grate in a small quantity of pecorino from the very hard fragment you have bought – you'll probably need 1 or 2 tablespoons but check and taste, as you don't want too much of its over-powering flavour. Finally, beat in the butter, sample and add more salt if you think it necessary. The result should have a wonderful green colour and garlicky flavour.

The beauty of a rolled soufflé is its versatility and transportability. You can slice and serve it cold for an outdoor picnic – it slices more neatly that way than when hot; or if near an oven, you can reheat it foil-wrapped, at 180°C, 350°F, Gas Mark 4 for 15 minutes, then slice and serve hot. The tomato sauce can be heated too, but do not reheat the *pesto*. Serves 6.

MARINATED VEGETABLES

The acid in this marinade makes the vegetables piquant and crisp; best eaten in small quantities and garnished with a soft cheese like Dolcelatte.

---

350 g (12 oz) fat, flavourful carrots,
    peeled
salt
350 g (12 oz) medium courgettes
2 large cloves garlic
dried oregano
black pepper
2 tablespoons red wine vinegar
olive oil
175 g (6 oz) Dolcelatte cheese

Cut the carrots into 5 cm (2 inch) lengths and drop into a pan of boiling, salted water. Simmer about 3 minutes; they should only half cook. Remove carrots, refresh under cold water to arrest cooking, and dry.

Wash but do not peel the courgettes, top and tail, cut into 5 cm (2 inch) lengths, and drop into boiling, salted water. Simmer for about 2 minutes, drain when half cooked, refresh and dry.

Cut both vegetables lengthwise into slices about 5 mm ($\frac{1}{4}$ inch) thick, and then cut slices into square sticks. Dry on paper towels and put into a deep bowl.

Bruise the garlic cloves with the handle of a heavy knife, peel and quarter them and add to the vegetables. Sprinkle on a large pinch of oregano and season with salt and pepper. Add wine vinegar and enough olive oil to coat the vegetables completely when turned repeatedly in the mixture.

Cover and refrigerate for at least 12 hours, turning periodically. The vegetables will become very crisp and the garlic and oregano permeate the vegetables. Remove the garlic before serving at room temperature, garnished with crumbled Dolcelatte. Serves 6.

MACKEREL, FENNEL AND ANISETTE

Another marinade, which in this dish features the complementary flavours of mackerel and aniseed in vegetable and alcoholic forms.

---

1 kg (2 lb) mackerel fillets
3 medium bulbs fennel, with leaves if possible
½ teaspoon coriander seeds
¼ teaspoon celery seeds
8 black peppercorns
1 teaspoon sea salt
6–7 tablespoons vegetable oil
juice of 1 lime
scant 1 teaspoon anisette liqueur (I use Marie Brizard, available in miniatures)

Skin the mackerel fillets and remove all bones; cut into bite-size pieces. Wash and trim the fennel, saving the leaves and green of upper stems as a garnish. Cut the bulbs into small pieces and put with mackerel into a wide glass or porcelain dish.

Pound the coriander and celery seeds, peppercorns and salt in a mortar with a pestle and strew the results over fish and fennel. Dribble on the oil, lime juice and anisette; turn mixture well in marinade, cover and refrigerate overnight, turning periodically. The acid in the marinade will partly 'cook' the fish and the anisette will reinforce the taste of the fennel.

Line the grill tray with foil and strew it with fish, fennel and enough marinade to moisten well. Don't try to crowd on too much at once, but grill the fish and fennel in several batches, about 2 minutes per side. Remove the mackerel, and grill the fennel longer, until slightly charred. When everything has been cooked, serve, with juices unchilled, within a few hours of grilling. Garnish with the reserved fennel leaves and the thinly sliced green of the reserved fennel stems. Serves 6.

RICE FLOUR SHORTBREADS

Ground rice and a lot of butter gives these a rich crispness. They are a delightful accompaniment to the cava jellies.

---

225 g (8 oz) unsalted butter, softened
grated zest of large lemon
100 g (4 oz) caster sugar
225 g (8 oz) plain flour
100 g (4 oz) rice flour (ground rice)
pinch of salt

Cream butter and lemon zest, gradually cream in the sugar; sift together the flours and salt and beat into the butter.

Break off bits of dough and roll into balls the size of marbles. Flatten into circles about 4.5 cm (1¾ inches) in diameter on heavy baking sheets, score with a fork and bake in a preheated oven at 190°C, 375°F, Gas Mark 5, for 10–15 minutes, until just beginning to brown. Leave the biscuits on baking sheets for 2–3 minutes before removing with a spatula. Cool on racks and store in airtight tins. Makes about 48.

CAVA JELLIES WITH SOFT FRUITS

Champagne jelly is a luxury, but champagne is a needless extravagance when cava, the Spanish *méthode champenoise*, is both a cheaper and a more successful alternative because of its grapey flavour. It must, however, be a dry and fruity one – run-of-the-mill sparkling wine will not do. Delightfully, bubbles prickle on the tongue as you eat the jelly.

---

5 leaves gelatine
450 ml (¾ pint) water
100 g (4 oz) sugar
zest and juice of 1 lemon
300 ml (½ pint) cava, chilled – Conde de Caralt seco gives a good result
soft fruits to garnish: bananas, kiwis, strawberries, raspberries

---

Soften the gelatine in a jug of water and drain. Heat the water in a saucepan, add gelatine and dissolve. Stir in sugar, pared and pithless lemon zest cut into strips and lemon juice. Heat mixture to just below boiling point, draw pan off the heat, cover and let steep for 30 minutes. Strain the liquid into a bowl through a fine sieve lined with a double thickness of muslin; discard the zest.

Cool jelly almost to the setting point and stir in cava, retaining as much of the bubble as possible by not over-beating.

Spoon or pour into ramekins or other small moulds; clear ones will show the jellies' translucence to advantage. Refrigerate until set; don't make more than a day in advance because jellies will then begin to lose their sparkle.

Serve them with the soft red fruits, and with sliced bananas and kiwi fruit, which can be cut up in advance, turned in lemon juice and transported to the site of your picnic in small containers. Makes 8.

CHOCOLATE

I can think of few self-indulgences as versatile, or satisfying, as chocolate. It comforts and impresses, from the Bourneville bar, eaten on a Friday evening train to the country, to the most sophisticated Parisian bitter chocolate cake. The recipes given here are based on a small number of ingredients, which must be the best: chocolate made with cocoa butter, not vegetable oil; double cream, unsalted butter; vanilla and almond essences, not 'flavourings'; Kirsch, Grand Marnier and good dark rum. It's luxury, and worth it.

CHOCOLATE-CHEESE BROWNIES

CHOCOLATE LAYER
175 g (6 oz) semi-sweet dark
  chocolate, broken up
40 g (1½ oz) unsalted butter
2 eggs
175 g (6 oz) caster sugar
75 g (3 oz) plain flour
¼ teaspoon salt
½ teaspoon baking powder
½ teaspoon vanilla essence
few drops almond essence
50 g (2 oz) walnuts, shelled and
coarsely chopped

CHEESE LAYER
50 g (2 oz) unsalted butter, softened
175 g (6 oz) Ricotta or softened cream
  cheese
50 g (2 oz) caster sugar
2 eggs, beaten
1 teaspoon vanilla essence
2 tablespoons plain flour, sieved
¼ teaspoon salt

Melt the chocolate and the butter in a small, heavy saucepan which you have set, covered, in a larger pan of just-boiled water. Beat the chocolate until smooth and set aside to cool.

For the cheese layer, cream the butter with the cheese, gradually beat in sugar, beaten eggs and vanilla, creaming thoroughly after each addition. Blend the sifted flour and salt. The mixture will be quite runny. Set aside.

For the chocolate layer, beat the eggs, gradually adding the caster sugar, until very thick, light, and increased in bulk. This is best done with a hand-held electric mixer. Sift together the flour, salt and baking powder and blend into the egg, beating with a wire whisk if necessary to eliminate lumps. Blend in the cooled chocolate and butter, the essences, then the walnuts.

Spread half the chocolate mixture into a well-buttered 22 cm (8½ inch) square pan. Top with cheese mixture and spoon the remaining chocolate on top. Zig-zag a wide-bladed knife through batter to get a marbled effect.

Bake at 180°C, 350°F, Gas Mark 4 for 25–30 minutes until *just* cooked – a knife inserted in the centre should come out clean and the top will have begun to crack. Let the tin cool on a wire rack and cut contents into 20 small brownies.

CHOCOLATE-DIPPED STRAWBERRIES

20 perfect strawberries, with stalks
about 350 g (12 oz) best semi-sweet
dark chocolate, 175 g (6 oz) finely
chopped, 175 g (6 oz) finely grated

Make sure that the strawberries are ripe, firm, clean, and completely dry before dipping in chocolate, otherwise the chocolate will not adhere.

Put the finely-chopped chocolate into a small heavy saucepan with a tight-fitting lid that will keep out moisture. Set this into a pan of just-boiled water and melt the chocolate as for the chocolate-cheese brownies; be sure to keep steam away from the chocolate, as it alters the consistency.

When melting is achieved, remove the pan from water and beat until smooth. Test the temperature with a thermometer; it should be 45°C, 113°F. If lower, return pan to water and cover until this temperature is reached. Take off the heat and beat in the finely-grated chocolate, a spoonful at a time, until the temperature is lowered to 26°C, 79°F. Return briefly to the hot pan, and stir with the thermometer in, until the temperature reaches 32°–33°C (90–92°F). These temperatures are important and should be accurately judged. By tempering the chocolate in this controlled way you are reforming the correct emulsion of cocoa butter and chocolate solids, necessary to give the dipped strawberries a hard surface with a sheen and no white streaks.

Holding each strawberry by its stem, dip quickly into chocolate to cover about three-quarters of its surface, and place on greaseproof paper on a baking sheet. The chocolate should harden in about 5 minutes, but if not, put the strawberries briefly into a refrigerator. Remove and store in cool, dry place (not the refrigerator). Don't allow the strawberries to touch each other. They do not keep and should be eaten on the day made. Makes about 20.

PAIR OF CHOCOLATE CHESTNUT ROLLS

CHOCOLATE SPONGE CAKE
6 eggs
200 g (7 oz) caster sugar
65 g (2½ oz) unsweetened cocoa
 powder
pinch of salt

CHESTNUT BUTTER CREAM
90 g (3½ oz) sugar
3 tablespoons water
4 egg yolks
about 175 g (6 oz) unsalted butter,
 softened
about 175 g (6 oz) unsweetened
 chestnut purée

TO FINISH
icing sugar

Line two Swiss roll tins, each measuring 32 × 22 cm (12½ × 8½ inches), with greaseproof paper large enough to extend above sides.

Using the ingredients for the cake, separate the eggs and beat the yolks, gradually adding 150 g (5 oz) of the sugar, until very light, thick, and increased in bulk. Sieve in the cocoa and salt and beat mixture with a wooden spoon until well blended.

Half-beat the whites, adding the sugar until stiff peaks form. Beat about a third of whites into cocoa mixture to lighten it; pour this on to the rest of the whites and fold together quickly.

Divide the batter between the cake tins, spreading evenly, tap each tin

Clockwise from top: Chocolate chip cookies, Chocolate chestnut rolls, Chocolate-cheese brownies, Chocolate-dipped strawberries, Frozen chocolate mousse, Chocolate and walnut cake, Le Paradis

smartly against work surface to settle the contents. Bake in a preheated oven at 190°C, 375°F, Gas Mark 5 for about 25 minutes or until the cake on the top shelf tests done (the cake on the lower shelf will take longer). Turn each out on to a separate tea towel which has been covered with a sheet of greaseproof paper. Peel the paper carefully from the back of each cake, and lay a fresh sheet over it. Roll up each sponge and cool.

While the cakes are baking, prepare the butter cream. Make a syrup by heating sugar and water up to 118°C (245°F), while beating yolks until thickened and light. Whisk the syrup into the yolks and beat the mixture for several minutes until thick and cool. It will grow significantly in volume. Beat in the soft butter bit by bit, until the butter cream suddenly comes together and is firm and spreadable. You may need to add a little more soft butter than the 175 g (6 oz) in order to achieve this. Sieve the chestnut purée directly into the butter cream, and beat to incorporate.

Unroll each sponge, remove the inner greaseproof paper and divide the butter cream between the two, spreading thickly to edges. Roll up each cake and don't worry if they crack a little. Trim the ends with a serrated knife, sieve a light coating of icing sugar over both. Serve thinly sliced. Serves 8.

CHOCOLATE CHIP COOKIES

225 g (8 oz) unsalted butter, softened
100 g (4 oz) caster sugar
175 g (6 oz) soft dark brown sugar,
 sieved
2 eggs, beaten
1 tablespoon vanilla essence
275 g (10 oz) plain flour
1 teaspoon baking soda
1 teaspoon salt
175 g (6 oz) walnuts, coarsely chopped
225 g (8 oz) chocolate chips

Cream butter well, gradually add the two sugars, the eggs and vanilla, creaming thoroughly after each addition. Sift together the dry ingredients and fold into the rest, followed by the walnuts and chocolate chips.

Drop small spoonfuls on to heavy baking sheets; flatten slightly and leave space between the cookies.

Bake in a preheated oven at 190°C, 375°F, Gas Mark 5 for about 10 minutes until just browning and still chewy. Remove from the oven, but leave on baking sheets for about 1 minute, then cool on wire racks. Makes about 48.

FROZEN CHOCOLATE MOUSSE

250 g (9 oz) semi-sweet dark
 chocolate, broken up
150 g (5 oz) unsalted butter
1 tablespoon dark rum
4 egg yolks
6 egg whites
scant 25 g (1 oz) icing sugar

TO SERVE
chocolate coffee beans
caramel custard (see page 122)

Oil the sides of a loaf tin measuring 21 × 7.5 × 7.5 cm (8½ × 3 × 3 inches) and line the bottom of the tin with a strip of unoiled greaseproof paper.

Melt the chocolate with the butter in a small, heavy saucepan which you have set, covered, into a larger pan of just-boiled water. Reheat the water as necessary to completely melt chocolate. When ready, beat smooth, remove the saucepan from the water, and beat the mixture for 1–2 minutes to cool slightly.

Add a dash of rum – no more than about 1 tablespoon – and the egg yolks. Beat again to thicken. When cool, beat the egg whites to soft peaks and beat in the icing sugar until firm peaks form. Beat about a quarter of the whites into the chocolate base to lighten it, then pour the chocolate on to the whites, folding them together quickly and deftly. Pour the mousse into the prepared tin and freeze overnight.

To serve, plunge the tin quickly into a basin of warm water, run a knife around the four sides, and turn the mousse out on to a platter. Peel off the greaseproof paper. Strew chocolate coffee beans around the mousse, and slice it thinly with a sharp, heated knife, adding a few coffee beans and the caramel custard to each serving. Serves 6–8.

CARAMEL CUSTARD

scant 175 g (6 oz) granulated sugar
8 egg yolks
vanilla pod, split
600 ml (1 pint) milk

Make a caramel with the sugar and a little water, bringing it up to a good colour (188°C, 370°F). Meanwhile, beat the yolks until thick and pale, while infusing the vanilla pod in the milk brought up to the scalding point in a heavy saucepan.

When the caramel is ready, remove from heat, take the pod from the milk, and, covering hands with a cloth, pour some of the hot milk into the caramel. It will bubble and froth alarmingly. Slowly pour on the rest of the milk and return mixture to the heat. Bring back to the boil and whisk thoroughly to dissolve any pieces of caramel which have stuck to the pan.

Pour this slowly on to yolks, beating fast, then put the mixture back into the milk pan. Over a high heat whisk vigorously, bringing the custard up to its first boil and sudden thickening. Immediately remove custard from the heat and sieve into a bowl to prevent curdling. Beat the custard afterwards to cool rapidly.

Chill the custard thoroughly and serve in a jug. Serves 6–8 with mousse.

LE PARADIS

CHOCOLATE SPONGE
3 eggs (size 1)
90 g (3½ oz) caster sugar
4 tablespoons unsweetened cocoa
  powder
pinch of salt

CHOCOLATE MOUSSE
290 g (10½ oz) semi-sweet dark
  chocolate, broken up
185 g (6½ oz) unsalted butter
5 egg yolks
dash of dark rum
1¼ gelatine leaves
6 egg whites
1½ tablespoons icing sugar

GENOISE
25 g (1 oz) plain flour
40 g (1½ oz) potato flour
pinch of salt
25 g (1 oz) unsalted butter
3 eggs
90 g (3½ oz) caster sugar

CREME CHANTILLY
1 leaf gelatine
375 ml (13 fl oz) double cream
about 25 g (1 oz) caster sugar
Grand Marnier
Kirsch

GLAZE
200 g (7 oz) semi-sweet dark
  chocolate, broken up
50 g (2 oz) unsalted butter
capful of vegetable oil

LEAVES
12–16 rose leaves
2 small bars plain chocolate

Make the chocolate sponge exactly as for Chocolate Chestnut Roll (see page 121) but using only one lined 30 × 22 cm (12½ × 8½ inch) Swiss roll tin. When baked, turn cake out on to tea towels and greaseproof paper, cover with another

towel and don't roll up.

While sponge is baking, make a chocolate mousse exactly as for the Frozen Chocolate Mousse with Caramel Custard (see page 121), but using the quantities stated here. After adding the yolks and rum to mixture, beat in soaked leaves of gelatine, which have been dissolved in a little hot water. Then proceed with the recipe. When the mousse is finished, refrigerate it in a mixing bowl until ready to use.

For the *génoise*, line the same size Swiss roll tin with greaseproof as for the sponge. Sift the flours and salt together twice and reserve. Melt the butter in a small metal cup and let cool. Put the eggs into a medium-sized heatproof mixing bowl and set bowl on top of a small saucepan of boiling water.

Begin to beat the eggs with a large wire whisk or with a hand-held electric beater set to high speed. After 1 minute gradually add the sugar and continue to beat until the mixture has grown thick and pale and begins to form a ribbon when the beater is raised. This takes about 5–10 minutes. Keep checking that the mixture is not getting too hot.

Remove the bowl from the pan and keep beating until the eggs and sugar are completely cold, by which time the volume will have tripled. This takes about 15 minutes with an electric beater, or twice that time by hand.

Gradually sieve the dry ingredients directly into bowl, folding them deftly with your hand – this is the gentlest and most thorough method of folding a *génoise*, with the least loss of volume. Fold in the melted butter, pour into a lined tin, spread evenly, rap smartly on work surface. Bake in a preheated oven at 190°C, 375°F, Gas Mark 5 for 20–25 minutes or until cake tests done. Turn out as for the sponge.

While the *génoise* is cooling, make *crème chantilly*. Dissolve the gelatine in a little hot water, cool slightly and add a few tablespoons cream. Whip the rest of cream to a soft shape, add the sugar and just a little Grand Marnier – this should be only slightly sweet and just suggest the flavour of Grand Marnier – whip in the liquid gelatine-cream mixture and whisk until firm but spreadable. Refrigerate until ready to use.

Choose a 22 cm (8½ inch) square cake tin with high sides, and line the bottom with unbuttered greaseproof paper, cut exactly to size. Cut the chocolate sponge and *génoise*, which should have cooled by now, to fit closely inside the tin. Split the sponge into two very thin layers with a long serrated knife. Cut *génoise* into three such layers (use the crusty top one for some other purpose). Do this as carefully as possible, but if the layers break up a bit, do not worry; they can be easily patched in assembling the cake.

Put the better of the two *génoise* layers on to greaseproof paper inside the tin, and lightly moisten with a little water that has been sparingly flavoured with Kirsch. Apply this mixture with a pastry brush, using just enough to moisten the cake. Reserve a little chocolate mousse – about 2 tablespoons' worth, with which to stick leaves down later – and spread half of the remaining mousse evenly over the whole of the *génoise*. Place the poorer of two chocolate layers on top of the mousse and moisten with Kirsch and water. Spread all of the *chantilly* over sponge, cover with second layer of *génoise*, moisten, and spread on remaining mousse. Cover with the second chocolate layer, and press assembly so that cake when turned out will be flat and even. Refrigerate for several hours to set.

Turn the cake out and make the glaze. Melt the chocolate and butter, add oil and stir. Allow the temperature of mixture to fall to 32°C, 91°F, then pour icing over top of cake and spread smoothly. Refrigerate.

Wash and dry the rose leaves. Melt plain chocolate on a plate over hot water. Take each leaf by its stem and drag it shiny side down, through the chocolate until thickly coated. Dry on greaseproof paper in a refrigerator until hard, then peel off rose leaves from stem end.

Remove the cake from the refrigerator when glaze has set, and with a long sharp knife, cut off the four sides to make an attractive square, heating the blade in the steam of a kettle before each cut and being careful not to drag the knife through the cake while doing this, lest you blur the lines of layering. Transfer to a flat serving plate, fill a small plain-tipped piping bag with the reserved mousse and pipe a little mousse on to four corners of cake so that three or four leaves can be stuck in clusters at each. Refrigerate cake until about half an hour before serving. Serves 8.

CHOCOLATE AND WALNUT CAKE

CAKE
175 g (6 oz) semi-sweet dark
   chocolate, broken up
175 g (6 oz) unsalted butter
3 eggs, separated
185 g (6½ oz) caster sugar
25 g (1 oz) finely ground walnuts,
   freshly prepared
40 g (1½ oz) plain flour
1 tablespoon potato flour
pinch of salt
1 extra egg white

GANACHE
225 g (8 oz) semi-sweet dark
   chocolate
250 ml (8 fl oz) double cream

TO FINISH
handful of walnut halves

Use a round cake tin, 20 cm (8 inches) in diameter and 4.5 cm (1¾ inches) deep, with a removable bottom. Butter the sides of the tin. Cut a circle of greaseproof paper to fit bottom exactly. Butter and flour it on one side, and flour sides of the tin. Separate the eggs.

Melt the chocolate and butter as for the Chocolate-cheese Brownies, while beating yolks and 175 g (6 oz) sugar with an electric beater, until very pale, thick, and increased in volume. Beat the chocolate and butter smooth, cool slightly and blend into the yolks and sugar. When this mixture is thoroughly cool, sift together the walnuts, the two flours and salt, and beat these into the base.

Beat the egg whites to soft peaks, beat in the 15 g (½ oz) of extra caster sugar and beat whites stiff. Fold with the base, pour into tin and bake in a preheated oven at 190°C, 375°F, Gas Mark 5 for about 40–45 minutes until the top has risen and begun to crack, and a fine metal skewer inserted into the centre tests oily, not dry. The middle should remain slightly undercooked. Cool in the tin on a wire rack. The top will crack a lot and separate from the body of the cake, which is normal.

When cold, push the cake up from the sides of the tin, reverse it on to a plate, remove the bottom of tin and peel off the greaseproof paper; reverse the cake on to a rack. Replace any parts of the top which may have come off, and make the *ganache*.

Break up the chocolate and put with the cream into a small, heavy saucepan directly over a low heat. As chocolate starts to melt, beat the mixture with a wire whisk. By the time the cream comes to the boil, the chocolate will have melted. Remove from the heat and beat smooth. Pour into a medium-sized bowl and cool, stirring occasionally.

When cool, beat at high speed with a hand-held electric beater for about 5 minutes, until mixture just holds soft peaks. It will lighten and increase in bulk. Don't overbeat, or *ganache* will stiffen. As it hardens fast apply *ganache* quickly to top, and the sides of the cake. Smooth the top, make pattern with a wide-bladed knife, and decorate with half-walnuts. Cut into small slices; this cake is rich and very filling. Serves 8.

A BIRTHDAY PARTY

My birthday is in May, and this is the sort of party I enjoy: green and snappy, with foretastes of summer in the flavours, textures and colouring.

SMOKED SALMON LASAGNE

This is light and exotic and easily made with the help of a food processor. I find Barilla lasagne is the best brand, available from good Italian grocers.

about 175 g (6 oz) green lasagne
about 175 g (6 oz) white lasagne
salt
vegetable oil
50 g (2 oz) walnuts
1 bunch of fresh coriander
450 g (1 lb) whole-milk Ricotta cheese
1 egg yolk
black pepper
75 g (3 oz) smoked salmon, very
*   thinly sliced and finely shredded*
350 g (12 oz) Mozzarella cheese,
*   grated*
50 g (2 oz) Parmesan cheese, freshly-
*   grated*
50 g (2 oz) butter, melted

Copiously butter a 1.5–2 litre (2½–3½ pint) heavy baking dish measuring about 23 × 30 × 5 cm (9 × 12 × 2 inches).

Boil the lasagne, a few pieces at a time, in two large pans of salted water with a good spoonful of oil in each, for about 10 minutes per batch. Remove the lasagne from the water with a wide spatula and drain, side by side, on paper towels.

Finely grind the walnuts and coriander leaves in a food processor. Beat the Ricotta cheese with the egg yolk, wal-nuts and coriander leaves. Season to taste.

Line the baking dish with a layer of white pasta, the pieces overlapping by about 1 cm (½ inch) and lining halfway up sides. With wet fingers, spread half the Ricotta mixture. Cover with overlap-ping pieces of green lasagne. Strew the salmon over the pasta.

Sprinkle half the Mozzarella over the salmon. Cover with half of Parme-san, dribble on half the melted butter and season.

Add a layer of white lasagne, spread on remaining Ricotta, cover with green lasagne and rest of cheeses and butter. Season well.

This dish can be assembled and refrigerated, foil-covered, overnight. Bring to room temperature before bak-ing. Bake, still covered in a preheated oven at 180°C, 350°F, Gas Mark 4 for 15 minutes. Remove the foil and return to the oven for about 35 minutes until lasagne is very hot. Brown under a preheated grill if necessary. Leave to rest for a few minutes before slicing. Serves 6.

Serve salmon lasagne with a green salad made with a mixture of leaves.

GREEN SALAD

I love the Smoked Salmon Lasagne served simply with salad. Arrange young cos lettuce leaves, oak leaf lettuce and corn salad or lamb's lettuce on a large glass platter. Purslane would be wonder-ful in the summer with one or two other kinds of leaves. Strew on snipped chives. Make up a vinaigrette dressing using 1 part lemon juice to 3 parts olive oil and several spoonfuls of Dijon mustard, plus seasoning and more chives. Pour over salad and toss to coat leaves.

BUTTERMILK VICHYSSOISE WITH WATERCRESS

I think that vichyssoise, a chilled soup, is much better – and lighter – finished with buttermilk instead of cream. A few leaves of watercress blended in shortly before serving intensify both the colour and flavour marvellously.

375 g (13 oz) potatoes, peeled weight,
*   thinly sliced*
225 g (8 oz) onions, peeled weight,
*   thinly sliced*
2 litres (3½ pints) home-made chicken
*   broth, as prepared on page 100,*
*   fairly weak; or half chicken broth of*
*   normal strength and half water*
salt
750 g (1½ lb) leeks, trimmed weight,
*   white part plus part of green*
black pepper
175–250 ml (6–8 fl oz) buttermilk
lemon juice
watercress

Put the potatoes and onions into a large, heavy pot (or two smaller ones), with the broth or broth and water mix. Add salt, half cover, and bring to the boil. Simmer for 5 minutes.

When trimming the leeks, save a little of the inner green for garnish, wash the leeks well and chop. Add to the broth, bring back to simmer, and cook for about 5–7 minutes until all the vegeta-bles are done. Cool the soup slightly, then liquidize until smooth, season to taste. Pass the mixture through a coarse sieve, forcing through all but the most fibrous and resistant parts of the purée. Add the buttermilk and a tablespoon lemon juice to sharpen the taste. Adjust the seasoning, remembering that soup

Clockwise from top: Hedgehog cake, Kiwis in syrup, Green salad, Initial biscuits, Vichyssoise, Vermouth cooler, Smoked salmon lasagne

thickens as it cools and that chilling dulls flavour.

Chill thoroughly. Shortly before serving, blanch a small handful of watercress leaves for 10 seconds in rapidly boiling water. Drain, refresh them and squeeze dry. Purée the watercress in a food processor, add a little soup and whiz again. Stir this well into the vichyssoise; its colour and flavour should intensify subtly. Adjust the seasoning. Ladle the soup into freezer-chilled bowls. Garnish with watercress leaves and a little blanched and refreshed julienned green of the the leek. Serves 6–8.

THE HEDGEHOG

The cake is a Swiss roll of sponge and strawberry butter cream, studded with strawberries and, naturally, candles. Like a hedgehog, it should look homely and rather lovable.

SPONGE
50 g (2 oz) potato flour
35 g (1¼ oz) plain flour
pinch of salt
25 g (1 oz) unsalted butter
4 eggs
120 g (4⅔ oz) caster sugar

SYRUP
1 tablespoon granulated sugar
2 tablespoons boiling water
Kirsch

BUTTER CREAM
250 ml (8 fl oz) milk, heated
3 egg yolks
75 g (3 oz) caster sugar
225 g (8 oz) unsalted butter,
  softened
100 g (4 oz) fresh strawberries, or
  frozen ones thawed and drained
red food colouring

TO FINISH
50–75 g (2–3 oz) fresh strawberries

Line a Swiss roll tin of 22 × 32 cm (8½ × 12½ inches) with an unbuttered sheet of greaseproof paper, cut to extend above the sides of the tin.

To make the sponge, sift the flours and salt together three times and reserve them on a piece of greaseproof paper. Melt and cool butter.

Break the eggs into a large heatproof bowl and whisk them briefly, using a hand-held electric beater. Set bowl over a small saucepan containing simmering water and whisk eggs at highest speed gradually adding sugar.

Beat the mixture until triple in bulk, remove the bowl from heat and continue beating until eggs and sugar are cold. Using a flexible rubber spatula, quickly start to fold in the sifted ingredients, tipping them gradually down their piece of greaseproof into the bowl. Fold in the butter until just combined. Pour the mixture across the surface of the paper-lined tin, smoothing it quickly. All movements should be deft.

Tap the tin against a work surface to settle and level its contents. Bake in a preheated oven at 190°C, 375°F, Gas Mark 5 for 20–25 minutes, reducing the oven temperature to 180°C, 350°F, Gas Mark 4 after 20 minutes if the top is browning too much. Test the cake with a thin trussing needle, and if done, turn out the cake on to a kitchen towel that has been covered with a sheet of greaseproof paper. Peel the paper carefully away from the cake. Lay a fresh sheet of greaseproof paper over the cake and, starting at one of the short ends, roll up the towel around the sponge. Leave the rolled-up sponge to cool.

To make the syrup, dissolve the sugar in the boiling water. When cold, add enough Kirsch to flavour.

To make the buttercream, prepare a very light custard with milk, yolks and sugar (beating yolks and sugar for several minutes before pouring on hot milk will achieve this). See page 126 for the basic method ignoring hazelnuts, vanilla, Kirsch. Strain and cool.

Cream the butter until very soft. Gradually beat and whisk in the custard until the mixture is the consistency of a spreadable cream. Purée the strawberries until smooth and add just enough to the butter cream to impart their flavour – probably less than the full amount. If necessary, beat in the tiniest drop of red food colouring.

Unroll the cooled sponge, remove the paper and brush the syrup over the entire inner surface of cake. Spread the buttercream thickly right to the edges. Reroll the cake and don't worry if it cracks slightly. Fit a 3–5 mm (⅛–¼ inch) plain nozzle on to a piping bag, pile in some butter cream and pipe the roll with diagonal stripes. Cut fresh strawberries into 'darts' and stud these over stripes.

Prepare and assemble cake within a few hours of eating. Serves 6.

KIWIS IN SYRUP

Someone asked me recently if I'd taken the pledge against kiwi fruit; I must have, unconsciously, as there are so few in this book. The question amused me so much that I actually began to think about this very agreeable 'gooseberry' which has been vulgarised by over-exploitation. The combination of flavours here goes well with Initial Biscuits.

Kiwis in syrup

250 ml (8 fl oz) fruity, but not sweet,
  white or rosé wine
3 tablespoons clear honey, not heather
  or lavender-scented
strip of lemon zest, without pith
6 × 75 g (3 oz) kiwi fruit

Simmer the wine, honey and finely-julienned lemon zest until the liquid has reduced to about 175 ml (6 fl oz) and tastes balanced and pleasantly sweet.

Top and tail kiwi fruits and peel away the skin in strips from end to end, using a small, sharp knife. Slice the fruit across, put into the syrup and leave to cool.

To serve, divide the drained slices among six dessert plates, garnish with a few strands of lemon julienne and spoon over a little syrup. The syrup can be prepared in advance, refrigerated and reheated when required.

Serves 6. For 8 portions, add two more kiwi fruits and increase the syrup quantities by a third.

INITIAL BISCUITS

When the cake has no inscription, these are the biscuits to follow it. Short and delicious.

225 g (8 oz) unsalted butter, softened
175 g (6 oz) caster sugar
2 eggs, lightly whisked
1 teaspoon vanilla essence, not
  'flavouring'
350 g (12 oz) plain flour
½ teaspoon baking powder
large pinch of salt
40 g (1½ oz) semi-sweet dark chocolate,
  melted and cooled

Cream the butter, gradually beat in the sugar, then the eggs and vanilla. Sift the flour, baking powder and salt, then beat into the butter and sugar mixture to form a dough. Weigh the dough, cut off three-quarters and work the chocolate into the

Initial biscuits

remaining quarter of dough.

Divide the vanilla dough in half, wrap the halves separately and refrigerate them until firm but not hard. Roll out one piece to 5 mm (¼ inch) thick on a floured board. Cut out circles with a 5 cm (2 inch) cutter and transfer those to heavy baking sheets; they will spread slightly in the oven.

Soften the chocolate dough by working it with a wooden spoon in a bowl set over a saucepan of very hot water. Mash and beat until dough becomes very malleable, like the consistency of pulled syrup, but not so hot that the butter oozes. Spoon into a piping bag fitted with a 3 mm (⅛ inch) plain nozzle, and pipe an initial on to each biscuit, tidying the shapes of letters with the tip of a sharp knife.

Refrigerate the biscuits for about 7 minutes to firm and preserve their shape. Bake them in a preheated oven at 180°C, 350°F, Gas Mark 4 for 10 minutes or until the edges brown. Cool completely on wire racks.

Keep the chocolate-filled bag in a warm place between usage. Roll out the remaining vanilla dough, reroll the off-cuts, and proceed as above until all the biscuits are baked. These biscuits keep for weeks in airtight tins. Serve with vermouth cooler. Makes about 72.

VERMOUTH COOLER

The mixture of liquors for this aperitif sounds rather alarming, but results are smooth and refreshing, with a welcome *pétillance*. Champagne can be served to those who like their drinks more orthodox.

175 ml (6 fl oz) Italian red vermouth
175 ml (6 fl oz) French dry white
  vermouth
85 ml (3 fl oz) crème de framboise
  (raspberry liqueur)
275 ml (9 fl oz) fresh orange juice
grenadine syrup
spiral of lemon zest, without pith
600 ml (1 pint) Perrier water, chilled
lots of ice

Whisk together the red and white vermouth, liqueur and orange juice. Add a little grenadine syrup to improve the colour, immerse the lemon zest and put to cool. Just before serving, pour the drink into a handsome jug, top up with Perrier to taste; you may prefer slightly more or less than 600 ml (1 pint). Stir, add more grenadine if the colour needs brightening, then drop in the ice.

Makes enough for 6 glasses-plus. To serve 8 people, or 6 more generously, make up to 1½ or even double quantities of the cooler.

Vermouth cooler

COOKING WITH WINE

Wine and its derivatives enhance the quality of food in as many ways as you would expect from a family in which champagne is a cousin to vinegar, and vermouth – a wine enhanced with barks, herbs and spices – is related to that famous wine-distillate, cognac.

In these recipes I have used wine and some of the members of its network of kin as condiments or as aromatic poaching liquids that turn themselves into flavourful sauces.

ASPARAGUS VINAIGRETTE

A classic, using oil and vinegar – the wine derivative *vin aigre*, or 'sour wine' – with sorrel and chopped egg, as unusual accents to the splendour of asparagus.

2 tablespoons red wine vinegar
salt
black pepper
120 ml (4 fl oz) olive oil
50 g (2 oz) very small, young sorrel
* leaves*
2 hard-boiled eggs
1 kg (2 lb) fresh green asparagus

Make the vinaigrette about 2 hours before serving by mixing together vinegar, salt and pepper, whisking in the oil. Stem the sorrel, wash and dry the leaves, shred them very finely and add to the oil and vinegar. Stir well and let sit, stirring occasionally.

Peel, halve and coarsely chop the eggs, doing yolks and whites separately. Cover and reserve.

Cut away the first 1–2.5 cm ($\frac{1}{2}$–1 inch) of the asparagus' tough stem ends and use a swivel peeler to pare each stalk. Make them up into string-tied bundles of

6–8 stalks each and immerse bundles in a large casserole of boiling, salted water. Simmer for 5–10 minutes, uncovered, until asparagus is just tender and still bright green. Put the bundles on to paper towels, cut the strings, drain and pat the asparagus dry.

Strew on the egg and serve at room temperature, the lower half of the stalks sauced with vinaigrette. Serves 4.

MACKEREL IN WHITE WINE

Another classic, this time from northern France, the fish poached in a very aromatic court-bouillon which jellies as the dish cools.

3 fresh mackerel, just over 450 g (1 lb)
* each, gutted*

COURT-BOUILLON
600 ml (1 pint) trocken or other dry
* white wine*
1 large wine glass of water
dash white wine vinegar
3 cloves
1 bay leaf
about 6 fresh coriander leaves
3 slices lemon
2 thin slices green pepper
1 large carrot, peeled
1 large onion, peeled and very thinly
* sliced*
pinch of salt
3 black peppercorns

TO FINISH
1 lemon
leaves of fresh coriander

Put court-bouillon ingredients into a saucepan – the carrot can be fluted after

peeling by running a lemon decorator called in French a *couteau à canneler* down its sides. Bring them to the boil and simmer 10 minutes.

Meanwhile, remove mackerels' heads and tails and cut the bodies across into 4 cm ($1\frac{1}{2}$ inch) sections. Wash away any traces of blood. Arrange pieces in one compact layer over the bottom of a wide heavy casserole or saucepan and pour on the court-bouillon and all of its trimmings.

Bring to the boil, lower heat to a bare simmer and poach the mackerel, uncovered, for about 10 minutes, or until just cooked through. Turn the pieces over once, very carefully, during poaching.

Transfer mackerel to one or two rimmed china dishes and pour over them the court-bouillon and its elements; they should cover the fish. Let cool and refrigerate, covered, overnight.

Remove from the refrigerator 30 minutes before serving, by which time the liquid will have jellied. Transfer fish to one or two serving plates. Discard lemon slices, bay leaf and coriander, plus cloves and peppercorns if you can locate them, and decorate the mackerel with onion, green pepper and carrot. Spoon on jelly and adorn plates with fresh slices from a lemon fluted before cutting, and fresh leaves of coriander. Serves 5–6 as a substantial first course.

Clockwise from top: Mackerel in white wine, Asparagus vinaigrette, Stuffed neck of lamb, Terrine of pork and prunes

TERRINE OF PORK AND PRUNES

Pork fillet or tenderloin with prunes is beloved of the Touraine French and the Danes. I've used these ingredients to make a pair of terrines, the gamey sweetness heightened by garlic and a few tablespoons of red Dubonnet.

275–300 g (10–11 oz) best prunes
1 tea bag
2 pork fillets or tenderloins, to yield a
    total of about 475 g (17 oz) after
    trimming
375 g (13 oz) rindless belly pork, to
    weigh 250–275 g (9–10 oz) after
    trimming
50 g (2 oz) rindless green streaky
    bacon
1 large clove garlic, peeled
50 ml (2 fl oz) red Dubonnet
salt
black pepper
about 350 g (12 oz) pork back fat,
    thinly sliced in sheets
butter
about 225 g (8 oz) lard

Put prunes into a saucepan. Use tea bag to make about 450 ml ($\frac{3}{4}$ pint) of very strong tea, pour this to cover the prunes, bring to the boil and poach fruit for about 1 minute. Turn off the heat and let prunes soak for 1 hour.

Meanwhile, trim the two cuts of pork of all nerve tissue – a little on the fillets, quite a lot on the belly – and cut them into small pieces, with the bacon. Run the meats through the coarse disc of a meat grinder, or food processor fitted with its steel blade, until coarsely chopped. Remove the combined meats to a bowl and pick out any nerve threads that may remain.

Drain the prunes well, stone and chop them, but not too finely. Mince the garlic and add to the meats with the prunes, Dubonnet and some salt and pepper. Mix thoroughly with your hands. Let the forcemeat marinate,

covered and refrigerated, for a few hours.

Line bottom and sides of two 900 ml (1½ pint) oblong terrines with the sheets of back fat, saving some for the tops.

Test forcemeat for seasoning by frying a small ball of it in butter until cooked through; add more seasoning if necessary, remembering that chilling will dull the subtlety of flavours.

Pack mixture into both terrines, rap them on the work surface to settle contents, and with a wet hand smooth over the tops. Cover with remaining back fat, a double thickness of foil, and the terrine lids. Place in a bain-marie. Bake in a preheated oven at 150°C, 300°F, Gas Mark 2 for 2 hours, removing the lid and foil for the last 15 minutes of cooking.

Lift from bain-marie, peel fat from the tops, and cover with foil-wrapped, weighted boards that can rest on the meat. When cool, refrigerate overnight, still weighted.

The next day, clean the rims of the containers, melt lard and pour it over the tops to seal meat completely.

Let the flavours mature for 3–4 days before slicing to serve with toast and butter. Remove the surrounding fat before eating. (The terrines will keep, refrigerated, for 2 weeks.) Each terrine serves 4–6.

STUFFED NECK OF LAMB WITH EARLY SUMMER VEGETABLES

Lamb from the scrag and middle neck is a firm, gelatinous meat that needs long, slow cooking to realize its succulent flavour. One of the least expensive cuts, it is subtle and delicious when boned and rolled round a stuffing of lemon, cheese and herbs, then poached in red wine. The acidity of the wine will help to tenderize the meat, which is delicious sauced with the poaching liquid and served with seasonal vegetables.

about 1.5 kg (3¾ lb) scrag and middle
    neck of young lamb, in one unboned
    piece
900 ml (1½ pints) lamb stock made
    from neck bones after removal, a
    peeled carrot and onion, pinch of
    thyme, bay leaf, parsley stalks, salt
salt
black pepper
2 carrots, peeled
1 large onion, peeled and stuck with
    3 cloves
2 cloves garlic, unpeeled
pinch of thyme
1 bay leaf
up to 1 bottle of fruity red wine
about ½ teaspoon arrowroot

STUFFING
100 g (4 oz) cream cheese
50 g (2 oz) butter, softened
50 g (2 oz) fresh breadcrumbs
1 large clove garlic, minced
chopped fresh herbs – parsley, tarragon
    or chives – to taste
grated zest of 1 small lemon
finely-minced meat trimmings from the
    neck bones
salt
black pepper
1 egg

VEGETABLES
about 150 g (5 oz) each young
    vegetables: spring onions, shelled
    broad beans, small turnips, tiny
    courgettes, new potatoes

Get your butcher to bone the lamb, taking care to pierce its flesh as little as possible (tell him it's to be stuffed). Also get him to chop up the vertebrae and give them to you with the rib bones. Or, if you are adept at boning, do this yourself and cut the vertebrae into two or three lengths.

Beat and knead together stuffing ingredients, season well and bind with enough egg to hold them firm.

Meanwhile, make a lamb stock in

Strawberry not-so-foolish

Strain and thoroughly degrease the poaching liquid, taste and reduce if necessary over a high heat; add a little red wine to refresh the flavour if need be. Simmer away the alcohol. Thicken slightly with arrowroot slaked in water; season and keep hot.

Simultaneously poach each vegetable until just tender in remaining lamb stock (which can subsequently be used for soup), and keep vegetables hot.

De-truss and unwrap lamb, 'seam' side down, and rapidly carve it into 1 cm ($\frac{1}{2}$ inch) slices. Arrange these over a hot platter, surround with the vegetables, spoon on a little sauce, and pass remainder in a warmed boat. Serves 4–5.

STRAWBERRY NOT-SO-FOOLISH

A fool with a difference: the strawberries are first soaked in *crème de framboise*, or raspberry liqueur, with which they have a true affinity, or in default of this, an orange-based liqueur such as Grand Marnier.

225 g (8 oz) ripe and flavourful strawberries, plus extra ones for garnish
3–4 tablespoons crème de framboise or Grand Marnier
25–50 g (1–2 oz) or more caster sugar, depending on sweetness of berries
120 ml (4 fl oz) double cream

Wash, hull and quarter strawberries and soak for 1 hour in 3 tablespoons Grand Marnier, plus 25 g (1 oz) sugar. Stir once or twice.

Purée the mixture in a blender, add more liqueur and sugar to taste; neither should be obvious, but should complement and give 'texture' to the berries.

Whip the cream, fold all together, spoon into glasses and chill, tightly-covered with cling film, for several hours. Serve very cold, on plates strewn with extra strawberries. Serves 3–4.

the usual way with bones and the aromatics listed, plus a little salt. Simmer for 3–4 hours, skimming often.

Open out the neck, boned side up, incise its thick parts and flatten the meat with your hands. Season it and cover it with stuffing. Fold over the long sides to enclose this, turn lamb over on to the centre of a double thickness of muslin measuring about 40 × 40 cm (16 × 16 inches), wrap muslin tightly round it to form a long roll. Tie one end of roll with string, loop the string five times round length of the roll, tie second end, loop string back underneath and tie it round the first knot. Trim the parcel ends.

When the lamb stock is ready, strain and degrease it. Put rolled neck into a heavy oval casserole into which it fits

snugly, add carrots, onion, garlic, herbs, enough wine to half-cover the meat, and 300–450 ml ($\frac{1}{2}$–$\frac{3}{4}$ pint) lamb stock. Sprinkle in a little salt, bring liquid to the simmer on the stove, and poach lamb in the lower middle of an oven preheated to 160°C, 325°F, Gas Mark 3 for $2\frac{1}{2}$–3 hours, with the lid of casserole slightly ajar until tender. Turn the parcel over every 30 minutes. Test by piercing meat carefully with a trussing needle.

Prepare vegetables by trimming onions, skinning beans, cutting turnips into small olives, and cleaning courgettes and potatoes. Reserve vegetables in bowls of cold water. When the meat is ready, remove it from the casserole and let it rest, still wrapped, in a warm place for 15 minutes.

SELF-INDULGENCE

Self-indulgence is all about pleasure and ease; a symbolic sun-bath with no particular high season. For me, such pleasure is based on the details of perfection: a flûte of well chilled pink champagne, or the cool segments of a tiny Cavaillon melon whose ripeness I savoured, one hot summer's day, with the house aperitif of a southern French restaurant.

Indulgence is based, too, on cooking and serving something well, for oneself and the delight of others. Below are some of my own candidates for the exercise of self-indulgence the year round.

GNOCCHI AND SALSA DI NOCI

On our working trip to Tuscany, my husband and I each ate a plate of pasta at the restaurant of the Fattoria di Montagliari, south of Florence. Hugo's plate was ravioli in a delicious *salsa di noci*, a walnut sauce for which Signor Giovanni Cappellii kindly gave me the recipe. I've put this with potato *gnocchi*, an Italian form of dumpling which I take great pleasure in making. If this kind of self-indulgent labour is not for you, have the sauce with some sort of ready made pasta; it's very agreeable with most pasta. My technique with *gnocchi* is based on Marcella Hazan's.

WALNUT SAUCE
185 g (6¼ oz) shelled walnuts
90 g (3¼ oz) pine-nuts
cold-pressed extra virgin olive oil
40 g (1½ oz) pecorino cheese, grated
20 basil leaves, chopped
85 ml (3 fl oz) single cream
black pepper
salt (optional)

GNOCCHI
750 g (1½ lb) floury potatoes
salt
plain flour

TO FINISH
15 g (½ oz) pecorino cheese, grated
basil leaves

Put both nuts into the food processor fitted with its steel blade. Process them, with olive oil to moisten, until the nuts are quite finely ground but are not an oily paste. Remove the nuts to a bowl, beat in the cheese, the 20 chopped basil leaves and the cream. Add more oil if needed; the sauce should remain quite thick. Season to taste, remembering that the cheese is salty. Cover the bowl with cling film and reserve. (The sauce can be made in a pestle and mortar.)

To make the *gnocchi*, boil the unskinned potatoes in salted water until tender. Drain and peel as soon as you can handle them. While still hot, purée through a food mill or ricer into a deep bowl. Sift on about 115 g (4½ oz) flour, work this into the potato and knead until smooth. You may need to add several more tablespoons flour if the potatoes are particularly absorbent, but stop when the mixture feels soft, smooth and still a little sticky. On a large floured board, form the dough into rolls the thickness of your thumb; leave to rest for 30 minutes.

Bring a large pan of salted water to the boil and begin to shape *gnocchi*. The method sounds involved but is actually not difficult; you'll quickly acquire the knack.

Use a floured knife, cut rolls into 2 cm (¾ inch) lengths. Throughout the process which follows, repeatedly flour, as needed, the *gnocchi*, the board, your hands and the fork with which you'll be working.

Choose a fork with long, slim, rounded tines. Hold the fork sideways in your non-dominant hand (left hand if you're right-handed), with the concave face towards you. With the index finger of your other hand, press a dumpling to the inside curve of the fork, just inside the points of tines; your index finger should be aligned to the fork's plane. When dumpling is in place, smartly flip it with the tip of your index finger along the tines of the fork, towards the handle. As it rolls to the fork's base, let the dumpling drop to the board. You'll get a sort of shell-like result.

Keep making these *gnocchi* – with increasing dexterity – until all the dough has been used. Heat four plates.

Uncover the walnut sauce, ladle and beat in enough of the boiling water from the pan to give the sauce a fairly loose consistency. Rapidly spoon a wreath of this on to each plate; keep the plates in a warm place.

Drop the *gnocchi*, about 24 at a time, into the pan of boiling water. They will rapidly rise to the surface. Simmer for 10 seconds more, lift them out with a slotted spoon, drain well and transfer directly to the plates. Boil all *gnocchi* in this way and, when plates are well-filled, season copiously, sprinkle over the pecorino cheese and basil leaves. Serves 4 as a first course.

Clockwise from top: Gnocchi and salsa di noci, Carrot and cucumber soup, Gateau Victoire au chocolat, Armenian lamb with rice pilaff

CRANBERICO

This cocktail uses cranberry juice, which should be sought in food shops with a sophisticated range of goods.

600 ml (1 pint) cranberry juice cocktail
175 ml (6 fl oz) white Bacardi rum
175 ml (6 fl oz) Perrier water
lemon juice
plenty of ice

Mix the cranberry juice cocktail, rum and Perrier water in a glass serving jug. Add lemon juice to taste, and ice. Pour out six glassfuls, including ice, and serve. Serves 6.

TRUFFLE TOAST

Each January, Jacques and Pierre-Jean Pébeyre and their wives host the Fête de la Truffe at Cahors in south-western France. The Pébeyres are to truffles what the Windsors are to royalty, and their hospitality is warm and generous.

At the family's truffle-processing plant during a recent fête, we inspected black and aromatic truffles of all sizes, and were served with fingers of hot, truffled toast. Ambrosial!

a whole black canned or bottled truffle
*   with its juice*
thinly sliced good quality bread
butter
salt and black pepper

Thinly slice the truffle, reserving its juice. Toast and butter the bread, remove crusts and cut into fingers. Lay several slices of truffle on each. Spoon the juices over the truffle. Season and eat.

BRIE TOAST

One night at the 21 Club in New York I ate nothing more than ripe peppery Brie on slices of toasted brown bread.

unpasteurized Brie, ripe and if possible
*   runny*
granary or wholemeal bread
butter
black pepper

Remove the rind from the cheese. Slice, toast and butter the bread. Spread with Brie, grind on pepper and eat.

FETTUNTA

During a working trip to Tuscany one recent spring, I tasted some admirable food. The *fettunta*, around Florence, is a garlic-rubbed and toasted slice of bread on which, in December, the newly-pressed olive oil is poured for sampling. In the summer, a *fettunta* – or *bruschetta*, as it's called in the neighbouring provinces of Umbria and Lazio – is often prepared with oil from the last year's harvest. Basil and tomatoes are added, and if all the elements are of the best, the result is magnificent.

white 'country' bread from an Italian-
*   run delicatessen*
cold-pressed extra virgin olive oil
salt
black pepper
1 clove garlic, peeled and halved
basil leaves
ripe, flavourful tomatoes, sliced

Thickly slice bread. Pour the oil into a deep dish and season well. Press both sides of each slice into the pool of oil. The oil should lightly soak each piece.

Lay the bread on foil on a heavy baking sheet. Toast in a preheated oven at 190°C, 375°F, Gas Mark 5 for 15–20 minutes, turning over once. Remove from the oven, rub each slice with the cut side of the halved clove of garlic. When toast has cooled slightly, cover with basil leaves and tomato slices.

Season to taste, pour on more oil and eat the *fettunta* without delay.

ARMENIAN LAMB WITH RICE PILAFF

I've used this recipe for ages, and am so familiar with it that I can't even remember its origins.

It has the excellent virtues of ease of preparation and improvement with age, reheating with superior results on the second or even third day after making. To the self-indulgent, such good nature can be an important quality in cooking; I highly recommend this comforting dish.

LAMB
1 boned shoulder of lamb
3 tablespoons vegetable oil
40 g (1½ oz) butter
2 medium onions, peeled and sliced
1 large clove garlic, peeled and sliced
2 teaspoons plain flour
1 teaspoon ground cumin
½ teaspoon ground cloves
450 ml (¾ pint) stock, made with bones
*   from the shoulder and a chicken*
*   quarter.*
2 tablespoons tomato purée
salt
black pepper

PILAFF
generous 15 g (½ oz) butter
a liberal pinch of saffron threads
1 small onion, peeled and finely
*   chopped*
225 g (8 oz) long-grain rice
150 ml (¼ pint) chicken stock, as above
salt
50 g (2 oz) pistachio nuts, shelled
50 g (2 oz) dried currants
black pepper

Trim the lamb of skin, excess fat and connective tissue. Cut into small cubes; if you have a devoted butcher, he may do all this for you.

Heat 1 tablespoon of the oil in a wide, flameproof casserole, add 15 g (½ oz) of the butter and, when foaming, lightly brown half the meat. Remove from the casserole. Add the same amount of oil and butter, brown the remaining lamb, then remove.

Melt the rest of butter with oil in the cleaned casserole, sweat onion and garlic until soft and golden. Stir in the flour and spices, stir over a low heat for 3–4 minutes. Remove from the heat, whisk in stock plus the tomato purée to form a smooth sauce; return to heat and bring the sauce to simmering point. Add the meat, some salt; stir well. Cook, partially covered, in a preheated oven at 160°C, 325°F, Gas Mark 3 for 2 hours, stirring occasionally, until the meat is tender.

Adjust the seasoning, cool, and refrigerate for 2–3 days.

When preparing to serve, remove the fat from the top of lamb and its sauce. Work a few tablespoons of water into the casserole and slowly reheat on top of the stove while making pilaff.

Cranberico, Toasts, Fettunta

To make the pilaff, melt the butter in a heavy saucepan, stir in the saffron and onion and sweat until the onion has softened. Wash and drain the rice, combine with the onion and stir over low heat for 2–3 minutes to begin cooking. Add the stock and salt, stir well, turn the heat very low, cover and leave undisturbed for 20 minutes. The rice should absorb all the stock and emerge cooked.

Blanch the pistachios for 1 minute in boiling water, then skin and shred. Fork the currants and nuts into the pilaff and season to taste.

Present the lamb flanked with the pilaff. Serves 4.

CARROT AND CUCUMBER SOUP WITH BUTTERMILK

I love cold vegetable soups finished with buttermilk, so this must be a logical self-indulgence.

---

500 g (1¼ lb) carrots, peeled weight
100 g (4 oz) onion, peeled weight
1.2 litres (2 pints) light chicken broth, made as on page 100
salt
250 g (9 oz) cucumber, peeled and seeded weight
black pepper
pinch of caster sugar (optional)
fresh dill
350–400 ml (12–14 fl oz) buttermilk
1–2 teaspooons lemon juice
smetana or soured cream

Put the carrots, onion and broth into a saucepan. Add salt, bring to the boil and simmer until the vegetables are just cooked. Cool slightly.

Meanwhile, grate the cucumber flesh; squeeze away as much of its liquid as possible.

When soup base has cooled, purée with the cucumber until smooth in a blender or food processor. Season, add a small pinch of sugar if you think the soup

needs it, plus some fronds of dill. If your blender is large enough, work in 350 ml (12 fl oz) buttermilk; otherwise remove the soup to a bowl and whisk in the buttermilk, judging whether to include the remainder. Add lemon juice to taste and adjust the seasoning.

Chill soup for several hours. Whisk before ladling into soup plates. Swirl a spoonful of smetana or soured cream in the centre of each portion and add a frond of dill. Serves 5–6.

GATEAU VICTOIRE AU CHOCOLAT

This is one of the ultimate chocolate cakes, a recipe from *Julia Child & Company*, made entirely without flour. I've adapted it slightly. The result is bitter and agreeably light, with a surprising, almost custard-like texture.

---

1 tablespoon instant coffee
4 tablespoons hot water
400 g (14 oz) semi-sweet dark chocolate, broken up
50 g (2 oz) unsweetened cocoa powder, sifted
2 tablespoons dark rum
6 eggs
100 g (4 oz) caster sugar
250 ml (8 fl oz) double cream
1 tablespoon vanilla essence (not 'flavouring')
icing sugar

TO SERVE
whipped cream
dark rum

Butter the sides of a 23 × 23 cm (9 × 9 inch) cake tin, about 5 cm (2 inches) deep. Line the base with buttered greaseproof paper.

Dissolve the coffee in hot water in a heavy saucepan. Add the chocolate, cocoa and rum. Cover the pan and set into a larger one of just-boiled water. Reheat the water to melt the chocolate.

Beat the eggs and sugar in a large bowl, using an electric whisk, for about 10 minutes, until the mixture has reached the consistency of lightly whipped cream. Whip the double cream until very soft peaks form, then whisk in the vanilla essence.

When the chocolate has melted, beat it with a wooden spoon; the result should be smooth, if a little resistant to the spoon. Blend the chocolate into eggs and sugar, folding rapidly and, when partially incorporated, fold in whipped cream until just combined.

Pour into the cake tin and place inside a bain-marie of simmering water to reach halfway up the sides of the tin. Bake in lower centre of a preheated oven at 180°C, 350°F, Gas Mark 4 for about 1–1¼ hours or until the cake has risen and cracked slightly, and a skewer inserted into the centre comes out clean.

Turn off the oven and leave the door ajar, allowing the cake and bain-marie to remain inside for 30 minutes. The cake will sink slowly and evenly back to its original volume. Remove from oven and leave to stand still in the bain-marie for 30 minutes before unmoulding.

The cake can be turned out and served at this stage, still slightly warm; you can also bake it a day in advance and reheat, still in the tin but minus the bain-marie, in a preheated oven at 115°C, 240°F, Gas Mark ¼ for 15 minutes.

Whichever plan you choose, turn the cake from the tin on to a board. Peel off the paper and turn back on to a flat serving plate. Work deftly but carefully, as the cake is very fragile. Dust with sifted icing sugar and slice into rectangles. Serve with lightly whipped cream flavoured with a dash of rum. Serves 10.

PASTRIES IN MINIATURE

When you present guests with an array of small cakes and tiny tarts, you are opening a jewel-box of temptations for the eye and palate. With some lemon curd, shortbread and pastry cream, fresh or dried fruits and a little sleight of hand, you will bring special elegance and charm to teas and wedding breakfasts.

SUCCES

This is a kind of light and chewy almond meringue sandwiched with coffee butter cream.

SUCCES BASES
100 g (4 oz) icing sugar
215 g (7½ oz) caster sugar
100 g (4 oz) finely ground almonds
6 egg whites
4 tablespoons milk

COFFEE BUTTER CREAM
90 g (3½ oz) granulated sugar
3 tablespoons water
4 egg yolks
175–225 g (6–8 oz) unsalted butter,
   softened
1 tablespoon good instant coffee
   granules, dissolved in ½ tablespoon
   boiling water

TOPPING
1 tablespoon unsweetened cocoa
   powder
25 g (1 oz) icing sugar
instant coffee granules

Cover heavy baking sheets with non-stick baking parchment. Using a pencil, trace about 40 circles, well spaced, on the parchment. Sift together icing sugar, 215 g (7½ oz) caster sugar and almonds.

In a second bowl, beat the egg whites until soft peaks form. Gradually beat in the remaining caster sugar and keep beating until the whites are very firm.

Add the milk to the sifted ingredients and knead together with your hands. Lighten this by beating in about a quarter of the whites. Pour almond mixture on to the remaining whites and fold together deftly. Fill a large piping bag fitted with a serrated 5 mm (¼ inch) nozzle with the *succès* mixture and pipe on to the circles on the baking sheets. Bake in a preheated oven at 140°C, 275°F, Gas Mark 1 for about 35–40 minutes until turning a pale biscuit colour (the meringues in lower part of the oven will take longer). With a spatula, carefully remove the baked bases from the parchment and cool on wire racks; they should be chewy, not hard. These bases will keep for about 2 weeks if they are stored, unfilled, in an airtight tin.

For the butter cream, make a syrup with the sugar and water and bring it up to 118°C (245°F). Beat the yolks until thickened and light. Whisk the syrup into the yolks and beat the mixture for several minutes until thick and cold. It will grow in volume. Beat in the soft butter gradually until the buttercream suddenly comes together and is firm and spreadable (you *may* need to add more butter than 225 g (8 oz) to achieve this). Beat in the dissolved coffee.

Fit a piping bag with a 5 mm (¼ inch) serrated nozzle and pipe a generous amount of buttercream on to 20 *succès* bases, slightly overlapping the edges. Cover with remaining rounds of *succès*.

For the topping, sift together the cocoa and icing sugar. Press 2–3 teaspoons coffee granules through a fine sieve and add to cocoa mixture to taste.

Cut greaseproof paper into thin strips and arrange on top of each *succès* in a criss-cross pattern. Sift over the cocoa mixture. Carefully remove strips and you will have an instant decoration. Some of cocoa will have settled alluringly on to the butter cream which shows around edges of each *succès*. Eat on the day of making. Makes about 20 *succès*.

LEMON CURD TARTS

SHORTCRUST PASTRY
quantities and method as in Jewel
   Tarts recipe on page 140

LEMON CURD
3 eggs
sieved juice and grated zest of 2 lemons
150 g (5 oz) caster sugar
50 g (2 oz) unsalted butter, softened

Bake, cool and turn out the small tart cases of various shapes as for Jewel Tarts (see page 140).

In a small bowl, whisk the eggs, beat in the lemon juice and zest, sugar and butter. Pour into a small heavy saucepan, set into a larger pan of simmering water. Whisk the mixture until it thickens to the consistency of a thick cream sauce. Pour into a bowl and beat well to ensure that there are no lumps.

Place the tart cases on to baking sheets and fill with the hot curd. Heat the filled tarts in a preheated oven at 180°C, 350°F, Gas Mark 4 for 1–2 minutes. Remove and cool.

Eat within a few hours of making. Makes 20–30 of assorted sizes.

An assortment of miniature pastries

CASINOS

A cheesy mousse between layers of *génoise* (sponge cake) and Swiss roll.

GENOISE
6 eggs
200 g (7 oz) caster sugar
50 g (2 oz) plain flour
75 g (3 oz) potato flour
large pinch of salt
25 g (1 oz) unsalted butter, melted and cooled

CREME AU FROMAGE
65 g (2½ oz) granulated sugar
4 egg yolks
3½ leaves gelatine
225 g (8 oz) fromage blanc
250 ml (8 fl oz) double cream

TO FINISH
175–225 g (6–8 oz) redcurrant jelly

Line two Swiss roll tins, each measuring 32 × 22 in (12½ × 8½) inches, with greaseproof paper in sheets large enough to extend above sides of tin.

For the *génoise*, place the eggs in a large china or metal mixing bowl set over a small saucepan of boiling water. Using a hand-held electric beater, whisk the eggs at highest speed, gradually adding the sugar. Continue whisking until the eggs become very light, thick, increased in volume and rather warm. Remove the bowl from the heat and whisk until the mixture is cold. The mixture will form a slowly dissolving ribbon when beaters are lifted.

Sift the dry ingredients together three times. Fold them into eggs and fold in the melted butter. Divide half the mixture between the two cake tins, spreading evenly. Tap each tin smartly against the work surface to settle and level the mixture. Bake on two shelves of a preheated oven at 190°C, 375°F, Gas Mark 5 for 20–25 minutes or until the cake on the top shelf is done. (The cake on the lower shelf will take longer.) Turn out on to separate tea towels covered with sheets of greaseproof paper. Peel the greaseproof paper carefully off the back of each cake, and lay fresh sheets of greaseproof over them. Starting at a short end, roll the towel around one of the two sponges and leave it to cool.

Repeat the process with the remaining *génoise* mixture, but do not make a roll with the fourth cake (use for another purpose).

Undo the rolled, cooled *génoise*, remove the greaseproof paper and spread it with a thin layer of hot, sieved redcurrant jelly. Roll up snugly, wrap in greaseproof paper cut to size and store for several hours in the refrigerator. Butter interiors of 16 round metal moulds, each of 75 g (3 oz) capacity, and line the bottom of each with a circle of buttered greaseproof paper.

For the *crème au fromage*, make a syrup with the sugar and a dash of water brought up to 118°C, 245°F. Beat the egg yolks until thickened and light. Soften the gelatine in a jug of water. Whisk the syrup on to the yolks and beat the mixture for several minutes until thick and cold. Drain the gelatine, dissolve in a little water over low heat and beat into the yolks. Whisk the *fromage blanc* until smooth and add to yolks. Whip the cream until soft peaks form and beat into the egg and cheese base. It will be thick and hold its shape.

Fill each mould almost to top with *crème au fromage*. Cut 16 circles of *génoise* to fit just inside the top of each mould and refrigerate for several hours.

When it is nearly time to serve, remove the Swiss roll from the greaseproof paper and, with a serrated knife, cut into slices about 8 mm (⅜ inch) thick. Paint the top and sides of each slice with heated and sieved redcurrant jelly.

Dip each mould briefly into hot water, turn out the contents on to a plate and peel the paper off what is now the top. Cover each top with a jellied slice of Swiss roll, which should just fit, and serve. Makes about 16.

MINIATURE FRUIT CAKES

The world's fastest and easiest.

1 egg
50 g (2 oz) caster sugar
1 teaspoon vanilla essence (not 'flavouring')
50 g (2 oz) unsalted butter, melted and cooled
100 g (4 oz) plain flour
¼ teaspoon salt
½ teaspoon mixed spice
120 ml (4 fl oz) buttermilk
¼ teaspoon baking soda
300 g (11 oz) mincemeat
75 g (3 oz) raisins
50 g (2 oz) candied cherries, quartered
40 g (1½ oz) candied citron, chopped
40 g (1½ oz) walnuts, coarsely chopped

Beat together the egg, sugar, vanilla essence and butter. Sift the flour, salt and mixed spice together. Mix the buttermilk with the baking soda and alternately with the sifted dry ingredients, beat this into the egg mixture. Fold in the mincemeat, fruits and nuts.

Butter 22 small brioche tins, measuring 4 cm (1½ inches) across the base. Fill three-quarters of each tin with the cake mixture and place on baking sheets. Bake in a preheated oven at 180°C, 350°F, Gas Mark 4 for 20–25 minutes. Leave to cool a few minutes before sliding a knife around the edges of the tins and carefully removing the cakes. These keep for months in airtight containers. Makes about 22.

JEWEL TARTS

Each tart is filled with a dollop of *crème pâtissière*, or pastry cream, to keep the moisture from the fruit from softening the pastry. Makes about 20–30 small tarts of varying sizes, which should be assembled within a few hours of eating.

SHORTCRUST PASTRY
275 g (10 oz) plain flour
4 tablespoons caster sugar
large pinch of salt
175 g (6 oz) unsalted butter, softened
yolks of 2 hard-boiled eggs, sieved
1 egg

PASTRY CREAM
3 egg yolks
50 g (2 oz) caster sugar
275 ml (9 fl oz) milk
vanilla pod, split
1 tablespoon plain flour
1 tablespoon potato flour

TO FINISH
50 ml (2 fl oz) double cream
1 tablespoon icing sugar
Kirsch
seasonal fresh fruits such as kiwi fruit,
*   blueberries, blackberries,*
*   redcurrants, raspberries,*
*   strawberries*
100–175 g (4–6 oz) apricot jam
100–175 g (4–6 oz) redcurrant jelly

To make the pastry, sift the flour, sugar and salt on to a pastry board. Make a well in the centre, put the butter into the well and make a trough in the butter. Add the sieved yolks and whole egg. With one hand, work the butter, yolks and egg swiftly together into a sticky mass. With a spatula, toss and chop the flour gradually into butter and egg until it begins to look like pastry. With both hands, bring the dough together. Add a few drops of water if necessary to make it adhere, knead briefly and form into a ball of dough. Wrap in greaseproof paper and a polythene bag. Refrigerate overnight.

To make the pastry cream, beat the yolks and sugar to the ribbon stage. Put the milk into a pan with the vanilla pod and scald. Sift the flour and potato flour (the latter makes for lighter pastry cream) on to the egg yolks and caster sugar. Beat well, then pour on the strained milk (minus the vanilla pod) and transfer the entire mixture to a small heavy saucepan.

Over a very low heat, whisk the pastry cream until it thickens and boils, beating vigorously to avoid the slightest lump. Boil for 30 seconds, whisking, then turn out on to a plate. Cover the top with cling film to prevent the formation of a skin. Cool completely.

Bring the pastry to room temperature, roll out and line small pastry tins of varying sizes and shapes. Chill for 30 minutes.

Place pieces of greaseproof paper weighted with dried beans inside each tin. Bake blind in a preheated oven at 180°C, 350°F, Gas Mark 4 for 15–20 minutes, removing the paper and beans when the pastry has set. Continue baking the tart shells until golden, browning and completely cooked. Cool and remove the tarts from the tins.

Take 225 g (8 oz) pastry cream and beat to aerate. Half whip the double cream, whisk in the icing sugar with a

Jewel tarts

scant dash of Kirsch. Whisk into pastry cream. Beat until completely smooth and light – if there is even a suspicion of a lump, pass through a fine sieve.

Fill each tart shell with pastry cream and top with fruit. I often use uncooked blueberries and 3 mm ($\frac{1}{8}$ inch) thick slices of kiwi fruit.

Brush the tops of the kiwi and blueberry tarts with simmered and sieved apricot jam. The tops of the black or red fruit tarts should be brushed with simmered and sieved redcurrant jelly. Makes 20–30 tarts.

HEARTS

Crumbly and buttery shortbreads.

100 g (4 oz) unsalted butter, softened
50 g (2 oz) caster sugar
grated zest of 1 small lemon
$\frac{1}{2}$ teaspoon vanilla essence (not
*   'flavouring')*
200 g (7 oz) plain flour
pinch of salt
milk

Cream together the butter, sugar, lemon zest and vanilla. Sift together the flour and salt and mix gradually into butter mixture, beating well after each addition.

When all the flour is incorporated, knead the dough diligently until it ceases to cling to the hand. Add a few drops of milk if necessary to moisten. Divide into two balls, wrap separately in greaseproof paper and refrigerate for 1 hour.

Roll each ball 2 cm ($\frac{3}{4}$ inch) thick on a floured pastry board. With a small heart cutter, cut out biscuits, flouring the cutter each time, until all the dough has been used.

Place on a heavy baking sheet. Bake in a preheated oven at 180°C, 350°F, Gas Mark 4 for about 20 minutes or until just turning golden brown. Cool on wire trays. These biscuits keep for months in an airtight tin. Makes about 48.

Succès

Hearts and cornets

GANACHE CORNETS

These are made with a mixture for *cigarettes russes*, each biscuit turned round a tapering cornet mould instead of the handle of a wooden spoon. An excellent use for leftover egg whites!

CORNETS
75 g (3 oz) unsalted butter, softened
75 g (3 oz) icing sugar
50 g (2 oz) plain flour
pinch of salt
3 egg whites
½ teaspoon vanilla essence, (not 'flavouring')

GANACHE
150 g (5 oz) semi-sweet dark chocolate
150 ml (¼ pint) double cream

Cover heavy baking sheets with baking parchment. Cream the butter and sugar. Sift the flour and salt together. Gradually beat the egg whites into the butter mixture, then fold in the flour. Beat in the vanilla essence.

Drop by teaspoons on to the baking parchment at well-spaced intervals. Spread into very thin circles of even thickness and about 7.5 cm (3 inches) in diameter. Bake in a preheated oven at 200°C, 400°F, Gas Mark 6 for 5 minutes or until the edges turn golden brown. Remove one baking sheet from oven and, working quickly, flip a biscuit off the paper, turn over and roll around the pointed tip of a metal cornet mould, 13 cm (5 inches) in length. It helps to have asbestos fingers, because the biscuit must be soft and hot to roll properly. Remove from mould and cool on a wire rack. Quickly proceed with the remaining biscuits, one by one. If they harden before being rolled, return briefly to the oven to soften.

To make the *ganache*, break up chocolate and put with cream into a small, heavy saucepan. Place directly over a low heat. As the chocolate starts to melt, beat the mixture with a wire whisk. By the time the cream comes to boil, the chocolate will have melted. Remove from heat and beat until smooth. Pour into a small bowl and cool. When cold, beat at high speed with a hand-held electric beater until the mixture holds soft peaks, has lightened and increased in bulk.

Spoon into a piping bag fitted with a 5 mm (¼ inch) serrated nozzle and pipe a rosette into the open end of each cornet. Refrigerate to firm the *ganache*. Remove from refrigerator about 15 minutes before serving. Eat on the day assembled. Makes about 36.

INDEX

ACKNOWLEDGEMENTS

I would like to thank the editors of *House & Garden*, particularly Leonie Highton and
Vicky Jones, for making this work both possible and enjoyable, and the many
generous suppliers and organizations who are listed below.

LONDON

Stephen Long Antiques

Edward Goodyear Flowers

Portmeirion Antiques

Bayly's Gallery

Linen Hire

Mollie Evans Antiques

Elizabeth David Kitchen Utensils

Souleiado

The Lacquer Chest

J.M. Turnell

John Baily & Son, Poulters

Frank Godfrey, Butchers

The Conran Shop

Sue Norman Antiques

Kenneth Turner Flowers

Valimex

Table Props

Britannia Antiques

The Golden Horn Restaurant

Robert Young Antiques

Tobias & the Angel

The Craftsmen Potters Shop

Knoodles

Schwartzsackinandcoltd

Lillywhites

Paperchase

Henry Willis Antique Silver

Jones Jewellers

Liberty

Divertimenti Cooking Utensils

Lonsdale Advertising

The Tunisian Tourist Board

Anthony Blake Studio

John B Benson, Architect

Tables Laid

PROVINCES AND ABROAD

Stuart Cousens
The Village Pottery
West Chiltington
West Sussex

Audrey Wilkerson
Admington
Warwickshire

Gwyn Davies
The Dairy Crest Creamery
Felinfach, Lampeter, Dyfed

Raven Products
Daws End
Marlow Common
Buckinghamshire

Johnny Grey
Grey and Co, Kitchen Furniture
  Designers
Wool House, Stedham
Midhurst, Sussex

Chocolaterie Valrhona
14 avenue du Président Roosevelt
26600 Tain l'Hermitage
France

PHOTOGRAPHERS' CREDITS

Clive Frost: pages 87, 88, 90, 91, 92

Christine Hanscomb: pages 2 (bottom
left), 11, 12, 13, 25, 27, 28, 56, 58, 59, 95,
97

Graham Kirk: pages 2 (top left), 2
(bottom right), 7 (top), 69, 71, 79, 80, 81,
83, 84, 85, 112/113, 133, 135

James Mortimer: pages 15, 16, 17, 18, 20,
21, 22, 23, 31, 32, 33, 35, 37, 38, 39, 41,
43, 44, 46, 51, 53, 54, 65, 67, 73, 75, 99,
101, 104, 106, 107, 109, 111, 115, 117,
120, 125, 126, 127, 129, 131, 138, 140,
141

George Seper: pages 2 (top right), 61, 63

Clive Streeter: front cover, pages 6, 7
(bottom), 8/9, 48/49, 76/77